A Reader's Companion to Mikhail Bulgakov's *The Master and Margarita*

Companions to Russian Literature

Series Editor: Thomas Seifrid
(University of Southern California, Los Angeles)

A Reader's Companion to Mikhail Bulgakov's *The Master and Margarita*

—— J.A.E. CURTIS ——

BOSTON
2019

Library of Congress Cataloging-in-Publication Data

Names: Curtis, J. A. E. (Julie A. E.), author.
Title: A reader's companion to Mikhail Bulgakov's The master and Margarita /
    J. A. E. Curtis.
Other titles: Companions to Russian literature.
Description: Boston: Academic Studies Press, 2019. | Series: Companions to
    Russian literature | Includes bibliographical references and index.
Identifiers: LCCN 2019026989 | ISBN 9781644691335 (hardcover) | ISBN
    9781644690789 (paperback) | ISBN 9781644690796 (adobe pdf)
Subjects: LCSH: Bulgakov, Mikhail, 1891–1940. Master i Margarita.
Classification: LCC PG3476.B78 M33335 2019 | DDC 891.73/42--dc23
LC record available at https://lccn.loc.gov/2019026989

ISBN 978-1-644691-33-5 (hardcover)
ISBN 978-1-644690-78-9 (paper)
ISBN 978-1-644690-79-6 (electronic, pdf)

Cover design by Ivan Grave.
On the cover:
'Variety Theatre', from a series of drawings and paintings on *The Master and
Margarita* by the artist Laura Footes; image by kind permission of the artist and
the Blavatnik Family Foundation.
Book design by PHi Business Solutions.

Published by Academic Studies Press in 2019
1577 Beacon Street
Brookline, MA 02446
press@academicstudiespress.com
www.academicstudiespress.com

In loving memory of Adam Curtis
(1950–2017)

Contents

Foreword   ix

1. Bulgakov's Life: Formative Years and First
   Successes—1891–1928   1
2. Bulgakov's Life: Battling the Censor, and Writing
   The Master and Margarita—1929–40   14
3. Drafts of *The Master and Margarita*   24
4. Publication History of *The Master and Margarita* in Russian   41
5. A Tale of Two Cities: The Structure of *The Master
   and Margarita*   49
6. Woland: Good and Evil in *The Master and Margarita*   61
7. Pilate and Ieshua: Biblical Themes in *The Master
   and Margarita*   72
8. Political Satire in *The Master and Margarita*   86
9. Literature and the Writer in *The Master and Margarita*   97
10. "So who are you, then?" Narrative voices in *The Master
    and Margarita*, Followed by a Stylistic Analysis of Extracts
    from the Text   109
11. English Translations of *The Master and Margarita*   132

Afterword—A Personal Reflection   143

Acknowledgements   149

Notes   151

Bibliography   167

Index   173

Foreword

It is over fifty years since Mikhail Bulgakov's novel *The Master and Margarita* burst upon the literary scene in Soviet Russia and in the West in the late 1960s, its impact only heightened by the fact that its manuscript had been kept secret, carefully hidden out of sight from the Communist authorities, for over a quarter of a century since Bulgakov's death in 1940. But the novel's success was due not only to the sensational surprise of its rediscovery, so many decades after its author had hoped that it might reach its intended audience. *The Master and Margarita*'s unique blend of exuberant satirical humour, demonic pranks, and a poignant love story, together with a solemn investigation into the nature of good and evil through a revisiting of the encounter between Jesus Christ and Pontius Pilate, constituted a startlingly original contribution to the twentieth-century Russian literary canon. Since then, it has become a literary classic, and for many Russian readers a cult text. It has been translated from Russian into dozens of languages, and has generated an extraordinarily wide range of literary and cultural responses in Russia, and across the entire world.[1]

Occasionally a writer appears whose works, while being inevitably shaped by the cultural legacies of previous eras, are nevertheless characterized by a unique degree of inventiveness and bold imagination. Mikhail Bulgakov is one such writer, as was the nineteenth-century Russian writer whom he most admired, Nikolay Gogol', of whom it is said that he succeeded in inaugurating European Modernism several decades before its time. To take just the example of Gogol's most famous short story *The Nose* (1836): its author contrives a bizarre plot out of a fractured, almost absurd narrative structure, launches the theme of the "unreal city" with his surreal depiction of St. Petersburg, and offers the reader a tale which lends itself most fruitfully to a Freudian reading. All these things would become key features of literature of the Modernist era. Nothing in the books that Gogol' had read, nor in his literary environment, could have prepared contemporary readers for the shock that *The Nose* offered them. Bulgakov described Gogol' as his favorite writer and his teacher, and observed that "no one can compare with him."[2] And just like Gogol', Bulgakov created in *The Master and Margarita* a novel quite unlike anything that had come before it in the Russian tradition or any other tradition, a text all the more startling for its utter indifference to the prevailing discourse of its time of writing in Soviet Russia, the discourse of Socialist Realism.

Bulgakov's greatest novel has reverberated in literary culture not just since its belated publication, but maybe even before that moment finally arrived in the 1960s. A text that has not yet been published might be considered incapable of inspiring other works; but as fuller archival documentation has begun to emerge it has become increasingly apparent, for example, that the poet and novelist Boris Pasternak, who admired Bulgakov and got to know him well in the final months of his life, would have discussed *The Master and Margarita* with his dying friend, and probably read the entire text in 1939 or 1940. We can therefore start to look at his own *Dr Zhivago* (completed in 1956) with different eyes. Both novels have as a central protagonist a writer living in the Soviet era whose creative gifts insulate him in some respects from the turmoil around him, but who as an individual is flawed and weak. Pasternak's device of attaching to his own novel a complete cycle of poems written by Yury Zhivago, and reflecting on the yearly unfolding of Christian celebrations, is a structural innovation comparable in its originality—but also in its central preoccupations—to Bulgakov's "novel within a novel" in *The Master and Margarita*. Lesley Milne quotes a passage from *Dr Zhivago* which reveals just how much the two authors' views on the role of religion in the modern world overlapped: "One can be an atheist, can doubt the existence and purpose of God, and yet know at the same time that man lives not in nature but in history, and that history as we understand it today is founded by Christ, that the Gospel is its foundation." She rightly concludes that: "In their novels the two writers stand firmly together, expressing shared cultural assumptions: the significance in European art and literature of the Christian idea and the validity of the ethical paradigm therein enshrined, in the face of an epoch which systematically negated these paradigms in word and in deed."[3] Pasternak died twenty years after Bulgakov, in 1960, and his great novel similarly had to wait another quarter of a century before first being published in the Soviet Union in 1988.

Once *The Master and Margarita* had appeared in print in the late 1960s, it began to play a quite different role in sparking innovative creativity. Since then, the range of its impacts within Russia has been immense, whether in inspiring the novelist Chingiz Aitmatov to interpolate a vision of the encounter between Christ and Pilate in his ground-breaking *glasnost'* novel *The Executioner's Block* (1987), or in prompting the opening lines of the first volume in Boris Akunin's immensely successful series of detective novels, the title of which in Russian is *Azazel'* (*Azazello*, 1998). Elsewhere, and in an entirely different culture, the British Indian author Salman Rushdie acknowledged the work as an inspiration for his controversial novel *The Satanic Verses* (1988). Rushdie has spoken of two very disparate texts inspiring the concept and the content of *The Satanic Verses*: William Blake's *The Marriage of Heaven and Hell* and Bulgakov's *The Master and Margarita*. In an interview with the English scholar Colin MacCabe, Rushdie described how he had combined three disparate story-lines into one novel and added: "It was also helpful to have as a model Bulgakov's *The Master and Margarita*, which does something similar."[4] There have been many scholarly accounts of what shaped Rushdie's seminal contribution to the genre of magical realism, with its uninhibited blending of the everyday with the fantastic, but Bulgakov is now often referred to as an early practitioner of the genre—albeit long before the term was first invented.

The Master and Margarita has also had various impacts in the sphere of popular culture. The singer Marianne Faithfull gave a copy of the English version to Mick Jagger of the Rolling Stones almost as soon as it was published, and in 1968 he released his successful samba rock number "Sympathy for the Devil." The song's opening lines echo the arrival of the Devil, Woland, in Moscow: "Please allow me to introduce myself . . .," while its chorus reflects one of the key enigmas of the text: "Pleased to meet you, hope you guess my name, / But what's puzzling you is the nature of my game. . . ." Mick Jagger's later girlfriend Jerry Hall, when she heard of a plan to make a film version of *The Master and Margarita*, was convinced that Jagger would be the ideal person to play Professor Woland in his "favourite" book.[5] Other celebrities have mentioned it as one of their favourite novels too. The Harry Potter actor Daniel Radcliffe has described it as ". . .just the greatest explosion of imagination, craziness, satire, humour, and heart. [. . .] . . .it's the greatest exploration of the human imagination, and it's about forgiveness and life and history, and it's just the most incredible book that I've ever read; I read it once and then I read it almost immediately again."[6] The American writer Annie Proulx has commented that: "The ambiguity of good and evil is hotly debated and amusingly dramatized in this complex satirical novel about the threats to art in an inimical material world and its paradoxical survival (symbolized by the climactic assertion that 'manuscripts don't burn')."[7] David Mitchell, the British author whose novels have twice been shortlisted for the Booker Prize, frequently selects it as a book he likes to offer as a gift: "If someone hasn't read Mikhail Bulgakov's *The Master and Margarita* I try to foist a copy on them. They either love it, or bail when they meet the talking cat with a machine gun."[8] The rock musician Patti Smith describes it as "very simply [...] one of the masterpieces of the Twentieth Century," and in 2012 she released an album *Banga*, in which the title track refers to Pilate's dog Banga as a quintessential symbol of love and loyalty.[9] This small sample of strong responses to Bulgakov's novel comes from a very disparate range of voices, and they each pick up on very different aspects of the text: but they all speak of a powerful, original piece of writing, which rarely leaves any reader indifferent.

One of the most characteristic features of the Russian cultural tradition, shaped as it has been since the early nineteenth century by both censorship and oppression, is its disconcerting blending of ingenious wit with chilling bleakness. Many works of Russian literature engage with utmost seriousness with the political and social challenges confronting the nation, while at the same time drawing upon fantastical humor. Bulgakov is a true heir to this unusual tradition, which begins with Pushkin and Gogol' and extends via Dostoevsky into the modern age, towards the ambiguities of the musical landscape of a composer like Dmitry Shostakovich. In works of breathtaking compositional boldness and narrative invention, Bulgakov and these other artists tread a fine line between comedy and tragedy, grotesque humor and horror.

In writing this Companion for readers wishing to find out more about Bulgakov's *Master and Margarita*, I am conscious that there already exists an enormous body of distinguished scholarly writing on the subject, in Russian and English as well as in many other languages.[10] In this volume I have attempted to outline some of the principal lines of debate and disagreement about the text, while offering some thoughts of my own about key issues. My aim has been to provide a general introduction to Bulgakov's life and to the novel for the first-time reader of the book, as well as offering additional chapters which may be of interest to a somewhat more academic readership. I begin with two chapters providing an overview of Bulgakov's life, highlighting events and circumstances which proved particularly relevant to the composition of *The Master and Margarita*. The tribulations of a life lived in Russia during the early decades of the twentieth century did much to shape his intense concern for the role of the writer in society, and enhanced his preoccupation with the autobiographical. The first chapter covers the years from Bulgakov's birth in 1891 in Kyiv (Ukraine) up until 1928, the year when the very first sketches for *The Master and Margarita* were drafted. The second chapter takes up the story from 1929 until Bulgakov's death in 1940, a decade full of professional challenges, political difficulties and even personal dangers for the writer, during which time he continued to draft and redraft the novel in the secrecy of his Moscow apartment.

The next two chapters describe the complex, and to some extent disputed, history of the writing of the novel, and then trace its publication history. Chapters 6 to 10 offer an interpretative reading of the text, considering in turn: the structure of the text; the enigmatic figure of Woland, the Devil; the novel within the novel, set in the ancient world, and its Biblical themes; political satire; and the figure of the writer, together with the theme of literature. I have assumed that the reader does not know Russian, but for the benefit of those who do I have included some extracts from the novel in Russian alongside their translations into English in chapters 11 and 12, where I consider narrative and stylistic features of Bulgakov's writing, and then move on to discuss the competing claims of the various available translations of *The Master and Margarita*. The Afterword includes a personal reflection on my own experience of having studied Bulgakov and his works over several decades, from the Cold War era to the Putin regime, and considers the present-day reconfiguration of attitudes towards a text which has continued to provoke impassioned debates and controversy even into the twenty-first century.

CHAPTER 1

Bulgakov's Life: Formative Years and First Successes—1891–1928

The world described in Mikhail Bulgakov's novel *The Master and Margarita*—Soviet Moscow in the late 1920s and 1930s—was very far removed from the city of Kyiv in which he had grown up as a child and lived as a student, just as far removed geographically as it was culturally, socially, and politically. But at the same time, certain preoccupations which derived from his upbringing and early experiences would prove crucial in shaping the concept of the work, and many of its central themes.

Bulgakov was born in May 1891 in Kyiv, capital of the present-day nation of Ukraine, the first child of a couple who both came from families of priests.[1] His father Afanasy had broken somewhat with family tradition by becoming an academic lecturer and researcher at the Kyiv Theological Academy, rather than a full-time priest. In another slightly unconventional step, Afanasy Bulgakov focused his academic investigations beyond and outside the precepts of Russian Orthodoxy, and was the author of studies of aspects of Methodism, and of developments in Catholic thought and Freemasonry, all work undertaken within the Theological Academy's Department for the Study of Western Christianity. This openness to alternative ways of approaching the Christian faith may have helped to shape his son Mikhail's religious sensibilities as well.

Bulgakov's mother Varvara would go on to have six more children after Mikhail—four girls and two boys—and presided over her lively brood with intelligence and good humor. The family was not particularly wealthy, but they were highly educated: the children were all widely read in the classics of Russian and European literature, they studied ancient and modern foreign languages, they took an impassioned interest in the scientific and political debates of their day, and they all loved going to the theatre and to concerts. The young Mikhail picked up the piano with great ease, sang in a pleasant baritone, and was a great fan of the opera. In particular, his sister once totted up the tickets he had pinned to his wall, and established that he had been over forty times to see Gounod's 1859 opera *Faust*, based on the original verse text (1828–9) by Goethe.[2] On some of those occasions it would have been the great Russian bass Fedor Chaliapin who performed the role of the charismatic devil Mephistopheles. In his later writings, and most notably in *The Master and Margarita*, themes and images from the Goethe original as well as from its musical setting by Gounod would acquire a kind of talismanic significance for Bulgakov, and were often associated with evocations of home, and of the civilised culture of the past.

The Bulgakov family led lives that were typical of the educated Russian middle class in Kyiv, which at the time was one of the great cities of the Russian Empire. Kyiv had a very significant Russian population, but issues of Ukrainian independence and the use of the Ukrainian language were not for the time being as controversial as they have become in modern times. Young Mikhail's childhood appears to have been very happy and carefree up to the age of fifteen. A succession of traumatic events, however, soon supervened to sweep away his familiar world.

First amongst these distressing experiences was the sudden illness which afflicted his father Afanasy, who in 1906 developed malignant nephrosclerosis, a disease affecting his kidneys and his eyesight. Afanasy Bulgakov died in March 1907, when he was still only in his late forties. There appears to have been a hereditary susceptibility to the disease, since in 1940 the same affliction would carry off Bulgakov himself, also before he had reached the age of fifty.

There is nothing surprising in the fact that an adolescent boy, the eldest of a large group of siblings, would find this painful loss a traumatic experience. It coincided with a rebellious phase in his youth, which manifested itself over the next few years not only in difficult behaviour, especially towards his mother, but also in his turning away from the Russian Orthodox faith in which he had been brought up. His sister Nadezhda (Nadya), who was particularly close to him, observed that he became fascinated with Darwin's theories, and that he had resolved the question of religion for himself "with non-belief." Family tensions were compounded when it became apparent that his mother's warm friendship with the family doctor who had tended Afanasy during his illness had gradually grown into something more; and although they did not marry for some years, Dr Ivan Voskresensky effectively became the young Mikhail's stepfather.[3]

In 1909, despite having told Nadya at an earlier point that he expected one day to become a writer, Mikhail applied to the University in Kyiv to study medicine: in this he was following in the footsteps not only of two of his maternal uncles, but also of his new stepfather. His studies did not run entirely smoothly, however, and he had to retake some of his exams, doubtless because of his all-absorbing love affair with an attractive young girl called Tat'yana (Tasya) Lappa from the town of Saratov, whom he met while she was visiting Kyiv. The two became inseparable, and despite the considerable reservations of both families, the pair married in April 1913. Mikhail was not quite twenty-two years old. He buckled down to his medical studies more seriously after that and finally managed to qualify in 1916—with quite respectable scores in the end—as a doctor.

By that time, the First World War had been devastating Europe for two years. As soon as he qualified in the summer of 1916, Bulgakov was sent to serve in a front-line field hospital, where Tasya, who had volunteered as a nurse, assisted him in numerous operations on wounded soldiers of the Russian Imperial Army, many of them involving amputations. She accompanied him again when he was assigned that same autumn to take over the running of a small rural hospital back in Russia, while more experienced medical officers took over at the front. This daunting experience of responsibility from the age of twenty-five for the full range of medical general practice, which lasted for eighteen months from the autumn of 1916 until early in 1918, formed the backdrop to Bulgakov's first set of short stories, written up in the mid-1920s as *Notes of a Young Doctor*. It was during this same period, spent by him and his young wife mostly in remote solitude, that the Russian nation, still fighting enemies abroad, experienced the cataclysmic internal changes brought about by the two revolutions of 1917. In February that year Tsar Nicholas II was forced to abdicate, and a Provisional Government of moderate socialist hue took over in order to oversee a transition towards constitutional democracy. But in October 1917 this too was swept away in the revolutionary coupled by Lenin and Trotsky, which brought the Bolsheviks to power in Moscow.

The young adults of the Bulgakov family had been brought up as loyal citizens of the Tsarist empire, and their natural inclination was to support monarchism. They therefore regarded the Bolsheviks with wary suspicion, rightly assuming that people of their class could expect no favours from the new regime. But political events in Kyiv were in any case becoming exceptionally complicated and confusing. In March 1918 the new Bolshevik government pulled Russia out of the war and signed the peace treaty of Brest-Litovsk with the Central Powers (Germany, Austria-Hungary, Bulgaria, and the Ottoman

Empire). This was essentially a capitulation, in order to obtain respite as they struggled to consolidate power after the October Revolution. The price for peace exacted by the Central Powers was extremely high: great swathes of territory on the western borders of the Russian Empire—and the populations who lived there—passed over into German control. These included the whole of Ukraine, which was to be ruled by a puppet government, the Ukrainian Hetmanate, now subordinated to those same Germans who had been the Empire's wartime enemy for four years. And at the same time, a fervent new Ukrainian nationalist movement had emerged, fighting partisan battles under the leadership of Symon Petlyura. Between 1918 and 1921, which became a period of Civil War in the aftermath of the October Revolution, the city of Kyiv was tussled over by Russian monarchist forces, by the Germans and their representatives the Hetmanate, by Petlyura and his Ukrainian nationalists, and by the Bolshevik Red Army advancing from Moscow to seize back the territory they had ceded in 1918. People disagree about how many times the city changed hands during this period, but Bulgakov affirmed that there had been fourteen changes of power, "and what's more I personally lived through ten of them."[4]

In the early months of 1918, Bulgakov and Tasya returned together from the rural medical practice in Russia to start living again in the family home in Kyiv. For ten years or more, this home had been a comfortable apartment occupying the top floor of a house on Andreevsky Hill, a broad, cobbled and exceptionally steep street snaking its way up from the lower city towards the gloriously gilded eighteenth-century onion-domed church of St Andrew. When the Bulgakov siblings and their spouses began to gather back in their home as the First World War ended, Varvara and her youngest daughter moved up the hill to live with Dr Voskresensky, and it was at this point, evidently, that the middle-aged couple were formally married. Between early 1918 and the later part of 1919 the household on Andreevsky Hill consisted therefore exclusively of a group of young adults, all of them aware that their political fortunes hung in the balance. The White monarchist movement was in retreat, and their cause was dealt a further bitter blow with the assassination by the Bolsheviks of Tsar Nicholas II and his entire family in July 1918. The Bulgakovs despised the Germans and the Ukrainian Hetmanate alike; were fearful—as Russians—of the populist violence unleashed by the Ukrainian nationalists; and as bourgeois monarchists could expect no sympathy from the Red Army. This is the situation described in Bulgakov's profoundly autobiographical first novel, *The White Guard*, in which a family of young adults who share the values of the Bulgakov family, living in an apartment exactly like the one on Andreevsky Hill, set in a city which is unmistakably Kyiv, waits with alarm to see how events will turn out. This novel, written shortly after Bulgakov had received the shocking news of his mother's sudden death in 1922, was a paean of love to the values of home and family, inspired by her memory.

By the time Bulgakov completed *The White Guard* in the early 1920s, his life had undergone a whole series of fundamental transformations. In circumstances which are still not entirely clear, he seems to have left Kyiv in mid- to late-1919 as a military doctor, mobilised by the pro-monarchist White Army as they retreated east and south towards the Black Sea. His two younger brothers Nikolay and Ivan left Kyiv at about the same time: the family lost contact with them for over two years as they travelled on into emigration, and neither of the two younger boys ever saw the rest of their family again. During 1919, Bulgakov suffered at least two deeply shocking experiences which he revisited later in his fiction and his drama. Briefly and forcibly mobilised in February by Petlyura's army, notorious for their anti-Semitism, he witnessed the beating and murder of a Jewish man one snowy night in the city, and felt powerless to intervene. After he had left the city with the monarchists, he was also present at the preparations for the hanging of a workman by a White general on suspicion of being a Bolshevik sympathiser: he could not bear to watch the death itself. These experiences not only reflected his growing disillusionment with the disintegrating cause of the Whites, but also engendered in him a lifelong preoccupation with issues of guilt and of cowardice. These would become central themes in many of his works, including *The Master and Margarita*.

Bulgakov's journey away from Kyiv with the White forces took him southeast as far as Vladikavkaz, a small town in the northern Caucasus, where Tasya was soon able to join him. It was here that he made a firm decision to turn his back on his career in medicine, and started to pursue instead his youthful ambition to become a writer. To begin with, he wrote short articles for the local press. These included an indictment of Bolshevism dating from November 1919 and entitled "Prospects for the Future," in which he contrasted the post-war programmes of reconstruction in the West with the plight of Civil-War Russia, still ravaged by fighting and threatened by the mob violence instigated by the Bolsheviks. Early in 1920 he wrote some pieces for a short-lived journal called *The Caucasus*. But his fate took another unexpected turn at this point, when he succumbed to a serious bout of typhus fever, which confined him to his bed for several weeks. During this time the Red Army advanced into the Caucasus, the Whites retreated, and by the time Bulgakov recovered and was back on his feet he found himself perforce living in Soviet Russia.

His recently adopted professional identity as a writer enabled him to suppress the evidence of his past as a doctor, which could have exposed him to risky questions from the newly installed Soviet authorities about just which military forces he had allied himself with during the previous months. At this time Bulgakov did consider seriously the option of fleeing into emigration, like so many of his contemporaries, and in the summer of 1921 he went so far as to travel to the Black Sea port of Batum, in Georgia, to see whether he could secure a passage for himself on a boat. His relations with Tasya had worsened by this stage, and he initially thought about travelling alone, although later on he summoned her to join him. However, he was unsuccessful in his attempts. And at this point he took a momentous decision about his future, and decided to travel north to Moscow to try and establish himself in a literary career.

Several considerations probably helped to shape this step he took, once he had contemplated the apparent impossibility—for financial and practical reasons—of escaping from Soviet Russia. First amongst these was the fact that the Civil War had finally petered out earlier that year, bringing to an end seven years of chaos and destruction inaugurated in 1914 by the outbreak of war, and extending through the revolutions of 1917 and the subsequent turmoil which had ravaged the country. The new Soviet regime offered an unknowable future, but there were some indications that the extremes of violence and class hostility which had characterised the Civil War period were soon to be moderated. In Moscow, earlier in 1921, Lenin had proclaimed a New Economic Policy (NEP), which was perceived as something of a concession to the economic norms which had prevailed in Tsarist times. The country was in such a desperate state after the years of upheaval that Lenin concluded that it was necessary to permit some private trade and commerce once again, to give the nationalised economy a kick-start as it began to rebuild. Infrastructure, transport, and heavy industry remained under the control of the state, but small-scale enterprises to provide food and other services began to flourish once again. These included privately owned journals, newspapers, and publishing houses. The signs were that the ferocious era of class warfare had given way to a certain reinstatement of bourgeois values in everyday life and culture. As Bulgakov weighed up his future, he calculated that the opportunities for him to make a living as a writer would be considerably greater if he stayed in Russia than if he were to try to find a Russian readership in emigration. But if he was to fulfil his considerable ambitions as a literary figure, he needed to be at the centre of things. He therefore left the Caucasus, visited Kyiv briefly to see his mother and sisters in September 1921, and then travelled on to Moscow, a city he barely knew, to seek his fortune there.

Bulgakov and Tasya, still just about holding their marriage together, endured some difficult years as they started life in the Soviet Russian capital. They occupied a single room with shared kitchen and bathroom facilities in a communal apartment on Bol'shaya Sadovaya Street, which Bulgakov cordially detested. He took on a succession of small writing and editorial jobs to scrape together an income during a period of raging inflation in the early 1920s, and the couple suffered extremes of cold and even hunger. By the time things had settled a little and he began to write his first novel, *The White Guard*, essentially completed between 1922 and 1924, his childhood must have seemed to belong to a different universe. As he entered his thirties, he could reflect that in the space of less than a decade he had lost almost everything that had shaped his earlier life: first of all his father, and more recently his mother; but also his brothers, his childhood homes, his native city, his religion, his profession as a doctor, the political regime, and even the nation he had grown up in. *The White Guard* was written essentially as a tribute to that past life, to the cultured values of his original social class and milieu, and, above all, to honour and celebrate the memory of his mother.

By the mid-1920s, Bulgakov had secured a reputation in Moscow as a writer of humorous sketches (*feuilletons*) and topical, anecdotal short stories.[5] In the space of just a few years he adopted the guise of a well-informed Muscovite citizen, with an intimate knowledge of the city's topography and a close understanding of the way life had evolved for the city's inhabitants under Soviet rule during the 1920s. He also started to move in literary circles, where his talent was increasingly recognised. Early in 1924 he went to a party for the Russian writer Aleksey Tolstoy, who had recently returned from emigration. Tolstoy and a number of others were seduced back by the Bolsheviks' apparent willingness to be reconciled with those who had left, by the energetic rebuilding of the country, and by the relatively tolerant attitudes of the authorities towards literature during the NEP years (1921–28/29). On this occasion Bulgakov got to know another recently returned émigrée, a lively and sophisticated young woman called Lyubov' (Lyuba) Belozerskaya. They soon began an affair, and by the end of the year he had left Tasya and moved in with Lyuba; they were married in April 1925.

The first few months of 1925 appeared to be full of promise. Bulgakov wrote a novella which decades later would become one of his most admired satirical works, the highly entertaining *Heart of a Dog*. A research scientist performs an experiment on a harmless dog, in which his sexual glands are replaced with those from the corpse of a drunk; inadvertently the professor succeeds in creating a new, thoroughly unpleasant humanoid who soon acquires the vulgar and obstreperous traits of a low-grade Soviet official. It was not difficult to discover the mocking analogy Bulgakov seems to be drawing here with the great social experiment the Bolsheviks had practised upon the common people of Russia. Readings of his new story to a literary circle were promptly reported to the OGPU (the secret police), with the recommendation that this subversive work should not be published under any circumstances. Meanwhile, a courageous journal publisher had begun to publish his novel *The White Guard* in serialized form, despite the obvious provocation offered by the very title of the work, not to mention its affectionate depiction of a middle-class intelligentsia which had long ago been branded the class enemy in Bolshevik ideology. But before the third and final part could appear, the Soviet authorities closed the journal down, and the publisher was arrested and forced to leave the country. Clearly, Bulgakov was not just acquiring a literary reputation, but he was also beginning to come to the attention of the police authorities. Nevertheless, the partial publication of *The White Guard* was to lead to one of the few genuine professional successes that Bulgakov would enjoy as a writer in his lifetime.

The Moscow Art Theatre had been renowned since the turn of the century as the theatre of the great director Konstantin Stanislavsky and of the playwright Anton Chekhov. The Theatre was keen to establish itself in the Soviet era with some contemporary drama, in order to demonstrate that it was not just a reactionary institution narrowly attached to the past. One of their literary consultants had read what had been published of *The White Guard*, and even on the basis of an incomplete text recognised that it had the potential to be transformed into a play. As it happened, Bulgakov, who had been writing plays, most of them not staged, for some years, had already begun considering this possibility, and he had even begun to sketch out a dramatic adaptation of the novel. The invitation that arrived in the spring of 1925 for him to call upon the literary consultant at the Moscow Art Theatre to discuss a possible dramatization represented the fulfilment of a long-cherished dream: the most prestigious theatre in the country had spotted his potential as a dramatist.

Bulgakov would go on to describe his experiences of working with the Moscow Art Theatre on the adaptation of his novel during 1925 and 1926 in a wickedly amusing autobiographical text, *A Theatrical Novel* (1936), which he wrote long after the events were over, and which was left unfinished. As a relative novice in the theatre, he did have a certain amount to learn about how to shape his plot into a stage piece of manageable proportions. He also had everything to learn about the histrionic temperament of those he had to deal with, from the Moscow Art Theatre's warring artistic directors Konstantin Stanislavsky and Vladimir Nemirovich-Danchenko, down to the bossy secretaries and the predatory finance and administrative managers. Nevertheless, there is a strong element of sincerity in the contented sigh given by Bulgakov's *alter ego* in *A Theatrical Novel*, the writer Maksudov, when he finds himself for the first time in the theatre's auditorium: "This world is my world . . ." [I, 455].

There were many difficulties to overcome as the play based on *The White Guard* took shape and rehearsals began, with vocal objections being raised by Communist critics who protested against the play's blatantly sympathetic portrayal of the middle-class Kyiv family who represented the now defeated White movement. The issue was taken to the highest level of the government, inaugurating a not infrequent set of discussions over the next fifteen years—right up to Politburo level—about Bulgakov's creative writing, and about the fate that was to be meted out to him. It was decreed that the play's title could not possibly repeat the provocative title of the novel, and this was therefore replaced with the anodyne title *The Days of the Turbins* (the fictional family's surname). The première of *The Days of the Turbins* in October 1926 was the theatrical sensation of the decade, with crowds flocking to watch it, a hysterical atmosphere in the auditorium as the actors portrayed the travails so many of the audience had themselves recently endured, and an ambulance stationed outside the theatre to care for those who were too overcome.

Bulgakov proved himself to be a remarkably quick learner, and his utter self-confidence about how he wanted this play to be staged, and how he wanted the actors to convey his intentions, rapidly earned him the reputation of a consummate man of the theatre. The Moscow Art Theatre promptly started negotiations with him about a stage adaptation of the still unpublished *Heart of a Dog*; and during 1925 he was approached by another leading Moscow theatre, the Vakhtangov, to write for them a comedy of modern life. His play *Zoyka's Apartment* describes a group of people blatantly unsympathetic to the Soviet system, who set up a dressmaker's salon in Moscow as a front for risqué entertainments, drug dealing, and, ultimately, murder as a means to raise money for their planned escape from the country. The setting, subject-matter, and tone of this play was utterly unlike its predecessor. *Zoyka's Apartment* was already in rehearsal well before the première of *The Days of the Turbins* took place, and it too premiered in October 1926. Bulgakov's sudden celebrity status had earned him yet another contract in the meantime, and he was soon beginning work during 1926 on a third new play, a skit on the events of the Russian revolution—framed by a satire on theatrical censorship—called *The Crimson Island*, scheduled to be staged by Moscow's Kamerny Theatre.

This astonishing and rapid sequence of successes was not being celebrated in all quarters, however, and the OGPU was watching him with increasing attentiveness. In all his plays he had been taking full advantage of the comparatively lax ideological atmosphere in the mid-1920s, during the NEP years, in order to offer sharply satirical observations about life in Communist Russia. But in May 1926 the OGPU turned up at his apartment, conducted a search, and confiscated some of his papers. In particular—and to his especial horror—they took away some private diaries he had written between 1921 and 1925. They also confiscated two typed copies of *The Heart of a Dog*, unequivocally putting a stop to any hopes that the Moscow Art Theatre had nurtured of staging the work. In September 1926, on the eve of a final run-through of *The Days of the Turbins* at the Moscow Art Theatre in the presence of Party officials, Bulgakov was summoned by the OGPU to an interview. He was questioned at some length about his personal history and his political convictions, questions he responded to with considerable courage and frankness. We need to bear in mind, naturally, that the Stalinist regime was in its early, relatively tame years, and that Bulgakov could not have anticipated just how brutal the repressions would be that would characterise the era of the Terror just a few years later. In answer to a suggestion that he might do better to write about Soviet-approved themes such as the lives of the workers or the peasants, he replied as follows:

> I am absorbed and keenly interested in the everyday life of the Russian intelligentsia, and I cherish it: I consider it to be a very important element in our country, even if it is weak. Its fate is close to my heart, and its experiences are precious to me. [...] But I have a satirical mindset. [...] I always write with a clear conscience, and I write things as I see them. The negative aspects of life in the Soviet state attract my constant attention, because I instinctively find a great deal of material there for myself. I am a satirist.[6]

This frank declaration of his beliefs constituted a *credo* which he would follow faithfully for the rest of his writing career. The OGPU, apparently satisfied that they had gained a good understanding of this potentially subversive figure, let matters rest there for the moment, and allowed him to go home without further obstruction. The staging of *The Days of the Turbins* went ahead. And a few years later Bulgakov was even allowed to have his drafts and diaries back, after

frequent protests about the confiscations and requests for influential acquaintances to intervene.

In the mid-1920s, therefore, Bulgakov was at the pinnacle of Moscow's theatrical establishment, lionised by theatre directors, adulated by his audiences,
and—to his own considerable satisfaction—one of the most controversial figures in Soviet-era culture. He was making rather a good living and had moved
with Lyuba into a spacious flat where he established a candle-lit study for himself, with a large old-fashioned carved wooden writing desk. He had three plays
in production, and soon started making plans for a fourth. Most of the writing
of this new play was completed during 1927, and into 1928.

This time he planned a play for the Moscow Art Theatre which would
serve as a kind of sequel to the 1918–19 events described in *The Days of the
Turbins*. *Flight* depicts the aftermath in 1919–20, as the pro-monarchist Whites
are finally defeated by the Red Army and flee through the Crimea into emigration in Constantinople and Paris. While the intelligentsia are portrayed with
some sympathy, as being noble-hearted if weak, the Archbishop of the Orthodox Church behaves with pusillanimous hypocrisy, and the military leaders of
the White Army are portrayed as vain and cowardly (in the case of its supreme
commander), or cruelly deranged (in the central character of General Khludov). The political message of this play confirms the disenchantment Bulgakov
and others of his social milieu experienced in the last years of Tsarism, while
not offering any kind of defence of Bolshevism. Its central preoccupation, as in
so many of his works including *The Master and Margarita*, is with the individual's personal code of honour, and the way that shapes his actions. As Bulgakov
was to reaffirm in his letter to the Soviet Government on March 28, 1930: "In
my plays *The Days of the Turbins* and *Flight*, and in my novel *The White Guard*,
I stubbornly depict the Russian intelligentsia as the very best stratum of our
nation."[7] Ultimately the intelligentsia in *Flight* choose to return to Soviet Russia,
unable to leave its culture—and the snow—behind. Khludov, now tormented
by guilt over his inhumane deeds, commits suicide in acknowledgement of the
barbarous cruelty he has shown towards the Russian people (or in a different
version of the ending, returns to the USSR to face his accusers).

At this moment of the peak of his success, Bulgakov seems in *Flight* to have
been revisiting the dilemma he faced in 1921, when he had contemplated emigrating via the Black Sea to Constantinople, as his protagonists do in the play.
On balance, he apparently concludes that emigration would have been a mistake: that it held misery and degradation for those who embarked on aimless
flight, whereas the true values of Russian culture lay back in the homeland. With

the advantage of hindsight, and our knowledge of what lay ahead in Soviet history, we may question that judgement. And he himself would very shortly have to confront the despairing realisation that he would never in fact be allowed to leave the USSR, even for short-term travel abroad. But in the mid-1920s Bulgakov had achieved the most he could ever have dreamt of, despite living under a regime whose ideology he found intensely unsympathetic. His plays were being put on despite opposition from establishment critics; his novel *The White Guard* had not been published in full, but its stage adaptation was doing very well; *The Heart of a Dog* had been confiscated, but he had been interrogated by the OGPU and still permitted to continue most of his activities, so he had some hope of getting the typescript back; and he had no real reason to suppose that he would not continue to thrive in Soviet culture, his reputation only enhanced by the *succès de scandale* that surrounded his name.

However, the question of whether the play *Flight* should be licensed for the stage became a matter for fierce public debate through the rest of 1928 and on into early 1929, when the matter was finally referred for consideration at full meetings of the Politburo of the Communist Party of the USSR. If anything, Stalin himself proved less fiercely opposed to the work during the discussions than some of his colleagues: he had, after all, rather unexpectedly proved to be one of the most devoted fans of Bulgakov's play *The Days of the Turbins*, which he had chosen to see at the Moscow Art Theatre on something like a dozen separate occasions. But in February 1929 Stalin wrote a letter replying to a critic who had denounced *Flight*, in which he in turn described the play as "anti-Soviet." As soon as the contents of the letter became known the Moscow Art Theatre, with what Bulgakov would forever regard as unforgivable haste, abandoned the plan to stage *Flight*. By the summer of 1929 all three of his other plays, *The Days of the Turbins*, *Zoyka's Apartment*, and *The Crimson Island*, had also hurriedly been removed from the repertoire by apprehensive theatre administrators. His brilliant career suddenly lay in tatters.

While the arguments raged over *Flight*, an entirely new project had nevertheless been beginning to take shape in Bulgakov's mind during the second half of 1928: this was a plan for his second novel, which would ultimately become *The Master and Margarita*. As he confirmed to his close friend Pavel Popov early in 1929, the stimulus for *The White Guard* had been the image of his mother. But this time it was his father, the theologian Afanasy, who was to prove the inspiration—a full two decades after his death—for Bulgakov's masterpiece.[8] Bulgakov may have lost his Christian faith as a teenager, but he was steeped in Christian culture, and his father's intellectual curiosity about the Western church as well as his loyalty to the Eastern Orthodox tradition had provided a model of open-mindedness about the practice of religion, as well as about its metaphysical significance. All this had been brought into sharp relief in Bulgakov's mind as he observed the Soviet state's philistine assaults on religion, scorned by Karl Marx in the 1840s as "the opiate of the people." He had recorded in his diary for early 1925 his horror at discovering that a new "Godless" publishing house had recently been established in Moscow, designed to support the state policy of militant atheism with publications that would denounce the figure of Jesus Christ as a swindler and scoundrel [VIII, 106]. The starting point for *The Master and Margarita* was thus a meditation upon the precarious status of the Christian religion in the Soviet state.

CHAPTER 2

Bulgakov's Life: Battling the Censor, and Writing *The Master and Margarita*—1929–40

Bulgakov's reflections during 1928 about the plight of the Christian religion under Soviet Communism represented just the beginning of a project in his mind, early jottings which would take several years to develop into the full novel as we know it. The following year, 1929, was a period which Bulgakov would describe as a "year of catastrophe" in his life, by which he obviously meant the disastrous and simultaneous collapse during that spring of all his theatrical undertakings.[1] However, it was also the year in which one new and transformative element would enter his life. Bulgakov's relationship with Lyuba had lost its intensity, and for some time they had been drifting apart. In February 1929 he went to a dinner party where he met Elena Sergeevna Shilovskaya, an extremely attractive married woman with two small sons; and they fell for one another immediately and irrevocably. As he put it in a clearly autobiographical passage in his novel, "Love leaped out in front of us, like an assassin jumping out in an alleyway, and struck both of us at once! It was like a lightning strike, like a blow from a dagger" (*The Master and Margarita*, chapter 13).[2] Elena's husband, who was a Lieutenant-General in the Soviet military establishment, happened to be away on a trip, and so they immediately started to spend all their time together. Elena recalled one night in May 1929 when Bulgakov came and woke her up at 3 am, took her to the nearby square known as Patriarchs' Ponds, pointed to a bench, and made a cryptic remark: "This is where they first saw him." From there they went on to a mysterious apartment, where two men she had never met before welcomed them with wine and caviar by an open fire. The older man, charmed by her, declared her to be a witch.[3] Readers familiar with *The Master and Margarita* will of course recognise elements of the love story between the novel's eponymous protagonists in this beginning of the relationship between Bulgakov and Elena, the great love of his life.

This hugely positive new departure in his life may have been what emboldened him to put up a something of a fight in defence of his four abandoned plays. In July 1929 he wrote the first of several letters to Stalin and to other members of the Soviet government, as well as to the writer Maksim Gor'ky, the most highly respected and influential figure on the Soviet literary scene.[4] In this letter he described his situation after ten years of life as a writer. He recounted the dismal tale of his banned plays and of his censored prose works, the monstrously aggressive and hostile critical reception he had received in the Communist press, the confiscation of his papers by the OGPU in 1926, and the response he had received when he applied to travel abroad for 2 months in February 1928: the application was simply turned down, and no explanation had been provided. As he put it: "At the end of ten years my strength is broken." Seeing no prospect now of being either staged or published in the USSR, he therefore implored the Soviet government to send him into exile abroad, together with his wife Lyuba (he evidently did not feel he could involve Elena in this sort of application at this stage in their relationship).[5] On July 30, 1929 he added: "The entire press has been determined to ensure that my work as a writer should cease, and its efforts after ten years have been crowned with complete success: with a suffocating clarity, based on these documents, I can tell you that I no longer have the strength to survive as a writer in the USSR."[6] While this letter and others he wrote around this time apparently received some sympathetic consideration in government circles, he never received any formal response—possibly because Stalin himself was actually away from Moscow that summer. Towards the end of August he wrote to his younger brother Nikolay, now living in Paris: "If my request is turned down, then I can consider that the game is over, it's time to put away the cards and blow out the candles. [. . .] Without any faintheartedness I am telling you, brother of mine, that the question of my destruction is just a matter of time, unless of course a miracle takes place. But miracles occur rarely."[7]

However, his new-found personal happiness also seems to have renewed his creative energies, and despite having four plays under a ban, he sat down in October 1929 to embark on an entirely new drama project. Calculating perhaps that he might have a better chance of getting staged if he turned away from contemporary—and therefore potentially controversial—subjects, he decided this time to write a play set far away in time and place from his own world. This was to be a biographical play about the seventeenth-century French playwright Molière. Once again presenting the Moscow Art Theatre with some rich challenges in terms of the complexity and the ingenuity of its structure, the play focused not so much on the genius of Molière as on the difficulties of his personal plight—not just his complicated and possibly scandalous love life, but above all his relations with the Sun King, Louis XIV, and with the deeply reactionary Catholic Church authorities, who regarded Molière's writings as subversive and offensive. This play about the relations between the intellectual and representatives of a repressive ideology inaugurates the theme of the writer in Bulgakov's works. In January 1930 he read his new work to the Moscow Art Theatre, who were thrilled with it; but in March the implacable Repertory Committee (the organ of Soviet censorship) placed yet another ban on his writings by refusing to license the play for performance. On January 16, 1930 Bulgakov wrote to his brother again: "I have neither protection nor help. I am telling you quite soberly: my ship is sinking, the water is rising towards the bridge. It is important to drown with courage. [...] If you have any means of sending me my royalties [for works published or staged in France] I'd ask you to send them: I don't have a single kopek."[8]

This new blow prompted Bulgakov to draft one further letter to Stalin dated 28 March 1930, an even lengthier diatribe than before, listing all his grievances, which he submitted to the authorities on April 2. By now things had begun to turn a great deal nastier on the cultural scene. Over the previous year an organisation of "proletarian" writers (RAPP) had seized the ascendant, and their influence had led to the persecution or banning of many writers who had been able to work in relative freedom during the previous few years. The NEP period inaugurated by Lenin in 1921, and marked by tolerant attitudes in the sphere of culture, had been replaced during 1928–9 by a reassertion of centralised government control in politics and economic life: this was the moment when Stalin, having essentially neutralised potential rivals such as Trotsky, began to establish supreme personal control over the Communist Party and over the nation as a whole. Bulgakov, evidently, still believed that it was possible and appropriate to submit a direct appeal to Stalin, in the hope that an intervention from him might reverse his fortunes. He was also still courageous enough to be quite outspoken:

> To struggle against censorship, of whatever kind, and whatever the government in power, is my duty as a writer, as are calls for freedom of the

press. I am a passionate supporter of that freedom, and I consider that if any writer should think of trying to persuade me that he did not need it, then he would be like a fish declaring in public that it did not need water. [. . .] M[ikhail] Bulgakov BECAME A SATIRIST at precisely the moment when true satire (the kind that penetrates into forbidden areas) has become absolutely unthinkable in the USSR.

He reported that the ban on the Molière play had caused him such despair that he had even destroyed drafts of some of his other projects: "And personally, with my own hands, I threw into the stove *the draft of a novel about the devil* [my italics], the draft of a comedy, and the beginning of a second novel, about theatre."[9] This, then, was the fate of the very first draft of *The Master and Margarita*, which he had been working on intermittently since 1928. Once again he asked to be allowed to leave the country, or else that he should be given the opportunity of some sort of employment in the world of theatre, since all of these bans had left him in such a straitened financial position.

An entirely external event was almost certainly the reason why on this occasion his letter to Stalin did receive a response. Vladimir Mayakovsky, the outstanding Futurist poet who had placed his art at the service of the Bolshevik Revolution, shocked the nation by committing suicide on April 14, 1930. This took place less than a fortnight after Bulgakov had submitted his desperate-sounding letter. Mayakovsky's funeral took place on April 17, and Bulgakov was present at the ceremony when the coffin was removed from the Writers' Club. The Government was very anxious to avoid any further embarrassing scandals taking place in the world of Soviet culture. On the very next day, April 18, 1930, Bulgakov received a personal telephone call at home, from Stalin himself.[10]

During their conversation (and once he had recovered from his overwhelming astonishment at this unheard-of manifestation of the head of state's interest in his affairs), Stalin asked him whether he really wanted to leave the country. Bulgakov was obliged to make a split-second decision, which involved him swiftly weighing up the risky consequences of giving an unacceptable answer. He decided to respond by observing that it was extremely difficult for a Russian writer to thrive outside his native land. He went on to tell Stalin that he had been unable to obtain a job at the Moscow Art Theatre, to which Stalin replied that he should apply again: he felt sure he would be successful this time. Stalin also told Bulgakov that they should meet and speak again, on some future occasion.

This 1930 intervention by Stalin in Bulgakov's fate was one of the most significant events in his life. Firstly, he had declined the opportunity to leave the country when it was apparently being offered: this was a choice he would come to regret, especially when he saw one of his closest friends, the writer Evgeny Zamyatin, leaving for Paris eighteen months later. Secondly, this did indeed lead to him being appointed to a post as an assistant director in the Moscow Art Theatre, which together with other posts of the kind provided him with a basic income during the 1930s. And thirdly, it opened up the prospect of further conversations with Stalin. To the end of his life, Bulgakov would be frustrated by the failure of that hope to materialise. For some years to come he would continue to write occasional letters, continue to believe that Stalin could and might do something to help him and other writers, perhaps even that Stalin did not really know about all the iniquities that were being perpetrated in his name. That hope would of course collapse as the Terror took hold.

The last decade of Bulgakov's life was shaped by further artistic projects such as the writing of further plays, including a biographical drama about the Russian national poet Aleksandr Pushkin, and of various prose works. And late at night, once his other tasks had been completed, he continued to work in secret throughout the 1930s on successive drafts of *The Master and Margarita*. But time and time again, his hopes would be frustrated, after periods when he briefly allowed himself to believe that one of his submitted works might actually reach the stage, or be accepted for publication. Furthermore, the exhilaration of his new liaison with Elena was abruptly interrupted when her husband Evgeny Shilovsky demanded that their relationship should cease—and from late February 1931 until the autumn of 1932 they didn't see each other at all. In April 1932 Bulgakov confessed his utter misery to his close friend Pavel Popov:

> Every night these days I look not ahead, but back, because I cannot see anything for myself in the future. In the past I made five fateful mistakes. Had it not been for them [...], I would be composing works, not by moving my lips soundlessly in my bed at dawn, but as one should do it, sitting at a writing desk. But there is nothing to be done now, you cannot retrieve anything.[11]

Amongst these five undefined "mistakes" that he felt he had made in his life were surely his choice not to emigrate across the Black Sea in 1921, nor again when he was offered the opportunity to do so by Stalin in 1930; and doubtless also his reluctant acceptance of Elena's decision that they should cease their relationship. However, the two of them did finally see each other again on September 1, 1932, and promptly agreed that they simply could not bear to live apart. Shilovsky bowed fairly graciously to the inevitable, and Bulgakov and Elena were married on October 4, 1932, the day after her divorce came through. Their lives together were characterized by great happiness and devotion. Elena's younger son Sergey moved in with them, and Bulgakov proved to be a loving and attentive stepfather. By 1934 they had moved into a larger and more comfortable apartment. From September 1933 Bulgakov insisted that Elena should keep a diary of their lives, a document which has proved an invaluable source of information about the most important phases of the writing of *The Master and Margarita*. "He himself, after his diaries were seized during the search in 1926, swore to himself never again to keep a diary. He finds the thought that a writer's diary could be confiscated appalling, unthinkable."[12]

Elena's diary also provides a discreet chronicle of Stalin's Terror as it unfurled around them, with arrests, trials and executions cutting great swathes through the circle of their acquaintances in the world of literature and the theatre. It was no longer just a question of not being published: a writer who fell into disfavour now risked his liberty, his physical safety, and even his life. On November 17, 1934, for example, a laconic entry in Elena's diary records a visit to them by the poet Anna Akhmatova: "She told us about the bitter fate of Mandel'shtam. We talked about Pasternak."[13] The poet Osip Mandel'shtam's arrest in May 1934—from the same building the Bulgakovs were now living in—and his initial sentence to forced labour on the White Sea Canal had traumatised the world of writers: his "crime" had merely been to write an epigram mocking Stalin. The poet Boris Pasternak had subsequently received a telephone call about Mandel'shtam out of the blue from Stalin, rather as Bulgakov had in 1930. During their conversation Pasternak learned that the sentence had been commuted to internal exile, which meant that Mandel'shtam could be joined by his wife Nadezhda (Mandel'shtam would nevertheless attempt suicide in the bleak town of Cherdyn' in the Urals, to which he was sent). Stalin asked Pasternak about Mandel'shtam's standing as a writer, and Pasternak would forever afterwards feel that he had somehow failed to defend his fellow-poet eloquently enough. Mandel'shtam's wife Nadezhda knew of Akhmatova's visit to the Bulgakovs that November: "Akhmatova went to the Bulgakovs and returned very touched by the reaction of Elena Sergeevna, Bulgakov's wife, who burst into tears when she heard about our exile and gave us everything she had."[14] A year later, in October 1935, Akhmatova would visit them again, in great distress, to seek advice on her own behalf about writing a letter to Stalin after the simultaneous arrests of her son Lev (whose father, the poet Nikolay Gumilev, had been shot by the Bolsheviks in 1921), and of her then husband, Nikolay Punin.[15] In the months after Mandel'shtam's arrest Bulgakov grew fearful, and began to suffer from nervous disorders: for long periods he felt unable to go out into the street unaccompanied. Some sessions of hypnotism eased his distress, and on November 22, 1934 Elena noted in her diary that he had gone out in the evening to visit a friend on his own, having not been outside alone for half a year.[16]

By May 1937, during one of the worst years of mass arrests, he was again in a terrible state and his fearfulness about being out on the streets alone had returned. In the bewildering roulette wheel of the Terror, even some of his former enemies were now being arrested or sacked. These included one of his most vocal opponents in the official literary press, the critic Osaf Litovsky: in *The Master and Margarita* he figures as the critic Latunsky, whose apartment is vengefully destroyed by Margarita. Litovsky lost his post running the censorship in June 1937, and was apparently arrested in early September. "That would really be too good," gloated Elena.[17] People had begun telling Bulgakov that his own prospects might be about to improve, and that he should ask for the bans on his plays to be reviewed, but he was not convinced: "'I won't go to see anybody. I'm not going to ask for anything.'"[18] In June he described to a friend how he and Elena would constantly talk "about one and the same subject—the annihilation of my literary life. We ran through all the options, and there is no means of rescuing it."[19] On October 5, 1937 Bulgakov summed up his recent literary career: "Over the last seven years I have created sixteen works, and every single one of them has perished except one, and that was an adaptation of Gogol'! It would be naïve to imagine that a seventeenth or nineteenth will get staged or published. I am working hard, but without any meaning or sense. Which leaves me in a state of apathy."[20] In these circumstances, his persistence in continuing to work away on his defiantly subversive *Master and Margarita*, unbeknownst to the outside world, seems like a considerable act of courage.

From time to time he would submit applications for himself and Elena to travel abroad, all of which were turned down:

> I have sent in an application for permission to travel abroad during August and September [1934]. I even began to have dreams about the waves on the Mediterranean, and the Paris museums, and a quiet "hôtel," and no acquaintances, and Molière's fountain, and the cafés, and, in brief, the opportunity to see all these things. For ages I've been talking to Lyusya [Bulgakov's pet-name for Elena] about the travelogue I could write. [...] Ah, if only it would come to pass! Then get ready for a new chapter—the most interesting one."[21]

The rejection of his application on this occasion was particularly distressing, since the couple actually saw their two passports for foreign travel lying prepared for them on a desk; but then the collection date was continually deferred, until they were told that permission had not been granted after all. By February 1937 Bulgakov would complain that he had become a prisoner in his own country: "This is a sore point for M[ikhail] A[fanas'evich]: 'I am a prisoner . . . they will never let me out of here . . . I will never see the world.'"[22]

There had been a further "year of catastrophe" for Bulgakov in 1936, when his Molière play, which had eventually been granted a licence for performance, reached the stage after painfully long years of rehearsal by the Moscow Art Theatre. Soon after it received its première—to great acclaim from the audiences who attended the first performances—an editorial on March 9, 1936 in the Communist Party newspaper *Pravda* offered a devastating condemnation of the work. It was described as a bourgeois play, which focused too much on Molière as a fallible individual rather than as a champion of social justice, and which deviated from the precepts of Soviet Socialist Realist drama. This was part of a new and widespread clamp-down in the arts, initiated with similarly destructive attacks on the composer Dmitry Shostakovich in *Pravda* during the preceding two months. Again, as with *Flight*, Bulgakov felt that the Moscow Art Theatre acted with unforgivable haste in immediately cancelling all further performances of his Molière play. Viktor Losev cites an example of a lengthy report to the OGPU on Bulgakov's state of mind after the publication of the *Pravda* article, which was evidently compiled by somebody amongst his circle of acquaintances:

> Quite apart from his bitter disappointment that his play, which had been rehearsed for four and a half years, was taken off after seven performances, he is also alarmed about his future prospects as a writer (another of his plays, *Ivan Vasil'evich*, which was due to be staged any day now by the Satire Theatre, has also been cancelled). He is afraid that theatres will no longer risk staging his plays, and in particular his *Aleksandr Pushkin*, which has already been accepted by the Vakhtangov Theatre. And not least he is preoccupied by the anxiety that he will jeopardise his financial security. [. . .] When my wife said to him that it was fortunate that the reviewers had kept silent about the political implications of his play, he asked with assumed naivety (deliberately): "Are there political implications in the Molière play?," and would say nothing further about it.[23]

And meanwhile their friends were still being arrested around them: Nikolay Lyamin, who had heard some of Bulgakov's private readings of portions of *The Master and Margarita*, was arrested on April 2, 1936 and initially sentenced to twenty-three years in a labor camp. He was allowed to come back in 1939, but still not allowed to live in Moscow, although he courageously visited Bulgakov there in secret during his final illness. Lyamin was arrested again at the beginning of the war and disappeared without trace.[24]

The Days of the Turbins had started to be staged again from the early 1930s, reputedly after Stalin had asked one day in the Theatre—perhaps disingenuously—why it was not currently on. In October 1936 the play marked its tenth anniversary, but the Moscow Art Theatre did nothing whatsoever either to celebrate the occasion or to congratulate the author. By then Bulgakov had in any case resigned from the assistant director post he had been awarded there after Stalin's 1930 phone call, and the final years of his life were spent instead working for the Bol'shoi Theatre. Here he made many new friends amongst the theatre's artistic directors, conductors and composers. His work editing and redrafting opera libretti was sometimes tedious, but he found it something of a relief to turn towards the world of music. And after all, works of art with few or no words could offer a less risky genre to work with than text-based drama in these dangerous years.

Bulgakov's friends and colleagues at the Moscow Art Theatre, however, still knew that he was uniquely gifted amongst contemporary playwrights, and in the late summer of 1938 their literary adviser Pavel Markov and others sought him out, frankly acknowledging the justice of his reproaches to them for his previous treatment at their hands. Even so, when it came to the Art Theatre's own fortieth anniversary celebrations that autumn, Markov would have an article published in *Pravda* in which he failed even to mention Bulgakov or his play *The Days of the Turbins* when listing Soviet-era authors, despite the fact that the play had been running for twelve years and been performed over 800 times, far more than any other Soviet drama they had staged.[25] Bulgakov's situation was becoming painfully surreal, as cultural circles seemed to be blanking out his very existence, whereas more pliable writers received medals, awards and financial bonuses. However, in December 1939 Stalin was due to celebrate his sixtieth birthday, and cultural institutions would be expected to devise new works to celebrate Stalin's achievements. Bulgakov's erstwhile colleagues from the Art Theatre had therefore come to him in the summer of 1938 to implore him to write the play they needed, a play about Stalin himself. After considerable initial reluctance, he agreed to take on the project: it offered him an opportunity to reflect on the political figure who had played such an important role in his own destiny as well as in the nation's history. Perhaps too it would become, at last, a play that would reach the stage. In his play *Batum* Bulgakov chose to write about the very beginnings of Stalin's revolutionary career, the years when he embarked on underground subversive activity after he had been thrown out of his school. This was a shrewd decision, as it meant Bulgakov could avoid talking about the ideologically tricky subject of Stalin's later role as a mature political leader alongside Lenin. The play manages not to be too obsequious, but paints a portrait in a fairly realistic style of Stalin's youthful charisma, as he outwits the Tsarist authorities and rallies the working people to the socialist cause. After Bulgakov's draft had received an enthusiastic response on a first reading, he and Elena were commissioned by the Moscow Art Theatre to take a trip south to the Caucasus in August 1939, to visit the town of Batum with the production team. This was a town he of course knew from his previous visit there in 1921, when he was thinking of emigrating. Shortly after they had set off, however, they received a telegram on the train summoning them back to Moscow: word had been received from the Kremlin that Stalin had after all decided against the play being staged.

As they drove back to Moscow, deeply apprehensive about what awaited them there, Bulgakov began to feel physically ill, and found it difficult to bear any bright light. Later in 1939, while they were visiting Leningrad to try and distract themselves from their now apparently hopeless plight, he realised that he was losing his sight. A conversation with a doctor confirmed his fears that he was succumbing to the same disease, malignant nephrosclerosis, which had carried his father off at such a young age. During his final months, and despite great physical suffering, Bulgakov continued to dictate to Elena alterations to *The Master and Margarita*. In his final days, and as he sank into delirium, Elena, believing that she could understand what he was trying to ask of her, made him a solemn promise that she would devote herself to the task of preserving his work and ensuring that the novel eventually got published. Mikhail Bulgakov died on March 10, 1940. Elena fulfilled her promise, assembling and maintaining Bulgakov's archive until over a quarter of a century later when, after she had survived the traumas of the Second World War as well as the later phases of Stalin's Terror, she eventually got it published. Its first, truncated publication came about a full twenty-six years after the author's death, when the journal *Moskva* published significant portions of *The Master and Margarita* late in 1966 and at the beginning of 1967.

CHAPTER 3

Drafts of *The Master and Margarita*

Given the difficulties of Bulgakov's personal life, and the frustrations of his public career as a writer in Stalin's Russia from the late 1920s onwards, it is scarcely surprising that the writing of his greatest novel—completed in conditions of deep secrecy, and over the course of more than a decade—became a far from straightforward task. Between 1928 and 1940, the writing was interrupted, and even abandoned at times, due to his personal crises, fearfulness about the danger of arrest, the demands on his time of other commissions and work, and eventually, grave illness. As Lesley Milne observes: "It is little short of miraculous that such a great comic novel should have been conceived and brought to completion in the Soviet Union in the 1930s. [...] Bulgakov alone remained merrily, anarchically, wickedly, seriously funny *on paper* throughout a decade when a verbal joke could cost physical freedom and life itself."[1]

In this chapter we will examine the evidence reflecting the development of the plot and structure of *The Master and Margarita* over a period of twelve years: this evidence is constituted by successive drafts, the precise categorisation of which has itself been a matter for scholarly disagreement as the archives in Russia have gradually opened up. These various drafts (or fragments of drafts) have been preserved in the archives thanks to the persistence and dedication of Bulgakov's widow Elena, as well as that of a number of his friends. As we have already seen, the publication of the novel in Soviet Russia after the author's death in 1940 was exceptionally delayed: substantial excerpts first appeared in the journal *Moskva* only in 1966 and 1967, and the full text appeared for the first time in the author's native country only in 1973. This is one factor significantly complicating the task of establishing a definitive text of the work. Elena's role in this story is absolutely crucial, both because of the personal testimony she could provide about the different stages of the novel's composition, and because of her own editorial role in finalising the text—not to mention her courageous efforts over more than a quarter century, both to preserve the material and to campaign for her husband's literary achievements not to be forgotten. Very few scholars—Marietta Chudakova of the Moscow Lenin Library's Manuscript Department being foremost amongst them—were able to interview Elena and record her account of the novel's evolution before the widow's own death in 1970. We are fortunate, therefore, that some written evidence contemporaneous with the composition of the novel has also survived: a few comments in Bulgakov's letters to friends, and Elena's diary entries from 1933 onwards, as well as the brief notes she kept during his final illness in 1939–40.

We should also bear in mind the fact that even after the novel had been published in a complete version in 1973 the Soviet authorities maintained a very cautious attitude towards full disclosure of materials relating to Bulgakov, clearly nervous of revealing the range and biting sharpness of his satirical responses to the Communist regime. For some fifteen years after the full publication of *The Master and Margarita*, and even as occasional further publications of his works continued to foster a cult following of him amongst Russian readers, access to his archives remained very strictly controlled, and actually became something to be struggled over. The rivalry and hostilities between Soviet-era scholars such as Marietta Chudakova, Lidiya Yanovskaya, and Viktor Losev persisted during the 1970s and 1980s, and beyond. But the late Soviet cultural policy of *glasnost'*, inaugurated by Mikhail Gorbachev from 1985 onwards, saw the long-awaited publication of certain other controversial texts by Bulgakov which had continued to be banned in Russia even though they had been available abroad for years in émigré publications, such as *Heart of a Dog* (first published in the USSR in 1987) and the play *Batum* (first published in the USSR in 1988). Archival access began to be freer, and to be regulated in a more open fashion: and some foreign scholars were also at last granted permission to work on the main Bulgakov archive in the Lenin Library's Manuscript Department.

This problematic context for the first decades of textual scholarship after the publication of Bulgakov's *Master and Margarita* led to a situation where different specialists began to affirm different schemes for understanding the history of the work's composition, and it remained very difficult to evaluate their competing claims. Certainly the publication of fairly full "complete editions" of Bulgakov's works has been very helpful. These include: the five-volume edition of Bulgakov's works published in 1989–90 (Moscow: Khudozhestvennaya Literatura), with the text of *The Master and Margarita* prepared by Lidiya Yanovskaya; and Viktor Losev's "full edition of the drafts and variants of the novel"

(Moscow: Vagrius, 2006), reprinted in his eight-volume complete edition of Bulgakov's works (St. Petersburg: Azbuka, 2011–13). Unlike the original publications of the novel, these editions have additionally offered the possibility of reading some of the earlier drafts of the text. However, 2014 then saw the publication of a weighty two-volume "full collection of the drafts of the novel" in an excellent and measured scholarly edition by Elena Kolysheva, based on over ten years' careful examination of all the available archival sources. This large-format edition, running to more than 1,600 pages, was published in Moscow by the Russian State Library (formerly Lenin Library)'s imprint Pashkov Dom, and immediately became a much sought-after bibliographical rarity, especially since the initial print run was of only 300 copies. Fortunately, there has been at least one reprint since that time. The Kolysheva edition, and her analysis of the competing accounts of the evolution of *The Master and Margarita*, can be regarded as definitive, and I will draw extensively upon it in my description below.

The publishers' introduction to the Kolysheva volumes reminds us that there are essentially two different versions of the novel in Russian which are still widely in circulation: the original one established by Anna Saakyants for the first full publication by Khudozhestvennaya Literatura in 1973, and a second version, originally published by Lidiya Yanovskaya in 1989.[2] Kolysheva's 2014 investigation seeks to analyse the drafts in such a way as to establish a version which—as far as possible—corresponds to the author's intentions, and it is this "definitive" version which she offers the reader in the second volume of her publication. She attempts to clarify several issues, ranging from the precise number of drafts of the text, to the "myth"—as she calls it—of the supposed disappearance or theft from the archive of a notebook containing one draft; or indeed the more prosaic question as to whether the protagonist Ivan's surname should be pronounced Pónyryev or Ponyryëv (she finds evidence to support the latter pronunciation).[3] There have been different schemes proposed by Chudakova and by Yanovskaya respectively for understanding the number of actual drafts for the novel—in Chudakova's case, in two studies dating to 1976, concluding that the novel had eight drafts;[4] while Yanovskaya, in a more recent 1991 study, considers that the text had six drafts.[5] Kolysheva's own conclusion is closer to that of Yanovskaya's, since she too suggests that there were six drafts, although she differs in her evaluation of certain supplementary notebooks and their significance in this scheme.[6] The factual basis for the following account of the evolution of the text is thus the scheme proposed by Kolysheva.[7]

FIRST DRAFT OF THE NOVEL (1928–30)

The start date for the first draft of the novel (1928–30) was confirmed in ret-rospect by Bulgakov, when he recorded the dates of its composition on later drafts of the text in 1937 and in 1937–8. We know that in the second half of the 1920s he had begun to plan a novel which would be inspired by the memory of his theologian father, rather than the image of his mother which had suffused and nuanced *The White Guard.* And we have already seen that in his well-known letter to the Soviet Government of March 28, 1930, in which he requested per-mission to leave the country, he explicitly described the work he had begun to write over the previous two years—and had recently burnt—as "a novel about the devil."[8] This distressing action apparently took place on March 18, 1930, the date when the shattering letter arrived from the Repertory Committee to inform him that his Molière play had not been licensed for performance at the Moscow Art Theatre.[9] The act of artistic self-harm is subsequently echoed in the novel itself, when the Master recounts to Ivan how he similarly tore up the notebooks containing his own much criticised novel and stuffed them into the stove, discovering as he did it that notebooks burn less easily than you might expect (chapter 13). Readers of Russian literature would immediately recog-nise that Bulgakov was consciously aligning himself here with the notorious action of Nikolay Gogol', who threw drafts of the projected second and third volumes of his novel *Dead Souls* into the fire at a moment of great personal dis-tress in 1852, just days before his death.[10]

Two notebooks have in fact survived the flames to offer us a glimpse of this first draft of Bulgakov's novel, although they have been very significantly damaged as well as having a large number of pages torn out. In 1977 Marietta Chudakova made an ambitious and fairly convincing attempt to recreate parts of the text using her scholarly intuition, and based upon a close knowledge of the later drafts. However, this undertaking has been scathingly criticised by her rival Lidiya Yanovskaya.[11]

In 1928–30 the novel apparently carried the title *The Engineer's Hoof,* and it opens with some extraordinary events taking place in Moscow, which a first-person narrator attempts to report to the police authorities. At an early stage the draft carried the subtitle "A Fantastical Novel."[12] In the opening scene involving a conversation between two writers, Berlioz has different first names, Ivan a dif-ferent surname from the later versions; but they do meet a wizard of the dark arts at Patriarchs' Ponds, and he tells them the story of Ieshua and Pilate, and of the crucifixion as well. This narrative was described with the chapter title "The

Gospel according to the Devil." However, at this stage the language and idioms used for the ancient world episode belong to the discourse of modern-day, post-Revolutionary Moscow.[13] The death of Berlioz, after which Ivan pursues the wizard and ends up in the sanatorium, is followed by a scene in a writers' club. A fourth chapter, dropped from subsequent versions, describes Berlioz's funeral. The scenes which follow involve prototypes of the hapless housing committee chairman Bosoy, and then of Likhodeev, Rimsky, and Varenukha, all members of the administration of what will become the Variety Theatre. There is also a significant character called Fesya, a man who is a learned scholar, but who shares few of the Master's eventual traits.[14] Chapter drafts which have survived in full include the interrogation of the Bosoy character, the misadventures of the manager of the theatre buffet, and the difficulties faced by Rimsky and Varenukha after the performance at the Variety Theatre. The second of the two surviving notebooks representing the novel's first draft contains variants of the previously drafted chapters. The first chapter, for example, unfolds with many of the details which survived into later versions. Towards the end of it, the stranger is asked whether he personally has seen Jesus, to which he responds by making a gesture representing a swallow flying; and at the start of his narrative he exclaims "This did happen!"[15]

One chapter which was worked up in some detail and given the heading "Mania furibunda" ["Raging madness"] was the chapter containing the satire of the writers' club, and describing Ivan being taken to the sanatorium. It also carried a proverbial epigraph in Latin: "Quos vult perdere Jupiter, dementat . . ." ["Those whom Jupiter wishes to destroy, he [first] drives mad . . ."]. Yanovskaya notes that the date of the action here is indicated as taking place some time after 1933 (a monument to a poet from the writers' club recalls his having died in 1933 from eating contaminated sturgeon); in other words, the novel at this stage involves a projection by Bulgakov into the near future, an attempt to anticipate how trends in contemporary Soviet society will develop.[16] Bulgakov actually offered this chapter for publication in an anthology at this time, submitting it under the pseudonym K. Tugay to the Nedra publishing house which had previously printed his stories *Diaboliad* and *The Fateful Eggs*, but he received no response.[17] This was the only attempt he made in his own lifetime to show the novel to anyone outside his immediate circle of family and friends, a few of whom did hear extracts from the text even at this early stage.

As Kolysheva concludes, this first draft is notable for being incomplete: it is primarily a satire on contemporary reality, and in this respect derives stylistically from his Moscow sketches and short stories of the very early 1920s; but it also contains some of his reflections about God and the devil. This version carries much more in the way of corrections and alterations than subsequent versions do.

One rather remarkable document which has emerged from the archives in the post-Soviet era confirms that the authorities were aware of the novel's existence even from the very beginning. This was a report by an unnamed man in Bulgakov's circle of acquaintants, submitted to the OGPU in 1928, which stated:

> I saw Nekrasova, and she told me that M[ikhail] Bulgakov had written a novel which he had read aloud to a certain group of people, who had told him that it would not be allowed to be published in its present form, since he was being very outspoken in his attacks; and so he had rewritten it and was thinking of publishing it, but at the same time he was going to circulate the original version to people in manuscript, and this would be at the same time as publishing it in a version which had been hacked about by the censors.[18]

In other words, it was already being suggested to the authorities not just that he had written something controversial, but also that he was contemplating disseminating it in an unauthorised manner. The OGPU must surely have kept an eye on subsequent developments.

NOTEBOOKS DATING FROM 1929–31 AND 1931

After the burning of the first draft in March 1930, Bulgakov returned to the project and worked on it intermittently, which is reflected in two further notebooks dating from 1929–31 and 1931 respectively. In Kolysheva's view, these do not in fact amount to a second draft. In the first notebook the chapter set at the writers' club (here called "Griboedov's Hut") and in the sanatorium is written out in full. In this notebook, and then in the second one, containing another tidied-up variant of the same chapter, the action is projected forward even further into the future than in the first draft, firstly to June 1943, and then to June 1945. In considering the specific date of June 14, 1943 for the concluding, quasi-apocalyptic events of the novel, Bulgakov may have been consciously mapping them on to the date predicted for the end of the world by the sixteenth-century astrologer Nostradamus.[19] The second notebook also contains sketches for a new chapter, "Woland's Flight," in which for the first time the figures of Margarita and of the

Master appear as fully developed characters: indeed, the ancient-world story has become a first-person narrative in the Master's voice. This version suggests that the story does end in a kind of cataclysmic collapse of the modern era in Moscow, with scenes of fire, death and destruction, people wearing gas masks, and air battles involving dirigibles.[20] Viktor Losev suggests that the entire plot of the novel was clear to Bulgakov at this point, and that only his physical and psychological weariness during his period of enforced separation from Elena in 1931–2 prevented him from completing it. This manuscript bears Bulgakov's handwritten words "Lord, help me to finish the novel. 1931."[21]

SECOND DRAFT OF THE NOVEL (1932–6)

Between 1932 and 1936 Bulgakov wrote a second, now complete draft of *The Master and Margarita* in seven notebooks. This was clearly associated with his great happiness after his marriage to Elena in October 1932, and especially during and after a trip he took with her to Leningrad in July 1933. On August 2, 1933 he described his renewed sense of inspiration to his friend Vikenty Veresaev: "A demon has taken me over. Starting in Leningrad, and now, stifling in my cramped rooms, I have begun to scrawl afresh page after page of that novel I destroyed three years ago."[22] Here and there, certain portions of the draft text have been removed with scissors. At this point he was considering a number of possible titles for the work, including "The Great Chancellor," "Satan," "The Hat with the Feather," "The Black Theologian," "He Has Appeared," "The Foreigner's Horseshoe," and "Fantastical Novel," as well as "Here I Am!" (*"Me voici!"* is the phrase Mephistopheles uses when he is first conjured to appear by Faust in Gounod's opera. This is normally translated into Russian using the same wording as here: «Вот и я!») The characters of Margarita and of a poet—named Faust at this stage—figure in this version.[23]

Bulgakov was also refining the structure of the text, and wrote out the sequence of chapters more than once: one of these outlines was dated October 6, 1933, and still had the events taking place in the month of June (rather than in May, as subsequently). One notable feature of this version is that Woland's narrative of the encounter between Pilate and Ieshua does not figure near the beginning of the novel, but is held back until chapter 10, when he appears to Ivan in the sanatorium. Another feature of this version is that Margarita's lover is retrieved by Woland's associates from a location which is unambiguously a Soviet labour camp, situated somewhere in a cold region, and he appears before Woland wearing rough clothes and in an unkempt physical state.[24] Between mid-September and mid-October 1933 Bulgakov read some portions of the novel which he had recently been working on to half-a dozen or more different friends, including the poet Akhmatova, the writer Vikenty Veresaev, his close friend Pavel Popov and his wife (Tolstoy's grand-daughter), and Elena's sister Ol'ga Bokshanskaya and her husband, who were both attached to the Moscow Art Theatre.[25] On October 12, 1933, however, Elena recorded in her diary the news that their friends, the playwrights Nikolay Erdman and Vladimir Mass, had been arrested for some satirical pieces they had written. Bulgakov "frowned," and that night he again burned part of his manuscript, presumably apprehensive that word of what he had been writing might get out.[26] In December 1933 an acquaintance invited Bulgakov to work with him on a rather different project, "a 'beautiful' theme—about the re-education of thugs in the labour colonies run by the OGPU." Bulgakov "suavely" refused.[27]

He had found that he worked well on the novel on his visits to Leningrad in 1932 and 1933, and he did so again in the summer of 1934, when he was there with the Moscow Art Theatre: "Oh, I have a lot of work to do. But in my head my Margarita is wandering about, and the cat, and flying . . ."[28] He wrote particularly intensively for 5 days, from July 12–16, as attested by the dates on the manuscripts. In a new notebook he wrote on the first page: "Novel. Ending. (Leningrad, July 1934)."[29] During the last week of September 1934 he was working on the penultimate and final chapters of the novel, entitled at this point "Night" and "Final Journey."[30] That autumn Bulgakov also wrote the chapter called "A Golden Spear."[31] This manuscript bears the handwritten words alongside the date "30.X.34": "To be finished before I die!"[32] There were further reviews of the numbering and titles of the chapters, one no later than October 30, 1934, and another no later than July 1, 1935, and possibly again by July 22, 1935, as indicated by the dates which he starts to enter now into the notebooks.[33] Bulgakov redrafts earlier sections or writes new ones, whilst also listing scenes that are still to come in the briefest of outlines. Likhodeev is transported in this version not to Yalta in the Crimea as in the published text, but to Vladikavkaz in the Caucasus, where Bulgakov had spent time during the Civil War. For the first time the narrative about Ershalaim is shifted away from Woland as being the sole and exclusive source for it: a fragment of the story about the crucifixion is presented as coming from a novel written by the Master. In July 1936 Bulgakov writes chapter 32, now called "The Final Flight." Kolysheva argues that this draft is the one that will shape all the ones that follow.

It should be noted that Yanovskaya differs here from Kolysheva's account. She believes there to have been a second, distinct draft of 1932–4 (and a separate third draft, correspondingly), in which the Ershalaim chapters were intended to be present, but where they did not as yet appear. She is very critical of Viktor Losev for publishing this in 1992 as a full draft by adding in the "Golden Spear" chapter from the following draft (the third draft according to Yanovskaya's system), and for elevating the phrase "The Great Chancellor" to the status of a possible title for the work.[34]

THIRD DRAFT OF THE NOVEL (1936)

The third draft of the novel (1936) was started no earlier than July 6, 1936 (a date which appears in a notebook from the previous draft), and was completed no later than 1937. The opening three chapters of *The Master and Margarita* appear here in a version which is very close to the final text. Other chapter titles are followed by blank pages, or by incomplete texts. Kolysheva suggests that the fact that the notebook's pages have been numbered indicates that Bulgakov originally intended to write this draft straight through from beginning to end.

FOURTH DRAFT OF THE NOVEL (1937)

That plan is partially achieved in the fourth draft of the novel (1937), to which Bulgakov provisionally gives the title "Prince of Darkness," and which also records the fact that the novel has been being drafted from 1928 up until 1937. Two notebooks with continuously numbered pages contain the first thirteen chapters of the novel, structured as in the final text, but still with some variations in chapter titles and in other details (Likhodeev still ends up in Vladikavkaz rather than Yalta). The narrative breaks off during the Master's story to Ivan about Margarita.[35] Bulgakov began reading this draft to some of his friends during May 1937, especially the stage designers Vladimir Dmitriev, and Petr Vil'yams and his wife, who described it as "a work of enormous power, interesting in its philosophy, as well as being entertaining in its plot and brilliant from a literary point of view."[36]

During 1937, that most terrible year of the Terror, Bulgakov and Elena received a number of visitors whose good intentions they somewhat doubted, such as Emmanuil Zhukhovitsky. They observed his behaviour and pestering with dismay: "... the full range: questioning, lying, and provocations. M[ikhail] A[fanas'evich] kept going off into his room to observe the moon through his binoculars, for the novel. There's a full moon at present."[37] There was also a young actor from the Moscow Art Theatre, Grisha Konsky, who kept pressing Bulgakov to read him "some of the novel about Woland":

> Konsky rang and said he was missing us, and could he come round? He came, but behaved strangely. When M[ikhail] A[fanas'evich] went to the telephone Grisha went into the study, walked over to the desk, took a scrapbook out of it and started looking through it, examined the desk in detail, and even tried to look inside an envelope full of cards that was lying on the desk. A right Bitkov [the police spy in Bulgakov's play about Pushkin].[38]

The autumn of 1937 was a period when Bulgakov was feeling rather desperate, toying with the idea of leaving the Bol'shoi Theatre, and unable to decide what would be the best course of action: "Tormenting attempts to think of a way out: a letter to the authorities [that is, Stalin]? Abandoning the theatre? Finish revising the novel and send it in? There is nothing to be done. It's a hopeless situation. During the day we went out on a river steamer—it settles the nerves. The weather was lovely."[39] In December 1937 Bulgakov started reading parts of the novel to his great friend the playwright Nikolay Erdman (who sneaked into Moscow to stay with them even though he had been officially sentenced to internal exile), and to Erdman's brother Boris, another stage designer.

FIFTH DRAFT OF THE NOVEL (1937–8)

The fifth draft of the novel (1937–8)—the revision mentioned above—is a complete draft contained in six notebooks with continuous page numbering, and with a concluding date of May 22–3, 1938. There is one additional notebook with materials for the text and the most up-to-date outline of the sequence of chapters. For the first time the novel is divided into two parts. In October 1937 Elena first refers to the novel in her diary as *The Master and Margarita*, and she confirms on 1 March 1938 that Bulgakov has now settled upon that title: "There is no hope of it being printed. And all the same M[ikhail] A[fanas'evich] is revising it, pressing ahead, and he wants to finish during March. He's working at night."[40] The section about Ieshua's crucifixion is now presented as Ivan's dream, whereas Pilate's conversation with Afranius and the murder of Judas now figure as part of the Master's novel. Particular attention is paid to the transitions into and out of the historical narrative, so that the final sentence of the preceding chapter also becomes the first sentence of each section of the Ershalaim story, and vice versa.

One new chapter is introduced, the story of Satan's ball. Yanovskaya points out that amongst the guests at the ball at this point were both Goethe and Gounod, the original sources of Bulgakov's Faustian intertexts. They are followed up the staircase by a character who is much more obviously recognisable in his facial features than he will be in later versions, as the disgraced head of the secret police (NKVD), Genrikh Yagoda, whose show trial began early in March 1938, and who is described here as "a great friend" of Woland's Abadonna, the exterminating angel.[41] The episode where Woland contemplates the city from the terrace of a beautiful building (the well-known Pashkov House, which overlooks the Kremlin) does not as yet include the arrival of the emissary from Ieshua, Matthew the Levite, to plead for the Master and Margarita's fate. During the spring of 1938 Bulgakov continued to read parts of the novel to Erdman and Vil'yams, but also to some medical acquaintances, one of the artistic directors of the Bol'shoi, another of his writer friends, and a journal editor. By now Bulgakov may have had little hope of the work being published, but he was determined that it should receive a hearing, at least amongst people whose opinion he valued. And it becomes impossible to believe that the existence of the novel remained a complete secret from the authorities in these circumstances.

SIXTH DRAFT OF THE NOVEL (1938–40)

The final handwritten draft of the novel—the fifth draft—had been completed, as we have seen, on May 22–3, 1938. The sixth draft of the novel (1938–40) is essentially represented by the typed version of the text dictated to Ol'ga Bokshanskaya, Elena's sister, during the summer of 1938: as a very skilled typist, who held a senior position in the Moscow Art Theatre administration, she completed the task within a month, on 24 June 1938. Bulgakov found her complete lack of interest in the actual novel somewhat irksome. The progress of this whole undertaking is entertainingly reflected in the letters he wrote to Elena, who—in a rare period of separation from her husband—was away with her son Sergey taking a holiday in the small town of Lebedyan', some distance to the south of Moscow. He made some changes and occasionally added new material as he went along. On June 2, 1938 he wrote to Elena: "The novel must be finished. Now! Now!"[42] But even as he was dictating, he was conscious that further revision would be required. By June 15 the work had been going well:

> 327 typed pages are lying in front of me (about 22 chapters). If I can keep healthy, the typing will be finished soon. And then the most important

thing still remains—the authorial editing, which will be extensive, complex, and attentive, and may involve the retyping of certain pages. 'And what will come of it?' you ask? I don't know. Probably you will put it away in a desk or a cupboard, where my murdered plays already lie, and occasionally you will remember about it. Although we don't know our own future. I have already formed my own judgment of this piece, and if I succeed in raising the ending a little more, I will consider that the thing is worth correcting, and worth putting away into the darkness of a drawer. At present I am interested in your judgment of it, and as to whether I will ever know the judgment of readers, nobody knows. My admired typist has greatly assisted me in ensuring that my judgment of the thing should be as stern as possible. In the course of 327 pages she smiled just once, at page 245 ("Glorious Sea". . .) [the scene where Woland's assistant magically compels a group of people to sing in unison]. Why precisely that should have amused her, I don't know. And I'm not sure whether she will succeed in tracking down some sort of main theme in the novel, but on the other hand I am confident that full disapproval of this thing on her part is guaranteed. This found expression in the following enigmatic phrase: "This novel is your own private business." (?!) By that she probably meant that she was not to blame![43]

This is, incidentally, the same letter to Elena in which Bulgakov prophetically characterises *The Master and Margarita* rather poignantly as his "final, sunset novel."[44]

This, the first actual typescript of the work, was then further annotated at various points between 1938 and 1940. Bulgakov had a notebook in which he himself wrote variants of the beginning of the first chapter, and of the Epilogue; there is also another notebook in which Elena wrote down variants of different parts of the novel under Bulgakov's dictation; and in 1939–40 Elena typed the novel out again, to create a revised typescript of the text.

According to Elena's diary, Bulgakov sat down to begin his revision of the sixth draft on 19 September 1938. Shortly afterwards he received the visit from his friends at the Moscow Art Theatre who wanted him to write the play about Stalin (*Batum*) for them, which may have distracted his attention away from *The Master and Margarita* for a while. During their visit Bulgakov read them the first three chapters of the novel. Subsequent references to this process of revision reappear in her diary only on February 28, 1939, and throughout March of that year. The actor Grisha Konsky was still pestering to hear the novel:

Misha said he would read him a scene from *Don Quixote* [Bulgakov's 1938 stage adaptation] instead. He read, and Konsky listened, and praised it. But it was clear that it wasn't *Don Quixote* he was interested in. And as he left he again began to ask if he could have the novel, if only for a single night. Misha didn't give it to him."[45]

But he did continue a series of readings for a group of his friends, who were enormously enthusiastic: "Over supper Misha was saying: so I'll submit it, so it can be published. Everyone giggled shamefacedly."[46] A few days later he read them the ending of the novel: "For some reason they froze as they listened to the final chapters. Everything frightened them. Pasha [Pavel Markov from the Moscow Art Theatre] was fearful, and out in the corridor he was trying to persuade me that under no circumstances should he submit it: there could be dreadful consequences."[47]

During May 1939 Bulgakov created new versions of the fates of both the Master and Margarita (in fact the published versions of the text still retain two different and conflicting accounts of their deaths), and of the finale of the very last chapter (32). At this point he also added the Epilogue recounting the confusion in Moscow after the Master and Margarita have departed, which, as Lesley Milne has pointed out, "instead of 'raising' the end of the novel, as Bulgakov had intended in June 1938, brings it back from visionary flight down to the muddles and incompleteness of life."[48] He dictated the alterations to Elena, who inserted additional sheets into the annotated typescript. This phase of work was completed on May 14, 1939. However, he was constantly struggling to find time to revise the novel further, as his obligations working at the Bol'shoi Theatre, correcting and redrafting opera libretti, consumed so much of his time and energy. And according to his friend Sergey Ermolinsky Bulgakov remained dissatisfied with the final sections, which continued to trouble him to the very end: "'There are places where it drags, some things which are unnecessary, and one or two important things which have been left out,' he would say, turning over the pages from time to time. But he was weary, very weary. And not just weary: he was already ill." Ermolinsky also tells us that this was when the enigmatic phrase which determines the Master's destiny was added to the text: "He has not deserved the light, he has deserved peace."[49]

In August 1939 came the catastrophe of the banning of his play about Stalin, *Batum*; and during a visit to Leningrad that September Bulgakov realised that he had fallen seriously ill. They hastily returned to Moscow. On September 26 Elena noted: "His gaze, turned deeply inwards. Thoughts about death, about the novel, about the play, about a revolver."[50] For several days he lacked the energy to work on the novel, although he asked her to take it out and to read extracts to him. But from 4 October 1939 he began to dictate new variants of certain phrases and episodes, which Elena took down in a new notebook. On October 17, 1939 she took delivery of a new American typewriter, but unfortunately, it was not easy to use at first.[51] He managed to keep working on the text up until November 9. His sister Nadya visited him at this time and found him "wearing his black Master's cap on his head."[52] Bulgakov persisted with the task of revision through until the end of the year, and on into 1940: "Misha, to the extent that his strength will permit him, is making corrections to the novel, and I am copying them down."[53] Visitors such as Ermolinsky and Bulgakov's youngest sister Elena came to read sections from time to time. The final mention of work on the novel comes on February 13, less than a month before his death on March 10, 1940.[54]

Kolysheva has undertaken an analysis of the various alterations which were made to the Bokshanskaya typescript between 1938 and 1940, which sometimes involve the correction of dictation or typing errors, or elsewhere certain alterations changing or reinstating moments from earlier versions. Sometimes, purple ink is used, elsewhere red or blue pencil. All of these tend to reflect intermittent rather than systematic revision, and it is particularly difficult to draw definitive conclusions about them. However, Kolysheva's careful tabulation of the variants in the second volume of her publication provide the reader with the clearest possible information about potential alternative readings.

Kolysheva argues that publications of the draft up until her own new version in 2014 have suffered from a number of errors in transcription; have not shown the dynamic transformation of the text through authorial amendments; and that preceding editors have failed to take into account the copy of the 1938 typescript which bears annotations made between 1938 and 1940. Viktor Losev, for example, in his 2006 publication of the drafts of the novel, is reproached for having occasionally combined together text from successive drafts to create what amounts to his own compilation. Kolysheva lists a number of his blatant misreadings, or omissions of words; and she points out that he has failed to understand, evidently, that a number of apparent errors of Russian grammar in the strange visitor's speech in chapter 1 in the second draft of the novel were put there deliberately, to represent linguistic mistakes he was making as a foreigner.[55] In her own edition Kolysheva has used a range of annotations to indicate insertions and crossings out of various types: whether Elena or Bulgakov made the amendments, and what colour of pen or pencil they used;

page and paragraph breaks; and places where Bulgakov used spellings of certain common words that were current in his own time but have now become obsolete (*galstukh* for *galstuk*; *chort* for *chërt* etc.). She notes that Bulgakov most typically made corrections as he went along, during the process of writing, so that crossings out are immediately succeeded by a different word, rather than subsequent corrections being inserted above or alongside a crossing out. All of these factors, she argues, have needed to be reviewed before a conclusive version of the text can be proposed on the basis of the various materials which constitute the sixth draft of the text.

In offering us her own "final" version of the text, Kolysheva argues that the two published versions currently in circulation (Saakyants, 1973 and Yanovskaya, 1989) are both seriously in need of review. She proposes Bulgakov's sixth draft as the most suitable basis for a definitive version, that is, the Bokshanskaya typescript modified by the various corrections, amendments and supplementary materials which she feels constitute part of the same basic draft. In particular she feels that the retyped version of the text created by Elena in 1939–40 has not been sufficiently taken into account by scholars, perhaps because the three extant copies of it found their way not into the state literary archives, but into the family archives of two of Bulgakov's sisters (Nadya and Elena), and into the archive of his close friend Pavel Popov. Each of these three owners made his or her own separate corrections (spellings, punctuation, grammar) to the typescript.[56] This later typescript (in its three variants) was therefore not readily available for earlier editors of the novel to consult alongside the various drafts in the main Bulgakov archive in the Lenin Library. His sister Nadya then created a further typescript on the basis of the one she possessed, which found its way into the archive of the literary editor and critic Evdoksiya Nikitina.[57] In all these versions the final chapter (chapter 32) concludes with Margarita's promise to safeguard the sleep of the Master, and it is only the Epilogue which concludes with the words about "the fifth Procurator of Judaea, the horseman Pontius Pilate."[58]

Kolysheva notes that a remark made by Elena to Marietta Chudakova, to the effect that Bulgakov broke off the corrections to the text at the point where Berlioz's funeral procession is being described (chapter 19), is accurate in respect of the handwritten amendments Bulgakov's wife was making to the 1938 Bokshanskaya typescript. But Kolysheva's evaluation of the typescript created by Elena in 1939–40 leads her to conclude that that part of her work on that version which was undertaken while Bulgakov was still alive extends just a little bit further, right up to the very end of that same chapter. She also argues that the disregarded retyping of the novel in 1939–40 explains the discrepancies between the 1938 version and the later (1963) version Elena prepared for publication, and that the speculation offered by Chudakova and Yanovskaya to the effect that one source of the text had been purloined from the archives or mislaid is therefore without foundation.[59] She surmises that Elena made a start on the retyping of the novel after Bulgakov had returned from a period spent having treatment in a sanatorium at Barvikhi, in the second half of December 1939: the first explicit reference to this retyping in Elena's "Notes on his illness" is dated December 25, 1939. Apparently, the last date when Bulgakov worked on the text was in February 1940.[60]

In the grief-stricken weeks which followed Bulgakov's death in March 1940, Elena could not bring herself to continue the retyping. However, with time she found the strength to start again, and the typing of this version was certainly completed well before June 1941, by the time of Hitler's invasion of the USSR and the beginning of Soviet military involvement in the Second World War. Bulgakov's niece Elena Zemskaya, later to become a distinguished Professor of Linguistics as well as the chronicler of Bulgakov's family history, recalled being given the typescript to read by her mother Nadya before they were evacuated at the end of 1941. Elena was herself evacuated to Tashkent, and during 1941–3 she gave the novel to a number of people to read. Amongst those who read or were made aware of the novel at this time were the film directors Sergey Eisenstein and Vsevolod Pudovkin, Nadezhda, widow of the poet Osip Mandel'shtam, and several writers, including Margarita Aliger, and Anna Akhmatova, who proclaimed Bulgakov to be a genius.[61]

However, Kolysheva warns us that although Elena was so devoted to her husband's memory and to his great novel, she nevertheless made a number of misjudgements or errors in editing his text on the basis of the 1938 typescript and the subsequent amendments. It has to be said that the examples Kolysheva identifies do little to change our reading of the text substantively, relating as they do to paragraph or sentence breaks, slight insensitivity to rhythmical patterns, her use of punctuation, particles and prepositions, her fondness for exclamation marks, minor changes in word order and so on. There are very occasional examples of minor changes in grammatical construction or choice of lexicon as well. It is nevertheless gratifying to have these tidied up once and for all in the version Kolysheva herself has prepared in her own edition.

In 1963 Elena once again retyped the novel, creating a typescript which came to be owned by Aleksandr Melik-Pashaev, a conductor and good friend of the couple's from the Bol'shoi Theatre. It was completed by April 1, 1963. Here there are new discrepancies between what she typed in 1939–40 and the later version, although many of them are of a similar order of significance to the ones noted above. Kolysheva tabulates all these discrepancies across more than fifty pages of her analysis. One detail which has attracted some comment is a switch (in chapter 13) in the exact adjectival term (the equivalent of "Pontius") used to describe Pilate in the anticipated final words of the Master's novel. In the corrected 1938 Bokshanskaya typescript, and again in Elena's 1939–40 retyping, he is described as "Pontiiskiy Pilat"; in the 1963 version this is altered to the less unusual "Pontiy Pilat."[62]

Although the finale to chapter 32 in the amended 1938 typescript had been crossed out in May 1939, when Bulgakov added the Epilogue, and was therefore omitted in the 1939–40 typescript, Elena reinstated in 1963 the paragraph which in 1938 had concluded chapter 32 of *The Master and Margarita*, the one with the reference to Pilate as the fifth Procurator of Judaea. This paragraph also highlights the role of Margarita in soothing the Master as she leads him to his final, charming home in the afterworld and promises him that his memories will vanish: Elena was evidently very fond of this passage.[63] The Epilogue which follows also ends with a reference to Pilate's name, but in a somewhat different formulation. For this and the other reasons cited above, Kolysheva argues that it is not acceptable to use the 1963 typescript as the definitive version of the text, as both Saakyants and Yanovskaya were inclined to do. Instead, Kolysheva offers us her own definitive text, created on the basis of the 1938 Bokshanskaya typescript, taking into account the author's subsequent amendments, and remedying the deficiencies of Elena's retypings of the text in 1939–40 and in 1963.[64]

All in all, the variations between the later manuscript and typescript versions of the text are not of fundamental significance, although Kolysheva's review of the successive drafts of the work seems to offer a reliable analysis of the issues involved. They do, however, allow us to trace in detail the evolution of Bulgakov's concept over the entire period of writing, away from the original satirical depiction of Soviet life at some point in the near future, and increasingly towards a focus on eternal spiritual values, love, and art. Nor is it really the case, as some have argued, that the text is "unfinished": Bulgakov had a clear sense of what he wanted to achieve in his *magnum opus* for some years before his death, and any inconsistencies that remain in the text are not sufficiently important to impede our understanding of his artistic purpose. On the other hand, it is probably true to say that there will never be an entirely "authorized" text of *The Master and Margarita*.

CHAPTER 4

Publication History of
The Master and Margarita
in Russian

Viktor Losev, editor of the eight-volume Azbuka edition of Bulgakov's works, has stated as recently as 2013 that "The history of the publication of the novel *The Master and Margarita* is not yet sufficiently well known, although it presents considerable interest. Unfortunately there are not that many documents preserved in the author's archive concerning this history, but even these have not been studied or published."[1] He nevertheless offers an outline of that history, drawing upon some hitherto unpublished documents, including diaries and letters of Bulgakov's widow Elena dating from the 1960s, and documents relating to the Soviet writer Konstantin Simonov, who played a key role at that period. This chapter offers a brief survey of the events which led up to the earliest publications of *The Master and Margarita* in the original Russian.

Elena had made a deathbed vow to Bulgakov that she would ensure that the novel would see the light of day. On March 6, 1940, when he was already in a semi-delirious state just four days before his death:

> I said to him on a hunch (I got the impression that he was thinking about it), I give you my solemn word that I will type up the novel, that I'll submit it, and you will be published! And he was listening, fairly alert and attentive, and then he said: "So that people should know. . . that people should know."[2]

But in December 1940, after a few months had elapsed since his death, one of Bulgakov's closest friends and confidants, Pavel Popov, wrote to Elena advising caution: "The less people know about the novel the better. The masterfulness of a genius will always remain masterfulness, but at the moment the novel would be unacceptable. 50–100 years will have to pass."[3]

Popov's choice of the term "unacceptable" is striking here: with Stalin's Terror still ravaging intellectual circles, the very existence of this satirical novel, especially with its religious preoccupations, might have proved extremely dangerous for those who knew about it. But perhaps Popov was in fact being pragmatic: he would have been aware that the police informers (Zhukhovitsky, possibly Konsky and others) who had swarmed around Bulgakov throughout the 1930s surely knew something about—or even of—the novel in any case. And Bulgakov had not hesitated over the long years of the novel's composition to give fairly frequent readings of portions of the text to those who were close to him, usually at home but occasionally even at friends' homes. Varlamov lists the following individuals who heard him read parts of *The Master and Margarita* during his lifetime: the Erdman brothers; the Vil'yamses; the composer Vissarion Shebalin; the Moscow Art Theatre actors Vasily Kachalov and Grigory (Grisha) Konsky; the writer Sergey Ermolinsky; Bulgakov's close friend Pavel Popov; the psychiatrist Samuil Tseitlin and the doctor Andrey Arendt (a direct descendant of the doctor who had treated Pushkin on his deathbed); the deputy director of the Bol'shoi Theatre Yakov Leont'ev; Vitaly Vilenkin from the Moscow Art Theatre literary department; the Bulgakovs' neighbour, the dramatist Aleksey Faiko; the publisher Nikolay Angarsky; the writing duo Il'f and Petrov; and of course the rather unimpressed Ol'ga Bokshanskaya, together with her husband.[4] To this list we could add Elena's older son Evgeny, still living with his father, Shilovsky, who occupied a very high rank in the Soviet military establishment; the wives of several of the men mentioned above; the poet Anna Akhmatova; Pavel Markov from the Moscow Art Theatre; and doubtless several others, including writers he warmly respected such as Boris Pasternak, who certainly got to know about the novel at the end of Bulgakov's life. With such a wide range of people knowing something of the novel, living in a repressive society where informants and denunciations thrived, it seems quite impossible that the authorities were not at least passively aware that Bulgakov had been working on a rather subversive text over a long period of time. On the other hand, Varlamov notes that there are apparently no official reports about Bulgakov to the NKVD (successor organization to the OGPU) preserved in the archives, dating from any point after 1936. In other words, we simply don't know (yet) what information was in fact reported to the authorities about Bulgakov thereafter, or whether even some decision had been made on high to lift the surveillance on him, while continuing to ensure that his works did not succeed in reaching a wider audience.[5]

There is one further issue that has been raised about the Bulgakovs' relationship with the organs of the secret police. D. G. B. Piper, one of the novel's earliest critics in the west, has ventured the controversial hypothesis that the "mysterious sense of kinship which exists between the Master, Margarita and Woland" represents an "aesthetic interpretation of the relationship between Bulgakov, his third wife and Stalin."[6] One of Bulgakov's most distinguished Soviet biographers, Marietta Chudakova, has even gone so far as to speculate that Elena played a role in Bulgakov's life that was shaped to some extent for her by instructions from the NKVD.[7] In other words, there have been suggestions that Elena was either deliberately placed by the authorities in a position where she could get to know Bulgakov more intimately, or was suborned by them to report on him during the course of their marriage. The rumours that tend to swirl around anybody who survived the repressions of the Stalinist era have tended to focus on Elena's somewhat surprising achievement in living a relatively luxurious and apparently fairly unconstrained life in Soviet Russia during its darkest years. Bulgakov's post-Soviet biographer Aleksey Varlamov, however, after scrupulously reviewing all the available evidence, has concluded that there is no basis whatsoever for believing in this theory.[8]

One notable development towards the end of Bulgakov's life was that he began to be visited by the writer Aleksandr Fadeev, an extremely complex figure who had joined the Bolsheviks as early as 1918 and now sat on the Central Committee of the Communist Party; he also occupied one of the top posts in the Union of Soviet Writers and would become a shameless apologist of Stalin in his later years. On August 3, 1929 in the Party newspaper *Komsomol'skaya Pravda* Fadeev had referred to Bulgakov and his friend Evgeny Zamyatin in unequivocally hostile terms, as "enemies of the working class."[9] Nevertheless, it would seem that he was genuinely struck and moved by his belated acquaintance in person with Bulgakov, who apparently asked him as he was dying to consult with Elena about any possible publications of his works.[10] He too certainly knew about the existence of *The Master and Margarita*, as is reflected in a diary entry by Elena on February 15, 1940: "Yesterday Fadeev rang and asked to see Misha, and he came today. He spoke on two topics: the novel, and a trip for Misha to the south of Italy, to recuperate."[11] Fadeev wrote to her five days after his death, describing Bulgakov as "a man of astonishing talent, who in his inner being was honourable and principled, and very clever. . . ."[12] Yanovskaya has alluded to persistent rumours that Elena had an affair with Fadeev not long afterwards, and argues that it was extremely likely that he read the manuscript of *The Master and Margarita* at that time. Fadeev ensured that in April and May

1940 she and her young son Sergey were enabled to go away to recover from the shock of Bulgakov's death in a Writers' Union sanatorium in Yalta, in the Crimea. Fadeev was also the person who made sure that she was evacuated, together with her literary archive, from Moscow in October 1941, after Hitler's shocking and unexpected invasion that June.[13] So perhaps what Pavel Popov was alluding to in his December 1940 warning to Elena was that the novel was certainly known about, by figures like Fadeev and therefore even in Writers' Union and government circles, before the Second World War—but that nevertheless nobody would be prepared to back its publication for the foreseeable future.

This state of affairs may help to explain Elena's bold decision after the end of the war to address a letter directly to Stalin, dated July 7, 1946, in which she requested that a collection of Bulgakov's works should be published. Rather astonishingly, her letter achieved a fairly favourable response, and an instruction was apparently issued to the Iskusstvo publishing house to explore the idea.[14] However, within a few months there was a renewed clamp-down on literary culture, and writers such as Anna Akhmatova and Mikhail Zoshchenko were savagely attacked in print; things became more repressive again, and nothing was in fact done to publish Bulgakov until well after Stalin's death in 1953.

As Nikita Khrushchev inaugurated what has come to be known as the Thaw period in 1956, marking a shift towards greater tolerance in cultural policy, an official commission on Bulgakov's literary heritage was set up, chaired by the relatively liberal writer Konstantin Simonov. Elena sent him a sample of works to read, holding back for the moment the more controversial texts such as *Heart of a Dog*, *The Master and Margarita*, and the play *Batum*. Simonov was enormously impressed to discover, albeit belatedly, that Bulgakov had been a writer of such quality. In consequence, a few of his plays, as well as his prose biography *The Life of Monsieur de Molière* and his *Notes of a Young Doctor* at last appeared in print between 1962 and 1965.[15] Elena wrote to explain these new developments to Bulgakov's brother Nikolay, who was still living in Paris:

> All those (some very important, and many different sorts of people), all those who have had the opportunity to get to know his creative work in full (I don't give that opportunity to everybody)—all of them precisely use the same expression: "a writer of genius." [...] And yet they are unaware (they've only heard about it) of what his prose is like. I know, I am absolutely sure, that soon the entire world will know his name ... [...] I am doing all that is in my power to ensure that not a single line written by him should get lost, that his exceptional personality should not remain

unknown. [. . .] This is the purpose and the meaning of my life. Before he died I promised him many things, and I believe that I will be able to fulfil it all. . . .[16]

It did not take fifty years, as Popov had feared, but it was well over twenty years before the very first allusion to the existence of the novel appeared in print in the Soviet Union. In 1962 the writer Veniamin Kaverin managed to include a passing reference to the existence of the manuscript of a "fantastical novel" called *The Master and Margarita*, as well as a 6-line account of its content, in his commentaries to the first publication of Bulgakov's prose biography, *The Life of Monsieur de Molière*.[17] 1962 was also notably the year when Aleksandr Solzhenitsyn's short novel *One Day in the Life of Ivan Denisovich* was published in a Moscow journal, sensationally breaking the taboo on acknowledging the existence of Stalinist labour camps, and reflecting a new Thaw-era attitude of tolerance towards controversial literary texts.

And so, as a full quarter of a century elapsed since Bulgakov's death, Simonov at last began to work with Elena on a plan to get *The Master and Margarita* published. Their initial idea was that the "historical" Ershalaim chapters should be published first of all as a separate "short novel" in one journal, with the main novel to follow in the journal *Moskva*. The two of them therefore started by preparing those chapters separately for publication. Simonov drafted a preface to the proposed publication:

> In essence this is not even one novel, but so to speak two novels, gath-
> ered together under a single cover. [. . .] The two novels combine and live
> alongside one another in an extraordinary way, but one could imagine
> them without difficulty—and to my eye, without artistic loss—separated,
> each of them existing on its own.[18]

He also proclaimed—somewhat unconvincingly, but perhaps bearing in mind the difficulties the project might still encounter in this period with the Soviet censors—that "Bulgakov's novel is entirely atheistic."[19] Their endeavour foundered, however. Nevertheless, as the other members of the literary commission began to discover *The Master and Margarita* for themselves, rumours about its existence became more widespread. As described in the previous chapter, Elena prepared and typed out a new version of the text in 1963, which she allowed several people to read, although very few materials have survived to shed light on the process of her editing of the text at this stage.[20]

And then at last the journal *Moskva* took the courageous decision in 1966 to publish the novel for the first time, with a Preface by Simonov and an Afterword by Abram Vulis. The first part of *The Master and Margarita* appeared in the November number (*Moskva* 11, 1966), with a print run of 150,000 copies; the second did not appear until mid-February 1967 (*Moskva* 1, 1967). Even so, the text had only been authorised for publication with very considerable cuts, many of them made with political and ideological considerations in mind: they concerned references to the secret police and their investigations and arrests, attacks on the Soviet literary establishment, Margarita's nakedness, and so on.[21] Belobrovtseva has calculated that these cuts constituted 12% of the total text, and involved 159 excisions, 138 of which related to Part II of the novel.[22] These two combined publications nevertheless caused a sensation. As Laura Weeks puts it, even though Bulgakov had begun to be known by a modern Russian audience in recent years as a satirical dramatist, and his novel *The White Guard* had also been published in 1966, "nothing could have prepared readers for the revelation that was *The Master and Margarita*."[23] One early enthusiastic response to the truncated *Moskva* publication came from Aleksandr Solzhenitsyn, who asked to visit Elena in April 1967 to express his excitement, and his determination to help see the work properly published.[24]

The critical debate immediately provoked within the Soviet Union by the two *Moskva* publications, pitting liberals keen to advance the de-Stalinisation ethos of the Thaw against the resistance of hardline Communists, has been thoroughly explored by Andrew Barratt.[25] But it should certainly be noted that several of Bulgakov's other works, such as *Heart of a Dog* and *Batum*, would still have to wait a further twenty years—until the *glasnost'* era of the late 1980s—to be published. In other words, the publication of *The Master and Margarita* was just about as far as even the new liberalism in the USSR in the mid-1960s was prepared to go. Nevertheless, the very fact of its having appeared had an enormous impact. As Stephen Lovell puts it: "Bulgakov's 'sunset novel' occupies a unique, and uniquely revealing, niche in Soviet culture, because it existed predominantly in three cultural domains: it was part of the official literary process, hence it was subjected to literary criticism, and attempts were belatedly made to institutionalise Bulgakov as a Soviet classic; it struck a powerful chord in the intelligentsia subculture; and it was eventually taken up by popular culture."[26]

The first full publication of the text of the novel in the USSR was strictly speaking achieved by the publisher Eesti Raamat in Estonia in 1967, but this was in an Estonian translation, rather than in Russian.[27] The first publication of the novel in the Russian language not to appear in a mangled and truncated form was in fact in Italy (Einaudi, 1967).[28] Yanovskaya recounts how Elena contrived to get official permission during 1967 for the book to be published abroad in full, using an ingenious argument to the effect that the cuts in the *Moskva* edition (amounting to thirty-five single-spaced pages of typescript) had not in fact been imposed by the censors, but simply reflected editorial choices instead. In October 1967 a letter was therefore sent to the Central Committee of the Communist Party from the Union of Writers, asking for permission to sidestep the usual rule that texts could only be published abroad in the exact form in which they had appeared in the USSR. This permission was granted in November, which was how the full text came to be sent to the Italian publishers Einaudi.[29]

In 1967 Elena was also at last allowed out of the country to visit Bulgakov's surviving relatives in France (his brother Nikolay had died in 1966), with the result that another full publication of the novel in Russian by YMCA Press followed: this included a preface by the Russian Orthodox Archbishop of San Francisco. In 1969 Possev-Verlag in Frankfurt am Main published another full edition of the Russian text, in which the cuts made for the *Moskva* publication were reinserted in italics. As was typical of the period, this version came out in a "pocket edition," a 3" × 4" volume printed in tiny print on very fine paper, ideal for slipping into a back pocket as a means of smuggling it back into the country through Soviet customs. However, these several publications abroad are not in fact precisely identical with one another, so that some questions about the exact sources they were each using still remain.[30]

In 1970 Elena died and was buried alongside Bulgakov in the grave she had selected for him in Moscow's Novodevichy cemetery. This meant that she never actually saw the first publication of the full text of the novel in the USSR in Russian, in an 812-page volume of Bulgakov's works simply called *Novels* (also containing *The White Guard* and the unfinished *Theatrical Novel*), published in Moscow in 1973 by Khudozhestvennaya Literatura. This 1973 edition was printed in 30,000 copies. Reprints in 1975 and 1978 amounted only to 10,000 and 50,000 copies respectively, followed by somewhat more generous ones in 1980 and 1984, of 100,000 copies each time.[31] That was scarcely likely to satisfy demand in such a highly literate country, with a population of well over 200 million people, especially since a high proportion of the first print-run was sent for sale abroad, to earn foreign currency, rather than being made available to the domestic market. Given the excitement about the text, it rapidly became one of the most sought-after literary volumes of the decade. As Hedrick Smith, the New York Times correspondent in Moscow, reported at the time: "The book's official price was 1.53 roubles, but the black market prices ran from 60 to

200 roubles."[32] Rumours even circulated in London alleging that copies of the *Novels* volume available there through the Flegon Press may have been pirated facsimiles (readers noted a price discrepancy, unheard of for a Soviet publication, between what was embossed on the back cover and what was printed amongst the other publication details on the back pages). The version of the text in the 1973 *Novels* edition was prepared by the literary editor Anna Saakyants who, with Bulgakov's widow no longer alive, allowed herself to make numerous small alterations and amendments to the version that Elena had typed up in 1963. Nevertheless, this became established as the canonical version of *The Master and Margarita* for the first, very numerous and avid generation of Soviet readers: people passed well-thumbed copies of the book from hand to hand and even copied the entire text out on their typewriters, with carbon copies, in order to share it around as widely as possible in the heyday of *samizdat* activity. Nothing could have been more unlike the literature of Socialist Realism, which even in the post-Stalin era still remained the prevailing official ethos of Soviet literary production.

Only in 1989 were the real debates over the integrity of the text inaugurated with Lidiya Yanovskaya's publication in Soviet Ukraine of a new edition of the novel with Dnipro, a publisher based in Kyiv. Her approach involved reinstating some of Elena's 1963 decisions, and amalgamating these with the 1973 Saakyants version. This version was also reproduced in the five-volume Khudozhestvennaya Literatura collection of Bulgakov's works which came out in Moscow in 1989–90, in the dying years of the Soviet state. And it has taken until the twenty-first century for scholarly attention to become specifically focused on the problems of establishing an authoritative text, by reviewing the Saakyants and Yanovskaya versions in the light of archival holdings of all the textual variants—as examined in the previous section of this book. Belobrovtseva rightly agrees with Viktor Losev that "the difficulties of the textology of this novel are extremely significant, and it is scarcely likely that they will ever find unambiguous resolution."[33] Irrespective of these scholarly debates, however, the novel has achieved enormous print-runs during the fifty years since it first appeared in Russian, with millions and millions of copies now printed and sold in Russia, as well as translations into dozens of languages. In their wildest dreams Bulgakov and Elena could scarcely have imagined the eventual reach of *The Master and Margarita,* as it established itself unequivocally as a twentieth-century classic of both Russian and world literature.

CHAPTER 5

A Tale of Two Cities: The Structure of *The Master and Margarita*[1]

It is a real challenge for those of us who have read *The Master and Margarita* more than once to reconstruct now our original impressions of the novel, as its plot unfolded for us for the first time. No subsequent reading can quite recapture that "innocence," as this extraordinarily complex work tantalizes and confuses us through its elaborate structure. A particularly striking effect is achieved at the very start, specifically in the breathtaking transition between chapters 1 and 2, where a comic encounter in Soviet-era Moscow between two ideologically conformist writers and an enigmatic stranger is abruptly succeeded by a realistic and moving account of the occasion when Ieshua Ga-Notsri, clearly recognisable as a Christ figure, is brought before Pontius Pilate for interrogation in the city of Ershalaim (Bulgakov's unexpected name for Jerusalem). This is followed by a bathetic return to the everyday setting in Moscow, achieved through the transition between chapters 2 and 3. The insertion of the Pilate story into the Moscow narrative is justified in straightforward terms—for the moment—by the fact that Woland, the stranger, offers to recount these events to his listeners, who have proclaimed their scepticism about all aspects of religion. But this conventional device of "story-telling" scarcely suffices to account for the astonishing divergence in narrative tone and power between chapters 1 and 2. Nothing in the character of Woland in chapter 1, neither in his language nor in the nature of his teasing and provocative conversation with Berlioz and Ivan, has prepared us for what comes next.

The narrative set in Ershalaim resurfaces again in Ivan's dream (chapter 16), neatly and precisely picking up from the point where Woland's story ends, in order to describe events later on that same day when Pilate spoke with Ieshua, and then moving on to the scene of the crucifixion. At this point the reader is forced to recognise that the function of this narrative within the frame story set in Moscow must indeed be much more complex than the simple "story-telling" device in chapters 1–2 had seemed to suggest. For how can a single, continuous narrative derive from two wholly different sources (Woland's words and Ivan's dream)? And indeed, the manuscript of the Master's novel, read by Margarita in chapters 25 and 26, then goes on to complete the story of Pilate and Ieshua, thereby confirming the internal unity and coherence of all four of the Ershalaim chapters. But it also adds a new, third component to the mystery of the story's sources. The version of events drafted by Margarita's lover, correlating as it does in every way with Woland's story and Ivan's dream, suggests conversely that these four chapters of *The Master and Margarita* equate exactly with the whole of the Master's "novel." The reader will wait in vain for any explanation within the text to this puzzle: the conclusion of the novel does not offer any elucidation or comment on its own structure. Bulgakov seems almost to expect his readers to revisit the text after their first reading, in order to unpick the significance of its intricacies with the benefit of hindsight. So one of the earliest problems raised in the novel is one of structure; and yet the author apparently leaves the issue unresolved.

But clearly our understanding of the novel's themes can only be complete once we have worked out the purposes of the interplay between its two settings separated by 2,000 years in time, early Soviet Moscow and historic Ershalaim. Most of the action takes place in one or other of these two distinct locations, although at the very end of the novel (chapter 32) characters from each city are brought together for the first time, thanks to supernatural powers. Erykalova has argued that the best way to read the novel is precisely as part of a single whole: "All three strata of the novel—Muscovite reality, the world of the Gospel chapters, and the world of Woland, Prince of Darkness [. . .] when all taken together, create a picture of the real world of Bulgakov's own time."[2] During our first reading of the text, however, we remain fascinated and puzzled by the way the plot shifts back and forth so unexpectedly between the raucous comedy of life in modern-day Moscow and the poised, subtle account of events in ancient Ershalaim.

A powerful additional element of suspense for the first-time reader is that the two protagonists who provide the book with its title are not so much as mentioned in the first dozen or so chapters, and only make their first appearance about half way through the text. But when we do finally meet the Master and learn that he is a writer who, like Ivan, is preoccupied with the story of Pilate, we begin to sense that the solution to the structural problem posed by the existence of the Ershalaim chapters will be found through this character. Acknowledging the complexity of the narrative's origins (in Woland's words, Ivan's dream, and the Master's text)—while accepting that it simultaneously constitutes the entirety of the Master's novel—will further help us to evaluate the ways in which the Ershalaim story and the Moscow narrative complement one another within the overall construct of Bulgakov's novel *The Master and Margarita*.

Although the Moscow and Ershalaim stories follow distinct trajectories, there are several ways in which the reader is actively invited to juxtapose them, through parallels and echoes in the chronology of events in both narratives, as well as in their imagery, and in the characterisations of the protagonists. But should one part of the novel, set in Ershalaim, therefore be read as a story which specifically anticipates what occurs in later history, in Moscow? On the whole, one should beware of exaggerating the links and similarities between Moscow and Ershalaim, as certain critics have been tempted to do.[3] The function of the internal echoes in *The Master and Margarita* is to bind the text together in suggestive and aesthetically satisfying ways, rather than to provide the basis for what can turn out to be rather limited and unproductive analogies. Reductive readings have been the bane of Bulgakov studies, in Russia as in the West, failing as they do to come to terms with the bold freedom of his use of leitmotifs in the novel. As Andrew Barratt puts it: "Devoid of symbolic meaning [the majority of the motifs] are perhaps best described as allusive refrains which draw upon a wide range of literary, mythical and religious texts to create an intricate network of interconnections, an aesthetic pattern which teases and delights the imagination by its associative fecundity."[4]

The chronological structure of the novel is certainly complex, but not excessively so.[5] There are moments from time to time when the chronology seems to become confused, sometimes intentionally and sometimes not. Intentional confusions arise from Woland's supernatural powers. His annual ball— "It is called the spring ball of the full moon, or the ball of the hundred kings" (chapter 22)—seems to last for several hours, although it both begins and ends at midnight on the Friday night. Another magical distortion takes place at the triumphant moment when the two lovers are at last accorded their final reward: "The Master and Margarita saw the dawn they had been promised. It began instantly, directly after the midnight moon" (chapter 32). Elsewhere there are unintentional inconsistencies, which presumably derive from the fact that the work was not completely polished and finalised before Bulgakov's death. Pilate tells Caiaphas that it is almost midday when he sets out to announce the verdicts on Ieshua and the others (chapter 2, echoed twice in the opening pages of chapter 16), after which the narrator perplexes us by declaring that it is still only ten o'clock in the morning of the same day (last line of chapter 2 and opening line of chapter 3). In Moscow the full moon which provides an atmospheric backdrop to the supernatural events is allowed to stretch over several days, and is described as appearing on Wednesday (chapter 3), Friday (chapters 20 and 22), and Saturday (chapter 32). Bulgakov may well have been deliberately choosing to be imprecise here, given that he had in fact made careful observations of the full moon for the novel in late June 1937, using his binoculars.[6] A full moon which does not begin to wane as it normally would helps to suggest the magical forces which have taken command of Moscow during Woland's visit.

One fundamental parallel between the two settings is established in the fact that the principal events which occur in Moscow and Ershalaim all take place over the latter half of a week, from Wednesday to Saturday in Moscow and largely from Friday to Saturday in Ershalaim. The full moon shines over both cities. We may in fact infer that events in Moscow are set during the Orthodox Holy Week, which can very occasionally fall as late as the month of May according to the modern, Gregorian calendar if Easter is very late in the Julian calendar (which is still adhered to in the Russian Orthodox Church). This would imply that Woland's spring ball takes place on the anniversary of the Crucifixion. However, as we shall see when we come to analyse the significance of Satan's ball in the novel, we should be wary of interpreting this occasion just as an aggressively blasphemous rite. As so often, Bulgakov ultimately subverts the expectations he has apparently set up in establishing this chronological echo between the two sets of events.

Another example of chronological echoing is used very effectively as a bridging device at the beginning of chapter 27, when Margarita finishes reading about how Pilate meets the dawn in Ershalaim on the fifteenth of Nisan (Saturday) just as she herself meets the dawn on Saturday in Moscow.[7] A more powerful image used to interweave the two narratives together in this manner is that of the impending storm, usually following upon a burning sun and stifling heat. There are actually three storms in the novel: the first is in Moscow on the Thursday evening as Ivan sits in the asylum trying to make sense of his encounter with Woland (opening of chapter 11); the second takes place in Ershalaim on the Friday evening, and hastens the end of Ieshua's sufferings (end of chapter 16); and the final one breaks over Moscow as the Master and Margarita bid farewell to Ivan on the Saturday evening, passing over before they set off on their final journey (end of chapter 30). Much of the action of the novel in both cities, therefore, can be said to unfold in a pre-apocalyptic atmosphere.

Echoing is used, however, not just in the chronological structuring of plot, but also in the selection of imagery. The contrast between the measured, intense and emotionally nuanced writing of the Ershalaim chapters and the more varied style of the Moscow chapters, which draws upon more prosaic rhythms and a more colloquial range of vocabulary, seems to establish a wide gulf between the two parts. Nevertheless, Bulgakov does occasionally use echoes or leitmotifs from the Ershalaim setting in the Moscow chapters, in order to lend the novel a greater cohesiveness. In a brilliant analysis David Bethea, for example, has shown how the imagery of horses and riders is threaded into the Moscow chapters, when we would normally expect them—for obvious historical reasons—to be largely confined to the Ershalaim chapters. He demonstrates that this device serves to infuse the Moscow setting with images which identify the modern world with the materialism of the fallen Whore of Babylon, and its temples—Berlioz's apartment, Griboedov House, and the Torgsin store—are burned down accordingly. Bethea also notes Boris Gasparov's point that Moscow becomes, at least in this respect, a splintered, reduced version of Ershalaim.[8] Gasparov in general sees the use of leitmotifs as the novel's most distinctive stylistic characteristic: "The fundamental device which determines the whole structure of meaning in *The Master and Margarita*, and which has at the same time a broader general significance, appears to us to be the principle of *leitmotif construction* in the narrative [. . .but. . .] all links turn out to be only partial."[9] Although this is a shrewd observation, Gasparov regrettably pursues this investigation to an exaggerated level. For instance, he attempts to find some sort of significance in the fact that J. S. Bach's initials in Russian would be I. S. B., which Bulgakov supposedly uses as an anagram in the address of Likhodeev's flat (302 *bis*), as well as in his selection of composers' names for his protagonists—(Igor') Stravinsky and Berlioz. All this forms part of a not very persuasive attempt to argue that Bulgakov was basing himself in his concept of the Ershalaim sections on the St Matthew and St John Passions by J. S. Bach. There is neither any logical nor any textual basis, however, for this kind of overinterpretation. Instead, we should accept Lesley Milne's finely argued case for comparing Bulgakov's techniques for handling leitmotif with the concept of the *figura*, as used in religious cycles of mystery plays and rites. In this context she quotes Erich Auerbach's 1946 study, *Mimesis*: "A connection is established between two events which are linked neither temporally nor causally—a connection that it is impossible to establish by reason in the horizontal [temporal] dimension." Milne goes on to suggest that: "If this concept of *figura* is employed in a structural analysis of *The Master and Margarita*, an elusive order and unity that the reader perceives, but as broken threads, can be revealed as woven into an extensive, ordered and finely-wrought canvas."[10]

There have been other rather far-fetched attempts, like Gasparov's, to read *The Master and Margarita* as a novel which has to be "decoded" before it will release its secrets. One of Bulgakov's earliest Western critics, Elena Mahlow, took it for granted that the work was written entirely in what is known in Russian studies as "Aesopian language," that is, an allegorical account of contemporary events disguised as something else. Mahlow accordingly reads the novel as a ciphered account of the Stalin era in Soviet history: Ieshua's old *chiton* (tunic) and sandals reflect the economic hardships endured by the Soviet proletariat in the 1930s; Matvey's dirty breadknife becomes a symbol for the unresolved problem of freedom versus necessity; and the fourteenth of Nisan is transposed through arcane arithmetical calculations to become February 27, 1917 (a key date in the first 1917 Revolution) according to this bizarre reading.[11] Similarly, D. G. B. Piper agrees with L. Rzhevsky that *The Master and Margarita* is basically a cryptographical novel, containing not-so-transparent references to political personalities and events from the early Soviet period. Piper sees echoes of the Bolsheviks Vyacheslav Molotov and Klim Voroshilov in Korov'ev and Begemot respectively, and of Stalin himself in Woland.[12] Such responses were very much of their time, following soon after the partial 1966–7 publication of the novel in *Moskva*, as readers, critics and censors alike during the early dissident era in Soviet literature sought subversive messages between the lines of what was actually written down on the page. Unfortunately these sorts of approaches disregard the novel's subtle messages and structural intricacy, not least in order to promote readings which assume that the two settings of Ershalaim and Moscow are virtually interchangeable.

Other echoes certainly do reach out from the Ershalaim sections into the Moscow ones. Sometimes these arise fairly straightforwardly. When, for example, Ivan compares the sanatorium chief Dr Stravinsky to Pilate (chapter 8), or when Margarita equates her failure to return in time to save the Master from arrest to Matvey's failure to spare Ieshua the torments of the crucifixion (chapter 19), these parallels can naturally be explained by their knowledge of the original story (Ivan through listening to Woland's narrative, Margarita through her reading). A different effect is achieved, however, when the narrator compares the shop-assistant's knife in the Moscow Torgsin store to Matvey's (chapter 28): this, we realise, can only reflect the more distanced overview of the author of *The Master and Margarita*. Andrew Barratt is surely right to celebrate in Bulgakov's writing this kind of "sheer playfulness, which enables the creation of unsuspected connections between seemingly discrete themes and episodes."[13] What such witty moments also do is to reassert the presence of the author in shaping our responses to his narrative, and to reaffirm the deeply personal and subjective vision which has created the novel in the first place. Other such "breachings" of the boundaries between the different levels of the narrative occur when the Master, newly restored to Margarita at the end of Satan's ball, addresses her as "Margot": this is not only an affectionate variant of her real name, but also conjures up an association with *La Reine Margot*, a popular novel of 1845 about Marguerite de Valois (1553–1615) by Alexandre Dumas, who was very widely read in Russia. In other words, long before the Devil's visit to Moscow the Master somehow seems to have sensed the "royal" lineage that Woland and his retinue, with their supernatural powers, have managed to discover in Margarita's antecedents (chapter 24). Equally, there are clear and deliberate resonances between the conversations Woland has in Moscow with Berlioz, and the one Ieshua has with Pilate in Ershalaim, about who ultimately controls men's lives, which essentially hang on a thread (chapters 1–3).

Many of the interpretations which lay most stress on the analogies between the two settings have based themselves on the pronounced similarities between the description of Ershalaim associated with Margarita's reading of the Master's novel and one of the descriptions of Moscow itself. Ellendea Proffer has, incidentally, drawn attention to further similarities between the two cities in Bulgakov's descriptions and his own birthplace, Kyiv, which also has a "Bald Mountain" (Golgotha) and is also divided, like Ershalaim, into an upper and lower part.[14] The passage in question is the one which Margarita reads over to herself after the Master's mysterious disappearance, and which is the only surviving fragment she possesses of the novel which he had thrust into the flames in the depths of his despair:

> She sat for almost an hour, holding on her knees the notebook damaged in the fire, leafing through it and reading over a section which, after the fire, had no beginning and no end: "...The darkness which had spread from the Mediterranean sea came down over the city the Procurator so detested. The hanging bridges linking the temple to the fearsome Antonia Fortress disappeared, a mass of blackness fell from the sky and streamed over the winged gods above the hippodrome, and the Hasmonaean palace with its

embrasures, bazaars, caravanserais, alleyways and ponds... Ershalaim, the great city, vanished as though it had never existed..." (chapter 19)

Azazello then recites part of this same passage back to her as proof that he has knowledge of the Master (chapter 19), and certain parts of it are repeated like a refrain as Margarita settles down to re-read the full text of the chapter while the Master, restored to her at last, sleeps (end of chapter 24). After this, it is the novel's overall narrator who seems to draw upon the Master's description of Ershalaim in his own description of Moscow, as Woland and his retinue are preparing to leave the city before the storm breaks: "This darkness which had spread from the West came down over the gigantic city. The bridges and palaces disappeared. Everything vanished, as though none of it had ever existed" (end of chapter 29). It would be tempting to read this as an emphatic identification of the two cities with one another, suggesting that what occurs in Ershalaim should be seen as directly prefiguring what happens in Moscow. But we should once again be wary of assuming that the extension and elaboration of a set of images in this fashion amounts to a somewhat crude "key" to the complexities of the novel. Bulgakov's highly poetic use of reminiscence in his prose more often than not celebrates aesthetically the visual or aural reverberations of a word or phrase, but he leaves the semantic connection unfulfilled and unresolved.

It should be added that the device of carrying a sentence over from the end of one chapter to the beginning of the next is used by Bulgakov to cover all the transitions from Moscow to Ershalaim, the first transition from Ershalaim back to Moscow, and to bridge several other chapters as well. In other words, Bulgakov's decision to reuse the sentence about the darkness coming down over the city is part of a broader pattern of emphatic repetition, which is used to underscore the trance-like state in which the visions of Ershalaim are perceived. This is most notable at the end of the first Ershalaim chapter, where Ivan's impression of Woland's narration is so vivid that he feels that he has been dreaming, rather than simply listening to a story (beginning of chapter 3). As Justin Weir observes: "The tale of Pilate and Yeshua is presented within the larger text of the novel *as primarily an experience* and *only secondarily a text*," because it is heard, dreamt and preserved in a much re-read fragment, rather than actually existing as a physical book.[15]

One further example of the verbal echoing of phrases across the different sections of the novel raises a subtle question about the relationship between the Master's novel (the Ershalaim chapters) and the outer novel represented not just by the Moscow narrative, but by Bulgakov's *The Master and Margarita* in its entirety. It arises from a remark made by the Master to Ivan as he relates to him the story of his past: "Pilate was flying, flying to a close, and I already knew that the last words of my novel would be: 'the fifth Procurator of Judaea, the horseman Pontius Pilate' ['pyatyi prokurator Iudei, vsadnik Pontiy Pilat']" (chapter 13). Chapter 26, the last of the Ershalaim chapters which make up the Master's novel, does indeed end with these words, except that the word "horseman" ("vsadnik") is omitted. But some confusion then arises when we reach the end of chapter 32, as well as the Epilogue which immediately follows it, which in the versions published until recently in Russia both conclude in exactly the same way, but introduce a new variant, since they both end with the words 'Pontii*skiy* Pilat.' We have already seen in our analysis of the drafts of the book that Bulgakov's own intention appears to have been to end chapter 32 with Margarita promising the Master eternal sleep, while only the Epilogue was to finish with the reference to Pilate; and that it was Elena who reinstated in 1963—and for the ensuing Russian publications—the paragraph which concludes chapter 32 with Pilate.

A number of hypotheses have been advanced about this device. Ellendea Proffer, presumably working with the partial *Moskva* journal edition of the 1960s, which has the Master's phrase appear exactly as he predicted at the end of chapter 32, proposes that the reader should therefore equate the Master's novel with the whole of *The Master and Margarita*.[16] Meanwhile, Laura Weeks concludes that it is Ivan who should be considered to be the author of the entire novel *The Master and Margarita*, on the grounds that he is witness to most of the important events in the text, and is therefore in a position to gather and disseminate the narrative once the events have reached their conclusion.[17] Lesley Milne similarly sees the novel about Pontius Pilate as a *figura* for *The Master and Margarita* itself, on the basis that Bulgakov is essentially evoking his own experiences in the literary world in his description of the Master's tribulations. She argues, somewhat controversially, that since chapter 32 (in the editions she was using) ends with the correct formulation, then: "The 'novel within the novel' is suddenly revealed as occupying the same space as the 'outer novel' minus Epilogue; the Epilogue re-establishes the separate identity of Bulgakov's *The Master and Margarita* from the Master's 'novel about Pontius Pilate.'"[18] The whole issue is beset with uncertainties, both about the author's final intentions, and about the importance—or otherwise—of the slight variations in the phrasing of the controversial sentence. It sometimes goes unnoticed that a first variation of the phrase in fact occurs even before the Master has identified it to Ivan as having a special significance, for the very first sentence of the Master's novel (that is, in Woland's narration in chapter 2) also ends with the words "the Procurator of Judaea, Pontius Pilate" ["prokurator Iudei Pontiy Pilat"]. The emphatic positioning of this phrase at the end of the hypnotically melodious opening sentence of the story of Pilate thus sets the Master's full narrative in a solemn and neatly symmetrical frame. However, to equate the Master's novel with the whole of *The Master and Margarita*, whether one includes the Epilogue or not, is surely to introduce a misleading blurring of distinctions. The Master's sense of alienation from the world of contemporary Moscow surely guarantees that he cannot even fictionally be supposed to have chosen to write about them; we have only to recall his adamant refusal when Woland suggests that he should have a go at writing about Aloizy Mogarych. (chapter 24) The sheer craftsmanship of the writing of the Ershalaim chapters is not in the least compatible with the relaxed and ironical style of the Moscow narrative. Perhaps Bulgakov, who invests the Master with a number of autobiographical traits without reducing him to a self-portrait, chooses to pay tribute to his writer-hero and affirms solidarity with him by echoing the Master's ending in the closing passages of his own novel. The Master cannot be regarded as the 'author' of *The Master and Margarita*: his concern is only with Pontius Pilate.

A further set of parallels has been drawn between the Ershalaim and Moscow sections of the novel in terms of the presentation of character. In particular, some critics have found points of identification between the Master and Pilate, while others have preferred to see the Master as a modern-day Ieshua. The case for equating the Master with Pilate is the less convincing, despite the evident sympathy with which Pilate is portrayed. Much has been made of the fact that both are guilty of the sin of cowardice, but the extent and nature of their cowardice is surely very different. Pilate will forever regret a moment of political fearfulness, a retreat into his role as a Roman Imperial official which leads him into a deep betrayal of spiritual and human values. In these respects Pilate has more in common with General Khludov, who is so burdened with guilt in Bulgakov's play *Flight*, than he does with the Master: like Pilate, Khludov too has ordered the execution of a man who spoke the truth to him, an execution carried out in the name of an Imperial cause which it has become increasingly difficult to defend and justify. The Master's cowardly weaknesses are less specific, and their consequences carry a less universal significance. When persecuted by the small-minded philistines of the Soviet literary establishment, and sensing the threat of arrest, he burns his novel rather than standing up for his art, his love and himself. But the Master's sacrifice of individual artistic and emotional integrity is scarcely comparable in scale with Pilate's despicable betrayal of Ieshua, his new philosophical and spiritual mentor, in the face of the menacing authority of Emperor Tiberius.

The parallels drawn between the Master and Ieshua are more compelling, although it is difficult to accept Skorino's view (based on the 1966–7 *Moskva* publication), when he claims that the two characters are virtually interchangeable: "In the novel *The Master and Margarita* there is one image which emphatically doubles and coincides with the image of Ieshua Ga-Notsri. That is the image of the Master."[19] Nevertheless, some links between the two men can be acknowledged, primarily in their shared experience of persecution for their ideas, their awareness of a higher reality, and their everyday human naivety. Ieshua is presented in the novel as the prophet of a new religion which will challenge the entrenched interests of all that both Pilate and Caiaphas represent, in favour of a faith based on simplicity, sincerity, and truth. He does little to save himself from pain and suffering, which he fears as any mortal would. The Master is confronted with personal challenges which cannot be considered equivalent to any degree, although he does suffer for his intellectual and creative activities. Nevertheless, the sense of an echoing pattern is reinforced by the fact that around Ieshua and the Master stand sets of parallel figures, in the persons firstly of Judas and Aloizy Mogarych, both betrayers of trust; and also in Matvey and Ivan, their imperfect disciples.

Not only is Ieshua the bearer of the Word, but as a man of words he brings about his own downfall as a direct consequence of his use of imagery:

> Hegemon, never in my life have I planned to destroy the building of the temple, nor have I incited anyone to such a senseless action. [. . .] I was telling them, Hegemon, that the temple of the old faith will collapse and a new temple of truth will be created. I said it like that so as to be more clearly understood. (chapter 2)

It is the literalism of his listeners, who take his words at their face value, which prompts his arrest. But rather than seeking to understand Ieshua as an artist figure, it is more fruitful to invert the comparison and to see the artist as possessing many qualities in common with the visionary and prophet. It is the Master, the author of the novel within the novel in *The Master and Margarita*, who gains in moral stature through the implicit parallel with Ieshua.

Overall, the direct parallels between the Moscow and Ershalaim portions of Bulgakov's novel are relatively limited. At the same time, the linguistic, psychological and situational echoes between events in the two cities contribute to the intricate richness and complexity of the central themes of *The Master and Margarita*. It is also striking that Bulgakov seems to have been fascinated in his writing with all the great and sacred cities of the Christian faith: *The White Guard* is set in his home city of Kyiv, the cradle of the Russian Orthodox church; his play *Flight* includes scenes set in Constantinople, the centre of Christianity in the East for nearly a thousand years; and *The Master and Margarita* encompasses the holy cities of Ershalaim as well as Moscow, home of Russian Orthodoxy since the fourteenth century, which Azazello compares unfavourably to Rome, the cradle of Christianity in the West (chapter 29). What many of these holy cities have in common, however, is that they were also governed by authoritarian or oppressive political ideologies. The Master's literary re-creation of the defining moment of Christian culture, and his persecution when he seeks to offer that narrative to his Soviet contemporaries in the beleaguered home of Russian Orthodox Christianity, is what confirms the significance of his achievements as a writer.

CHAPTER 6

Woland: Good and Evil in *The Master and Margarita*

In the Ershalaim chapters Bulgakov—or in the terms of the fiction, the Master—portrays central figures from the Gospel story in a way which, if it is not strictly speaking a "religious" depiction, nevertheless affirms the historical basis for the founding narratives of the Christian faith. He achieves this through the absorbing sense he communicates of the physical reality of the city, with its sounds and smells and heat and light, reinforced by the way the narrative is grounded in carefully researched historical *realia*—from architecture to sandals, dress, food and wine. All of this is rendered in an occasionally archaic vocabulary, which also helps to conjure up a vivid sense of period. Furthermore, the relations between the principal characters in Ershalaim—Pilate, Ieshua, Caiaphas, Matthew the Levite, Afranius, Niza, and Judas—are conveyed with rich psychological nuance: the power play between them, their motives, their manipulations or self-deceptions are all minutely observed. This further serves to reinforce our sense of the historical reality of what is being depicted: these are fully-rounded human individuals, emotionally convincing to us even across two millennia of time.

All of this makes the depiction of Woland all the more original and startling by contrast. Woland is clearly identified as a Satan figure: but at the same time he is not created with direct reference to a canonical religious tradition, as the Ershalaim characters are. He appears as a unique, *sui generis* figure, with no truly significant existence outside the confines of Bulgakov's fictional world. And indeed, Bulgakov consciously intended him to enter the novel as an enigmatic figure. This is reflected in a diary entry of Elena's dating from April 27, 1939, in which she describes how Bulgakov enjoyed challenging his close friends to guess Woland's identity:

> Yesterday we had both the Faikos round, with Markov and Vilenkin. Misha [Bulgakov] read *The Master and Margarita*—from the beginning. A huge

impression. They immediately and insistently began to ask for a day to be agreed upon for the continuation. After the reading Misha asked—so who is Woland? Vilenkin said that he had guessed, but that he wouldn't say it for anything. I suggested to him that he should write it down, I would write as well, and we would swap notes. So we did that. He wrote "Satan" and I wrote "the devil." After that Faiko also wanted to play. But he wrote on his bit of paper—"I don't know." And I fell into the trap, and wrote for him—"Satan."[1]

However, the extent to which Woland should be understood as the Devil of mainstream Christianity—or of any other kind of variant of the Christian faith—remains a highly contentious issue for readers right down to the present day. If Woland is the Biblical Satan, operating in relation to individuals by tempting them to undertake sinful actions, should he be regarded as unequivocally a force for evil in the novel? This is one of the most complex questions in *The Master and Margarita*.

Some critics, such as Andrew Barratt, have made an articulate case for considering the characterisation of Woland to reflect a specific position in theological debates, in this case as a representative of the Gnostic tradition:

Woland's twin roles of unorthodox evangelist and agent of deliverance cannot be accounted for by reference to any conventional notion of the diabolical, yet they can be accommodated within another tradition: that of the Gnostic religion. Woland's activities in *The Master and Margarita* fit him perfectly for the title of "gnostic messenger." The Messenger – also known as the Alien – is, according to Gnostic teaching, the supernatural being who comes to earth periodically bearing a message which, if properly deciphered, promises the possibility of divine illumination. Perhaps the most important feature of the Messenger, however, is that he will be recognized only be a very small number of people (or "pneumatics"), in whom the divine spark has not been totally extinguished by the conditions of earthly existence.[2]

This interpretation is convincing to the extent that it encompasses the roles of Margarita, the Master and, to some extent, Ivan—all of them members of the literary or literate intelligentsia—in uniquely recognising the significance of their encounters with Woland. We could point out, however, that the Master receives his "message" (the story of Ieshua and Pilate) quite independently of Woland, even if the message is the same one that Woland brings, and that

Woland's role is clearly much more authoritative than that of a mere messenger. Barratt's reading is also less persuasive if it is trying to suggest that Bulgakov was specifically commending a Gnostic vision of the world to his readers. Indeed, it is very hard to read *The Master and Margarita* as a text designed to promote any single approach to Christianity: quite the contrary.

More recent readings by a number of Russian critics, particularly those who write from the perspective of the modern-day Russian Orthodox Church, have been even more problematic. M. M. Dunaev, for example, suggests that the Master has "known" Woland for some time, and that he writes his "blasphemous" novel about Pilate directly under Woland's dictation, as an "anti-Gospel." This interpretation, which seems to take no account of the redemption themes in the novel—affecting Pilate as much as the Master—has been energetically promoted in a book and in television broadcasts by a charismatic deacon of the Orthodox Church, A. V. Kuraev.[3] Bulgakov's otherwise reliable and judicious biographer Aleksey Varlamov similarly slips into highly coloured interpretative territory when he argues that "All-powerful Woland is repellent, loathsome. In the final version of the text he shakes off some of this surface loathsomeness, but what about his inner being?"[4] Modern Western readers will recognise here a range of responses to Bulgakov's work which find the presence of black magic themes in the novel just as unpalatable as those which have caused J. K. Rowling's Harry Potter books to be denounced in certain circles. However, it is virtually impossible to construct any sort of coherent interpretation of *The Master and Margarita*—certainly when considered as a whole—from any of these highly partisan perspectives.

By contrast, one of the textual sources which Bulgakov annotated extensively in creating the character of Woland suggests that he need not be regarded either as the bearer of a very specific version of the Christian message, nor as the source of evil and of scurrilous blasphemy. This source was M. A. Orlov's *History of Man's Relations with the Devil* (1904), the introduction to which makes some observations about pagan views of good and evil deities which may shed some light on what Bulgakov was trying to achieve:

> The pagan not only believed in the existence of the malevolent spirit, but also served him. The evil deity was just as much a deity for him as the good spirit. What's more, there was no need for him to concern himself and make such special efforts with the good deity. Evil gods were another matter. They have to be persuaded to be well disposed towards you, otherwise all you can expect from them is malice and harm. For this reason the

cult of the evil spirit in primitive society was elaborated far more deeply, in much more detail, and more thoroughly than the cult of benevolent gods. [...] Christianity, on the other hand, took up an entirely different position with regard to the evil spirit. Whilst formally recognising its existence, and without thinking of denying it, Christianity turned this position into a dogma and declared the evil spirit to be "Satan" (that is, "opponent"), the enemy of the good deity, a sort of opposite to deity. God must be worshipped, while Satan is worthy only of horror.[5]

Bulgakov seems to incline towards this "pagan" approach in *The Master and Margarita*, with the virtuous Ieshua playing a relatively passive and muted role for much of the text (and any "God" remaining completely invisible), while the "prince of evil" turns out ultimately to be pursuing moral purposes: indeed, he needs to be propitiated if he is not to mete out stern punishment for misdeeds. For the society which Woland meets with in post-Revolutionary Moscow has proved perfectly capable of creating evil by its very own efforts. As Erykalova suggests: "Even the lowest representatives of the Christian universe, Woland and his companions, become righteous judges in the world of Moscow philistines who have destroyed the Master".[6]

Quite apart from his moral standing, his role in *The Master and Margarita* is to provide the structural linchpin which binds the different fictional worlds of the novel together. He does not seem to appear in the Ershalaim chapters, but there is no reason to question his claim to have been a witness in some sense to the events that took place there. We may recall that in the first draft of the novel (1928–30) there is a hint that he identifies himself with the swallow who flies in and out of Pilate's balcony at Herod's palace, and like a witness he insists in any case to Berlioz and to Ivan that "This did happen!"[7] He thus, quite uniquely, provides a direct link between Ershalaim and modern Moscow. He also takes the Master and Margarita with him at the end of the novel to the realm of the beyond, where their eternal destinies will be resolved. Woland is the one figure who travels between all the worlds of *The Master and Margarita*, and his authority is beyond doubt.

However, the most important thing to bear in mind is that Bulgakov's Woland is primarily a literary creation, inspired by poetry and opera rather than by conformity to religious doctrine. Bulgakov derived his essential inspiration for the character of Woland from Goethe's *Faust*.[8] However, it would only be an exceptionally knowledgeable reader who would spot straight away that Woland's name is in fact one of the variant names for the devil Mephistopheles in *Faust*, albeit a name that is only ever used in passing, and in just one single line of Goethe's verse drama (Mephistopheles refers to himself as "Junker Voland" ["Noble Woland"] in the Walpurgis Night scene of Part I, as he commands the witches to make way for him). It is therefore a mark of the Master's profound erudition that he unhesitatingly identifies the enigmatic Woland, simply on the basis of Ivan's description of their encounter. So Bulgakov has opted for a deliberately obscure correlation between his own Woland and Goethe's Mephistopheles, perhaps precisely in order to obstruct facile equations between one character and the other. Some of the standard Russian translations of Goethe's Walpurgis Night scene do not even trouble to include the detail of "Junker Voland" at all, and instead have Mephistopheles simply refer to himself in the line in question as "the devil."[9]

A further complication arises in the way that Woland's name is first introduced in the novel. When Ivan catches sight of the mysterious stranger's visiting card, he sees that he has a name beginning with a "W" (chapter 1). But Goethe himself spelled the name *Voland* in the German original, and it is still not quite clear what importance we should attach to Bulgakov's reworking of the spelling (in one of the earliest drafts he did in fact give the name on the visiting card as "Dr Theodor *Voland*"). Apparently, Bulgakov had been using A. L. Sokolovsky's notes to his 1902 translation of Goethe's *Faust* into Russian prose, in which it is explained that the name "Voland" in Goethe was a usage itself derived from the German noun *Faland*, a word broadly used in earlier times to denote a deceiver or demon.[10] Some interpreters have suggested that the letter "W" appealed to Bulgakov more than "V" because of the rich associations of its inverted form "M" with the names of *M*ephistopheles as well as the *M*aster and *M*argarita, not to mention his own Christian name *M*ikhail.[11] It is also possible to speculate that Bulgakov, using only Russian sources, simply got confused in the end by the Cyrillic transliteration of the Latin letter («B» in Cyrillic), and back-rendered it inaccurately, assuming in error that the name Goethe used must start with a "W," just as the word "Walpurgis" does.

Yet another clue to his identity is provided in chapter 1, when Woland unexpectedly offers the agitated Ivan a cigarette, and astonishes him and Berlioz not only by being able to offer Ivan his favourite brand, but also because these are proffered in an ostentatious gold cigarette-case marked on its lid with a triangle of diamonds. Yanovskaya has mockingly described the attempts by critics to "decode" the significance of this detail, from those who argue that it is a Christian symbol of God, or of the Holy Trinity, to those who have debated whether it is a clue to Bulgakov's supposed involvement (through his father) in Freemasonry. In notebooks dating to 1938–9 Yanovskaya came across some jottings by Bulgakov about the different names of the devil, including a reference to the word *Diavol* (in one of its Russian spellings), with the capital letter underlined; she notes that on the same page Bulgakov had sketched a roughly equilateral triangle. Her own conclusion is therefore that the triangle is a Greek letter "delta," which is quite simply the initial of the Devil himself (a roughly triangular «Δ» in Cyrillic). Yanovskaya also points out that Bulgakov had in fact hesitated over this question: in another draft of the novel a few months earlier the cigarette-case had carried the monogram "F" (for *Faland*?) in diamonds.[12]

From time to time further echoes of Goethe's *Faust* surface in *The Master and Margarita*. The image of a poodle head serves as the handle of Woland's cane (chapter 1), figures as a black outline on a pendant presented to Margarita during the ball, and reappears later in the same scene embroidered in gold on her cushion (chapter 23). This all recalls the fact that when Goethe's Mephistopheles first appears to Faust, it is in the form of a black poodle. The name Margarita also carries an association with *Faust*, since it is the usual rendering in Russian of the name of Gretchen (the diminutive form of the German name Margarete), Faust's beloved. However, Gretchen's seduction and her murdering of her illegitimate baby in *Faust* is not a story which is attached to Margarita: in Bulgakov's novel it is the unfortunate Frieda who shares Gretchen's fate. There is a further echo of Gretchen carousing on Walpurgis night in the detail of the scar which encircles the neck of Gella, the only female member of Woland's retinue. Woland even explicitly invokes Goethe's text when he suggests to the Master in chapter 32 that in his future life he might want to sit, like Faust, over a retort, fashioning a homunculus (in actual fact in Goethe's original it is not Faust but his assistant Wagner who manufactures the homunculus).

However, all these echoes precisely do not add up to a fully-developed system of references on Bulgakov's part to the content of *Faust*. Unlike Mephistopheles, Woland does not seek to tempt mortals towards sin in order to capture their souls: quite to the contrary, Woland exposes people's petty failings only in order to exact appropriate retribution and urge them towards more honest and virtuous behaviour. Most of their punishments (except those inflicted upon Berlioz and Baron Maigel') are in fact rescinded once the appropriate message has been conveyed. Margarita is a bold and self-assured modern woman, not a wronged maiden like Gretchen; and the Master, unlike Faust, does not thirst for knowledge and power. He is, however, the victim of the political and cultural ideologies which have spawned the likes of Berlioz and Maigel'. Bulgakov, who behaved with commendable restraint when those who had persecuted him in his life fell into disfavour, relishes the opportunity in his fiction to fantasise the retribution he would like his opponents to suffer. Ultimately, the images from Goethe's *Faust* gain a new, independent life in Bulgakov, and the reader need not seek fully developed analogies or parallels in order to appreciate their intermittent presence in the novel. As so often with intertextual references in Bulgakov's writing, the full significance of many connections remains allusive, even elusive, rather than direct.

We still need to consider the most explicit identification of Woland with Goethe's text, which is provided by the overall epigraph to *The Master and Margarita*:

"... And so, who are you then?"
"I am a part of that power which seeks forever evil, and does forever good."
Goethe, Faust

Viktor Losev has pointed out that Bulgakov extensively annotated the 1902 translation of *Faust* into Russian prose by A. L. Sokolovsky, which he owned. Nevertheless, the specific rendering from German into Russian of this passage which opens *The Master and Margarita* does not exactly match Sokolovsky's translation, nor any of the other commonly available published translations, and Losev concludes that Bulgakov must have redrafted it for himself.[13] The epigraph was actually a relatively late addition, and it only appears for the first time in a notebook which Bulgakov began writing in on May 29, 1938, that is, when he was about to embark on dictating the entire text to Elena's sister Ol'ga during that summer.[14] "This epigraph was thus not the novel's starting point but its summation," concludes Lesley Milne.[15] But the epigraph's account of the role of the devil Mephistopheles in *Faust* does fulfil the crucial function of inaugurating and providing a frame of reference for the discussion of the paradoxical relationship between good and evil which is so central to *The Master and Margarita*. It is also echoed and expanded quite explicitly by Bulgakov in the dialogue between Woland and Ieshua's emissary Matvey, sent to request that the Master and Margarita should be granted happiness in the afterlife. Woland mocks Matvey for his hostility towards himself:

> You pronounce your words as though you did not recognise shadows, nor evil either. Will you not be so kind as to consider the problem of what would become of your good if evil did not exist? And how the world would look if shadows were to disappear from its surface? (chapter 29)

In this vision of the world, as in Goethe's epigraph—and in certain pagan cults—the devil apparently exists to complement the forces of goodness, tormenting and provoking mankind towards the path of virtue. Woland's initial role is to pay a visit to modern-day Moscow, where people have been cut off from their spiritual heritage by the Bolshevik Revolution. Soviet man has ceased to see that upon his actions will hang consequences which may not even become apparent until the next life, that he is responsible for determining his own destiny through the choices that he makes. In this quasi-existentialist vision of the dilemmas of choice confronting the individual, Woland can only hope to give modern man salutary reminders of his spiritual responsibilities under a materialist political regime.[16]

Bulgakov's appreciation of Goethe's *Faust* was also significantly shaped by his familiarity, not so much with the original literary text as with its 1859 adaptation by Charles Gounod for the opera. He had got to know the opera, mostly in its Russian translation from the French, extremely well as a schoolboy growing up in Kyiv. In those works such as *The White Guard* in which he evoked his comfortable and cultured youth in Kyiv, the image of the score of *Faust* propped up on the piano expressed his nostalgia for a pre-revolutionary past that was irrevocably lost. In particular, he favoured Valentin's aria "Avant de quitter ces lieux . . ." ("Before leaving these parts . . .")—a baritone piece that he liked to sing himself—in which Gretchen's brother prays for her safety before he sets off to war. The aria celebrates the values of family, piety, loyalty, and honour. However, in his satirical play about Moscow under NEP, *Zoyka's Apartment* (1926), Bulgakov had conjured up the resurgent bourgeois materialism of the mid-1920s with a very contrasting musical accompaniment from Gounod's *Faust*. This quite different piece was Mephistopheles's frenzied celebration of human cupidity in a song called "The Golden Calf." As we have seen, one of the early titles Bulgakov considered for *The Master and Margarita* was the phrase "Vot i ya!" ("Here I am!"), the first words uttered by Mephistopheles to Faust in the Russian-language version of the opera.[17] In the finished novel, Woland uses this specific phrase to comic effect, to introduce himself to the very hungover Styopa Likhodeev (chapter 7). Bulgakov quotes the phrase again in his unfinished *Theatrical Novel*, where the "Mephistophelean" publisher Rudol'fi interrupts the writer-hero Maksudov as he prepares to commit suicide. It was thus in many ways Gounod's Mephistopheles, rather than Goethe's original, who provided the primary source of inspiration for the figure of Woland.

Perhaps unexpectedly, Woland is one of the characters in the novel who changes the most as the action unfolds. He initially appears at Patriarchs' Ponds in the comical guise of an eccentric foreigner, wearing an elegant grey suit with matching shoes and a dashing grey beret, and with somewhat troubling different-coloured eyes—one black, one green (chapter 1). These have become a black suit and beret with a gold and diamond pocket-watch by the time Likhodeev comes round from his hangover to find Woland in his apartment (chapter 7). In that first meeting at Patriarchs' Ponds, he briefly assumes in his appearance and mannerisms the prankster mode which will characterise several of his associates during their stay in Moscow, especially the enormous black cat Begemot and the mischievous Korov'ev. This association of the demonic with exuberant humour is well captured in the piece of music with which Bulgakov chooses to mark the hour of midnight in the restaurant at Griboedov House, the jazz foxtrot "Hallelujah" by the American composer Vincent Youmans (1927). It opens with the lines: "Satan, lies awaitin', and creatin', clouds of grey . . . but hallelujah, hallelujah helps to shoo those clouds away. . . ." This was a hugely popular piece which Bulgakov loved to play on the piano, at a time when the Soviet authorities had precisely singled out the foxtrot as the epitome of damaging and decadent western influences on Soviet society.[18]

However, by the time Woland makes an appearance during the magic show at the Variety Theatre, his physical appearance is no longer described: and although his retinue get up to all sorts of comical and scandalous tricks there, he plays little part in them and indeed vanishes before the end of the show. He himself is now referred to as "the wizard," a step towards solemn authority, which is reinforced by the respectful way in which Korov'ev now addresses him as "Messire" (chapter 12). When Margarita is presented to him as they prepare for the ball, he seems to have aged from the man of about forty we saw in chapter 1: he is now balding and deeply wrinkled, still with an apparently twisted face, and wearing a grubby black nightshirt while his painful knee is being massaged. But there is no doubting his awesome powers over life and death. And at the culmination of the ball, as he passes judgement on Berlioz and on Baron Maigel', his shabby garments are transformed into a classical black tunic with steel sword (chapter 23). This is the guise in which he will bid farewell to Moscow in chapter 29. When they quit the city—and the present-day world—on their black horses, Woland and his retinue all revert to their true forms. His minions acquire the human forms of a courtly prince or a demonic pageboy; but Margarita observes that she would be incapable of describing even what the reins of Woland's horse were made of: ". . . and she thought that perhaps they were chains made of moonlight, and that the horse itself was just a mass of darkness, the mane of the horse a stormcloud, and its rider's spurs the white sparkles of the stars." As he reassumes his supreme powers and prepares to plunge back into the dark abyss with his retinue, Woland has become increasingly incorporeal, less and less human in his physical presence. Instead, he has become once more a metaphysical entity, whose true realm is otherworldly (chapter 32).

The deeper seriousness of Woland's purposes also soon becomes apparent: his interest lies in weighing the moral standing of those he comes across in the modern age. He serves ultimately as a force for justice, reassuring Margarita at the end of the book that "Everything will be as it should be, that is how the world is made" (chapter 32). Lesley Milne has rightly observed "the frequently retributive nature of Woland's justice."[19] Berlioz suffers a swift and very drastic penalty for his obstinate scepticism about Jesus and the Devil, and for his role in promoting atheism: he is decapitated by a tram, and ultimately consigned to oblivion.[20] Many other Soviet citizens will be judged—largely for more petty misdemeanours—and found wanting, and will be punished accordingly. In the entertainment he lays on at the Variety Theatre, Woland is really pursuing one of his underlying aims for visiting Moscow in the first place, which is to observe how the people of Moscow have changed under Soviet-imposed atheism. After the shocking episode where Begemot rips off the head of the compère Bengal'sky, Woland allows himself to be swayed by the woman in the audience who pleads "for God's sake" for him not to be tormented any further. All in all, Woland concludes of the inhabitants of Moscow that:

> They're just like other people. They're fond of money, but then that was always the case ... [...] They're unthinking, but what of that ... and compassion does occasionally knock at their hearts ... they're just ordinary people ... and on the whole they remind me of the people before ... it's just that the housing problem has affected them. ... (chapter 12)

This seemingly unremarkable conclusion was the kind of remark that could in fact prove ideologically controversial. Much of the satirical writing of the 1920s (and many of Bulgakov's works, most notably *Heart of a Dog*) had highlighted this fact that human nature doesn't essentially change under a new political regime. Such a view was entirely contrary, however, to the Marxist theories promulgated by the Communist authorities, who justified their revolutionary upheavals of society by arguing that if you changed the material conditions and class relations in which people lived, you would transform human nature and bring into existence a new, collectivist society in which noble impulses would prevail. Satirists such as Bulgakov focused instead on the virtual impossibility of changing people's behaviour, and thereby tended to suggest a degree of backsliding in the bright future of the Soviet society that was supposedly being created.

It is notable that the attention of Woland and his retinue is primarily focused on the world of culture during his visit to Moscow: most of his victims belong to the world of literature (the writers' organisation MASSOLIT), or to associated realms such as the world of theatre. It is not hard to imagine why Bulgakov was especially preoccupied with these, given the frustrations of his own literary and theatrical aspirations in the late 1920s and 1930s. But Woland does not initially seem even to have any knowledge of, or interest in, the Master. He declares that he has come to Moscow merely to observe its inhabitants, and also to celebrate his annual spring ball, and it is only because of his arrangement with Margarita for her to host this ball with him that his attention is drawn to the Master, especially when he learns—to his apparent astonishment—that the Master's novel is about Pontius Pilate:

> "About what, about what? About whom?", Woland expostulated, ceasing to laugh. "At this time? That is astounding! And could you not find any other subject?" (chapter 24)

But as we shall see, this crossing of the paths between Woland, Margarita, and the Master will initiate a series of events which none of them have as yet anticipated, culminating in a deed of cosmic significance, the pardoning of Pontius Pilate. The encounter between the forces of mischief and the genius of the artist will be resolved into an event entirely spiritual in character, fully bearing out that paradoxical message in the epigraph from Goethe's *Faust*, which affirms the eventual triumph of good over evil.

CHAPTER 7

Pilate and Ieshua: Biblical Themes in *The Master and Margarita*

Pilate's question "What is truth?," which he addresses to Ieshua in chapter 2, naturally identifies him for the reader with the Pontius Pilate of the Gospels, where these words are attributed to him (John 18:37). The major protagonists of *The Master and Margarita* reveal their moral standing in the extent to which they rise to the challenge of Pilate's problematic question, and in how they demonstrate their faith in the truth. Bulgakov enables this to happen by presenting his characters not just with a nebulous notion of "truth," but with "the truth," apparently, a completely authentic account of what actually happened when Pontius Pilate was confronted with the necessity of passing judgement on Jesus Christ, who appears in the novel as the somewhat altered but nevertheless unmistakable figure of Ieshua Ga-Notsri. Bulgakov's version of the story is at once immediately recognisable, and yet also disconcertingly different from the Gospel versions in other respects too. He names the city in which the Master's novel is set "Ershalaim," a rendering which closely resembles the Hebrew form, "Erushalaim." This represents one of the instances in which he deliberately departs from the conventional Russian rendering of a name—which here would normally be "Ierusalim"—in order to emphasise that he is blatantly engaged in the creation of a fresh account of events. At the same time, the city undoubtedly remains the Jerusalem we associate with the birth of the Passion story. Bulgakov's interpretations of the figures of Pilate and Ieshua are, similarly, presented in an unfamiliar mode. This has the effect both of suggesting new insights into traditional images and myths, and of creating an entirely new "myth," with repercussions for the larger world of his novel.

The author requires the reader to accept that the four Ershalaim chapters in *The Master and Margarita* purport to represent the absolute truth of those events. This is why Bulgakov constructs the text in such a complex way: if three different sources are capable of telling, dreaming or writing successive parts of a single, integrated narrative, then the only logical explanation the reader can derive from such a conundrum is that this is an ultimate truth, something which exists on a higher plane, accessible to the artist (the Master) only through the power of his inspiration. As Donald Fanger put it in an early response to the publication of the work, commenting on the nature of the Master's novel: "By merging it with Woland's account and Ivan's dream, Bulgakov seems to be suggesting that truth subsists, timeless and intact, available to men with sufficient intuition and freedom from conventional perception."[1] The two writers, the Master and Ivan, are both 'rewarded' with glimpses of that higher truth, firstly because they are disposed to be receptive towards it, and secondly because they have a role to play in some supranatural destiny ordained by Ieshua, who ultimately does belong to the metaphysical realm.

Bulgakov's "true" account of these events is offered in the first instance as a counter-weight to the traditional versions embodied in the Gospels. In his conversation with Berlioz and Ivan, Woland dismisses these entirely: "'Nothing whatsoever of what is written in the Gospels ever actually took place, and if we were to start referring back to the Gospels as though they were a historical source . . .' he smiled again, derisively" (chapter 3). And Bulgakov does much to convince us that Woland is right about the Gospels being untrustworthy. He not only provides us with an alternative narrative of the events, but also displays the stages at which, even from the very start, distortions entered the Gospel stories. Specifically he shows how this affects the writing of Matvey's account. His Levy Matvey corresponds to the tax-collector referred to as Matthew in the Gospel according to Matthew (9:9), and as Levi in Mark (2:13–14) and Luke (5:27–8), and he is the only Evangelist to figure in Bulgakov's portrayal. This may have been precisely because the story of the writing of Matthew's Gospel is especially confused, which would serve Bulgakov's intentions here. There exists one school of thought, according to which the text now accepted as canonical is in fact a Greek version which is only based on—and adds to—an original Aramaic text by Matthew.[2] Bulgakov passes no comment on this specific issue, but it is worth bearing in mind that Matvey's account in *The Master and Margarita* (which corresponds neither to Matthew Aramaic, nor to Matthew Greek) should not really be *expected* to match the canonical text.

In Bulgakov's version, even the original notes jotted down by Matvey are discredited by Ieshua, who complains about this to Pilate:

> They haven't learnt anything, and they've muddled everything that I have said. Altogether I'm beginning to fear that this confusion is going to persist for a very long time. And all because of the fact that he takes inaccurate notes of what I say. [...] I once took a glance at his parchment, and I was horrified. I hadn't said a single one of the things that were written there. I begged him: for God's sake, burn your parchment! But he tore it out of my hands and ran away. (chapter 2)

It is never made clear what Matvey's motives might be for this misrepresentation, unless it is simply his limited grasp in understanding Ieshua's words. He seems to have had every opportunity to get things right otherwise, since he is close to Ieshua before his arrest, witnesses his death, and even learns the truth about the death of Judas from Pilate. In suggesting that this eyewitness material then gets lost from sight, Bulgakov underlines his view of all the Gospels being inherently untrustworthy. The reader, however, is privileged—through the Master's narrative—to have the "true" account of what happened. When Pilate foils Matvey's bitter anger by confessing to the murder of Judas, Matvey is sufficiently mollified to accept from him the gift of a clean piece of parchment. Only then, apparently, will Matvey's notes begin to be written up as a coherent text, which will perhaps become what we know as Matthew Aramaic, and which will thus represent just one step towards the canonical Gospel narrative that bears his name. The "true" story of the death of Judas is not included in these later drafts, however.

In offering the reader a kind of fifth Gospel—Max Hayward has described it as Bulgakov's "own splendid neo-apocryphal version" of the Passion[3]—the author adopts an entirely unorthodox approach to the sacred story. But he is ultimately less concerned with the precise details of the Master's heterodoxy, although this is naturally of some significance, than he is with the artist's duty to follow his own inspiration. Bulgakov undertakes the extraordinary project of rewriting the Gospels not because he wishes to contribute to some sort of arcane theological debate, but because this action fulfils an essential function in his portrayal of the artist.

One of the works which we know Bulgakov read during the composition of *The Master and Margarita* may have contributed to his ideas about the justification for such an undertaking. This volume, which Bulgakov apparently annotated in great detail, was Father Pavel Florensky's *Mnimosti v geometrii* (*Concepts of the Imaginary in Geometry*, Moscow, 1922).[4] It is not impossible that he was introduced to the book by his close friend Evgeny Zamyatin, who had read it during the summer of 1923 and been struck by the work's preoccupation with interlinked concepts of geometry and literary aesthetics which had helped to shape his own 1920 anti-utopian novel, *We*.[5] Inspired by the recent controversies over the theory of relativity, Florensky's study took the 600th anniversary of Dante's death as an occasion to investigate the innovative geometrical features and non-Euclidean perspectives employed by Dante in his vision of the structure of Hell in *The Divine Comedy*.[6] In the first part of his study Florensky uses an analogy from literature to illuminate his thesis about geometry, which may conversely shed some light on Bulgakov's attitude to the canonical texts of the Bible:

> We know [...] that, just as several translations of a single poetic work into another language or languages do not obstruct one another, but actually complement one another, even though no single one of them wholly substitutes for the original – so scientific diagrams of any given reality can and should be multiplied; and truth will not thereby suffer in the least.[7]

Not only should a single reality be capable of being represented in several aspects or interpretations but, as Florensky goes on to argue, any single interpretation ceases to be valid as soon as it starts to claim for itself a monopoly on authenticity. This view underpins the argument implicit in Bulgakov's handling of the Biblical story: that the absolute authenticity of the Gospels can be questioned without this obliging us to reject them, while the artist is nevertheless fully justified in offering an entirely new, personal narration of the story. And after all, even the four Gospels themselves offer competing accounts of a single story. Indeed, Bulgakov's "fifth gospel" perfectly illustrates the device of *ostranenie* ("defamiliarizing," or "making strange"), identified by literary scholars of the early twentieth-century Russian Formalist school as one of the techniques which writers deploy in order to avoid cliché. The Master offers a fresh reading of the Gospel story—and Bulgakov offers this same text as one portion of the novel he longed to make available to readers in 1930s Stalinist Moscow—in order, ultimately, to remind people of the Biblical sources. As we read the account in *The Master and Margarita*, we are startled by its unexpected blending of familiar and unfamiliar details into renewing our interest in the story, and in the eternal issues it raises.

The Master and Margarita was written over many years, during which time Bulgakov was also writing his biographical plays and other studies about remarkable writers such as Molière and Pushkin, both of them free spirits who similarly suffered much under the constraints of authoritarianism. In these works too, Bulgakov sought to create a picture of the past in which he would combine historical verisimilitude with creative licence. In Soviet Socialist Realist culture during the 1930s, such issues concerning the truth and realism of fiction had gained acute political and moral importance.

Clearly, Bulgakov was thoroughly versed in the scriptures and in the apocryphal writings which form the essential backdrop to his writing of the Ershalaim chapters. As the son of a Professor of Comparative Religion, he had not only been brought up as a committed member of the Russian Orthodox Church community, but was doubtless also familiar with at least some of the doctrinal issues and divergences which characterised various branches of Western Christianity, the topics Afanasy Bulgakov investigated for his scholarly publications. Bulgakov was wholly at ease with the imagery and narratives of the Bible, and extremely confident about deploying and elaborating them in his novel. In some moments his evocation of Biblical themes borders on parody.[8] One such instance is brilliantly explored by David Bethea in his book on *The Shape of the Apocalypse in Modern Russian Fiction*, where he considers the slightly puzzling (and perhaps not fully revised) ending of *The Master and Margarita*, with its storms, catastrophic darkness, voices like trumpets, and four horsemen. These details echoing moments from the Book of Revelation create a pre-apocalyptic mood, even though it is an apocalypse which never ultimately comes to pass, and which is resolved with a happy ending for the Master and his lover in the afterworld, and in comic confusion back in Moscow. Bethea has called chapters 31 and 32 "not only the most 'elaborate' but the most *explicit* parody of the Book of Revelation in Russian literature."[9]

As Yanovskaya has made clear, Bulgakov was equally well read in the debates which had swept the theological world during the later part of the nineteenth century, as a more rationalistic society attempted to confront the historical and logical problems raised by the Biblical texts. Bulgakov had, after all, lost his Christian faith in his teens, under the impact of these new, "scientific" ways of thinking.[10] When Berlioz gives Ivan his little lecture on the challenges which academic scholarship has offered to the Biblical stories in the past, he provides a fairly wide-ranging survey of the key arguments put forward by these nineteenth-century scholars. Zerkalov has pointed out that Bulgakov seems in actual fact to have extracted all the points he needed for Berlioz's atheist harangue from a convenient Soviet anthology, the fourth edition of *Antireligioznaya khrestomatiya* (*An Antireligious Anthology*, Moscow, 1930), edited by A. Gurev and published by the Bezbozhnik ("Godless") publishing house.[11]

As for his own religious views as an adult, Belobrovtseva reminds us of the fact that Bulgakov refused on his deathbed to have a funeral service held for him in church, suggesting that he did not want it.[12] Varlamov offers a different interpretation of this episode, quoting Elena's memoirs in which she says that when he was ill Bulgakov whispered to their friend Yakov Leont'ev that Elena would want to give him a religious burial, but that this risked causing her harm politically, and so it should be a civic ceremony. "And then many people reproached me for the way I had buried a believer. But this had been his wish."[13] And perhaps Bulgakov genuinely did have some residual religious feeling. In a 1923 diary entry he had commented on his recent purchase of Fenimore Cooper's *Last of the Mohicans*:

> What charm there is in that sentimental old Fenimore Cooper! His David, who is constantly singing snatches of the Psalms, was the one who turned my thoughts towards God. Maybe He's not needed by the bold and the brave of this world, but for such as myself it is easier to live with the thought of Him.[14]

Belobrovtseva also recalls a conversation she had with Elena in 1968, in which she asked her a direct question about Bulgakov's religious beliefs. His widow told her that Bulgakov was not religious in the traditional sense of the word and rarely went to church, although he did believe in God, and that the notion of a God amounted to the same thing for him as the idea of a supreme justice. According to her, Bulgakov envisaged posthumous existence as the ongoing experience of the spiritual state in which a man found himself, either at the time of his most terrible sin, or of his noblest undertaking. He expected to meet in the afterlife with those who had been close to him, irrespective of whether their epochs on earth had coincided or not.[15] These testimonials seem to concur in suggesting the emotional, aesthetic and spiritual importance that religion retained for Bulgakov, even if he no longer professed or practised the faith of his youth.

Apart from any conceptual ideas he may have gleaned from Florensky, Bulgakov also read more widely as he actively gathered material for the Ershalaim chapters. As well as referring for certain details to his much-loved companion, the classic Russian-language *Brockhaus and Efron Encyclopaedic Dictionary* (originally published in 1890–1907), he drew particularly extensively on four major works central to the nineteenth-century rationalist debates. The first of these volumes was D. F. Strauss's *Life of Jesus* (1835–6), a work arguing that the Gospels should be viewed as myth, even if some credence could be given to the idea of the historical existence of a man called Jesus. Bulgakov also made notes on A. Drews's book *The Myth About Christ* (1909), where even the existence of Christ was called into question.[16] Both of these texts are somewhat dry, and Bulgakov seems not to have drawn upon them very much for specific *realia* in the way that he certainly used F. W. Farrar's *The Life of Christ* (1874), which he read, like these other books, in Russian translation. This fascinating work was intended to present the Church's case in the debate, which it does by amassing an enormous amount of archaeological, historical, geographical and textual evidence to buttress the traditional religious view. Almost every page of the text is embellished with footnotes on points of fact and with illustrations, including views of Jerusalem and of the surrounding area. There are also pictures of coins, clothing, vegetation, the five-pointed "Colossal lamp," architectural plans of important buildings, furniture, architectural features, maps, and works of art. It is this work above all which contributed to the astonishingly tangible, realistic texture of Bulgakov's writing in the Ershalaim chapters, even though he is not necessarily concerned to reflect Farrar's principal aim, which was to demonstrate and confirm the historical plausibility of the Gospel narrations. This kind of extensive research into the most recent scholarly literature about Jerusalem at the time of Christ is one of the factors which lends Bulgakov's rewriting of the Passion story its exceptional aesthetic power.

It emerges from Yanovskaya's account of Bulgakov's sources that he drew on a fourth text in particular as the starting point for his analysis of the significance of Christ. This was Ernest Renan's *Life of Jesus* (1863), as well as, to a lesser extent, the same author's *Antichrist* (1873). When, for example, he drew up columns in which to jot down details about Christ from a number of sources, the first was headed "According to Ernest Renan," the second "According to F. W. Farrar," while the third was headed "According to other sources" and remained empty.[17] Renan's work, which by its very title emphasised that the author viewed Jesus as a human rather than a divine figure, also sought to investigate the Gospels as a historical document. This was not done, as he hastened to make clear in his prefatory words, out of a spirit of irreverence, but in order to cleanse religion of what he believed to be its abhorrent accretions of dogma and superstition. Renan's ultimate purpose was to support religion through his investigations. Certain points made by Renan, especially in his concluding chapter, seem to have found distant reflection in the whole concept of

The Master and Margarita. Fundamental among these is Renan's view that the very narrative of the Passion is in itself seditious: that by presiding over this tragedy the State struck a terrible blow against itself, since all the subsequent renderings of the story would stress the appalling role played by the Roman authorities, and would be understood and used to undermine the standing of the Roman Empire.[18] Bulgakov, in offering his own version of the Passion to the modern era, was of course similarly implying a challenge to the notion of State power. Renan's view that the sublime figure of Christ symbolises the pinnacle of man's striving towards the noble and the good is also important to the portrayal of Ieshua in *The Master and Margarita*. Yanovskaya argues that in general Bulgakov developed the personality of his Ieshua on the basis of Renan, but drew the historical detail and the depiction of Pilate from Farrar.[19]

A further source that Bulgakov drew upon was an 1891 article by N. K. Makkaveisky "On the Archaeology of the Story of the Passion of Our Lord Jesus Christ," which he came across in a set of *Publications of the Kyiv Theological Academy*, where his father Afanasy would publish many of his own research articles. In earlier versions of the Ershalaim chapter describing the crucifixion Bulgakov, following Farrar, had depicted Ieshua being nailed to the cross. But Makkaveisky had investigated the question and shown that victims in that period were often in fact tied to the crosses with ropes. Bulgakov made careful copies of Makkaveisky's drawings of the different types and forms of crosses used, and in his drafts of the novel from about 1936–7 onwards he opted to describe Ieshua being lashed, rather than nailed, to the cross.[20]

The stylistic ploys adopted by Bulgakov for the Ershalaim chapters underpin this technique of blending historically authentic details with features which "defamiliarize" the well-known story. El'baum's study shows convincingly how he selected his language in order to keep the reader poised between the familiarity of realistic detail and the strangeness which appertains principally to the Greek or Hebrew vocabulary used where a Russian reader would expect to find the Russianized terms s/he knows from the Bible (hence "Hegemon," "Ershalaim," "Ieshua Ga-Notsri," "tetradrakhma" and so on).[21] Milne notes that Christ's name, defamiliarized into "Ieshua," is in fact a phonetic rendering of the original Aramaic.[22] Over and above this device of "making strange" people or objects who possess more familiar and traditional Biblical appellations, Bulgakov also goes to considerable lengths to avoid such words as *raspyatie* ("crucifixion") or *krest* ("cross"), whose emotive symbolic power could distract from the individuality of his rendering.[23] All these strategies have the effect of drawing attention to the uniqueness and idiosyncrasy of the Master's vision.

The most striking innovation in the Master's text is the central role played by Pilate in the story, rather than the traditional focus on Christ. The text foregoes the relatively distanced perspective of the Gospels in order to create a tautly constructed psychological study of Pilate, and it is Ieshua who recedes into the background. Justin Weir notes that: "For a novel that delves so deeply into the reflective, creative side of selfhood, *The Master and Margarita* contains few passages that depict the inner mental world of its characters. They occur much more frequently in the Pilate story and indicate the close ties of that story with the Russian realist novels of the nineteenth century."[24] One of the many paradoxes in the conceptual framework of *The Master and Margarita* is that the fantastical is largely confined to the modern world of Moscow, while the imagined past of distant Ershalaim, where the miraculous events of Christian mythology first arise, seems more rooted in concrete reality.

Stylistically, this effect is achieved through the concentrated use of atmospheric imagery (light, colour, sounds, heat, the sun, the moon, the gathering storm) to evoke Pilate's heightened emotional sensitivity, his physical unease, his sense of foreboding, and his premonition of personal and universal tragedy. Bulgakov appears to have leant particularly heavily on Farrar's *Life of Jesus Christ* for the portrait of Pilate in chapter 25:

> Such was Pontius Pilate, whom the pomps and perils of the great yearly festival had summoned from his usual residence at Caesarea Philippi to the capital of the nation which he detested and the headquarters of a fanaticism which he despised. At Jerusalem he occupied one of the two gorgeous palaces which had been erected there by the lavish architectural extravagance of the first Herod. It was situated in the Upper City to the south-west of the Temple Hill. [. . .] It was one of those luxurious abodes "surpassing all description." [. . .] Between its colossal wings of white marble [. . .] was an open space commanding a noble view of Jerusalem, adorned with sculptured porticoes and columns of many-coloured marble, paved with rich mosaics, varied with fountains and reservoirs, and green promenades which furnished a delightful asylum to flocks of doves. [. . .] A magnificent abode for a mere Roman knight! And yet the furious fanaticism of the populace at Jerusalem made it a house so little desirable, that neither Pilate nor his predecessors seem to have cared to enjoy its luxuries for more than a few weeks in the whole year. They were forced to be present in the Jewish capital during those crowded festivals which were always liable to be disturbed by some outburst of inflammable patriotism.[25]

Although the settings shift away to Golgotha and down into the city, away from Pilate in his magnificent and oppressive palace, nothing is described in the Ershalaim chapters which has not been at least ordained by Pilate, or which does not reflect his frame of mind. Even the swallow which flies in and out of the balcony, considering whether to build a nest there (chapter 2), must be interpreted as a reflection of Pilate's fleeting and joyous hope of securing spiritual fulfilment, a hope dashed by the secretary's inappropriately regretful announcement that there are still serious charges of political subversion outstanding against Ieshua. As we have seen, Woland appears to have identified himself as this swallow in an earlier draft of the novel. Bulgakov presents Pilate's story as a tragedy of irresolution in a man sensitive enough to recognise a higher truth, yet who fails to safeguard it.

It is difficult to agree with the well-known modern-day Russian religious publicist Andrey Kuraev, when he describes the Pilate chapters as being quite simply blasphemous. Nor is it possible to accept the view of the highly-placed monastic priest Job (Gumerov), who has declared that the "demonism" of Bulgakov's novel is entirely self-evident, because the Gospel is narrated by Satan, and who has warned readers against simply enjoying the novel as a piece of fiction, on the grounds that: "We cannot avoid making a choice simply by invoking cultural values, artistic mastery and other such things. And people have to make a choice, between Jesus Christ and Woland."[26] What is really important about the Ershalaim chapters in Bulgakov's version is that essentially they lay the foundation for the theme in the finale of *The Master and Margarita* of Pilate's repentance and desperate longing for absolution. Lesley Milne has noted that once again one of Farrar's observations may have contributed to Bulgakov's characterisation of him: "Pilate was guilty, and guilt is cowardice, and cowardice is weakness."[27] She also argues persuasively that this theme represents the culmination of a series of studies of guilt and repentance in his works, beginning with *The White Guard* and some of his short stories, which appear to recount various personal experiences of witnessing and failing to prevent violence during the Civil War years:

> Only in *Flight* and *The Master and Margarita* did Bulgakov find the psychologically, aesthetically and ethically satisfying framework for his need to find a pattern that would 'undo' a violent crime. And in *The Master and Margarita* the victim is, again, a Jew. [. . .] In *The Master and Margarita*, the first drafts of which date from 1928, the year of *Flight*'s completion, the pattern of a dialogue interrupted by cowardice on one side is repeated; the

haunting of executioner by victim in both play and novel represents the stirrings of conscience."[28]

In other words, Bulgakov goes well beyond the traditionally more sympathetic view of Pilate held in the Eastern Church and in the Apocrypha. His Pilate bears the burden of suffering we would normally associate with a tragic hero.

By contrast, Bulgakov's portrayal of Ieshua has—not surprisingly—also aroused some controversy on the grounds that it diminishes the miracle-working divine figure and emphasises instead his most human traits. Certain relatively insignificant details familiar to us from the Gospels are presented as being simply untrue or inaccurate, thus compelling us to reappraise what we think we know about Ieshua, and allowing us to see him in a slightly different, fresh light. For example, all four Evangelists state in the Gospels that Jesus rode into Jerusalem on a donkey or colt; but in *The Master and Margarita* Ieshua firmly denies this to Pilate, explaining that he doesn't possess a donkey and that he simply entered the city on foot (chapter 2). More significantly, Bulgakov's Ieshua fears pain, hopes to evade death, and emerges in his own account of the events leading up to his arrest as a naive rather than a wise victim. While the Gospels allow Christ certain human weaknesses, notably in the Gethsemane narratives, Bulgakov renders these far more conspicuous by stripping all the mystical powers away from his portrayal. In particular, there is no anticipation of a resurrection, and the Messianic aspect is entirely absent. However, if Ieshua is only discreetly invested with an aura of the supernatural, his healing of Pilate's migraine is perceived—by the latter at least—as a miracle. Nevertheless, what Pilate most yearns for is the opportunity to continue his fascinating conversations with Ieshua, not further miracles. Ultimately, however, Ieshua's intervention on behalf of the Master and of Margarita towards the end of Bulgakov's novel, asking that Woland should take care of them, confirms for the modern reader both that he does indeed have a continuing existence in the realm of the transcendent, and that he commands supreme powers over life and death.

One consequence of the presentation of Ieshua as a particularly human Christ-figure is that the political significance of his actions is brought out more emphatically. Ieshua's views on the transience of earthly power finally seal his fate when he expounds them to Pilate:

> Amongst other things I said [. . .] that all power amounts to the coercion of the people, and that there will come a time when the power of the Caesars will no longer exist, nor any other power. Man will pass into the

kingdom of truth and justice, where no power of any kind will exist at all. (chapter 2)

In Bulgakov's works about Molière and Pushkin a similar theme had emerged in relation to the supreme value of art, with literary culture presented as being far more durable than the short-lived regimes of political rulers, however powerful and oppressive. The political sphere is a contingent one: it will be outlived by the eternal truths of morality, as well as by the literary artefacts which can embody them. The challenge to secular power which Ieshua articulates carries telling overtones for the twentieth century, where the rule of Stalin can be compared to the reign of Tiberius. But Ieshua should not be reduced solely to a symbol of democratic freedom struggling against tyranny and repression. Above all he is the bearer of a spiritual truth, a visionary.

This "truth," which it is the Master's destiny to transcribe is both a highly individual interpretation of the Passion on Bulgakov's part, and presented as an absolutely authentic account of what happened. The confrontation between a higher truth and oppressive ideologies is played out in two respects in Ershalaim, where Ieshua has to contend with the prejudices of the old religion led by Caiaphas, as well as with the political power of the Roman regime. This conflict is renewed in modern Moscow as the Master confronts the new philistinism of the literary establishment, and also of the political ideology which shapes it.

Although, as we have seen, Bulgakov certainly undertook extensive research in order to write the Ershalaim chapters, it would be a mistake to assume on his behalf an erudition which might suggest that he pursued the more abstruse niceties of Christology in order to argue a highly specialised case about the "real" story of the Passion. A number of studies of *The Master and Margarita*, such as those by H. El'baum and A. Zerkalov, have, with scant regard for the available archival information about Bulgakov's sources, made minute analyses of his interpretations in order to present him at the very least in the role of a shrewd Talmudic scholar, and certainly in the guise of a profound religious philosopher. Varlamov has suggested that one major contrast between *The White Guard* and *The Master and Margarita* is that his earlier novel culminates in a Christmas which is actually celebrated, despite the political turmoil in civil-war Kyiv, whereas in this text Woland and his retinue leave Moscow together with the Master and Margarita just before the celebration of Easter; and he even suggests that the anticipation of the Resurrection is precisely what actually drives them away. It is difficult to find much textual support for this reading, however. In this sense Varlamov reads *The Master and Margarita*, for all its fantastical and engaging qualities, as a work devoid of hope, one of the most tragic novels in Russian literature, and one which suggests that its author's turning away from his Christian upbringing had brought him pain: "This was not Bulgakov's fault, for it reflected the personal tragedy of his life and faith."[29] This not only disregards the issue of the role and function of the Ershalaim chapters within *The Master and Margarita* as a whole. It also fails to match anything else that we know about Bulgakov's intellectual preoccupations. And Varlamov himself ultimately modifies his conclusions: "However heretical this novel is, it is nevertheless illuminated by the glow of truth." He admits that the "ancient" chapters are not so much blasphemous as beautiful, and that Bulgakov did not ultimately encourage people to deny the true Christ and reject the Gospels, as sometimes people reproach him. In the end, Varlamov feels, Bulgakov's project amounts to a reflection on the intelligentsia's loss of God and their quest to rediscover him.[30]

Bulgakov drew upon his sources—and Farrar in particular—for the striking images and the precise details which would lend his text an air of historical verisimilitude. But this does not commit the reader—or himself—to accepting his particular account of events as a substitute for other versions, including the Gospels themselves. In the Master's novel Bulgakov offers us a version of the Passion story which in terms of the fiction of *The Master and Margarita* is demonstrably an absolutely accurate, genuinely "authorized" version of the events. But at the same time he does not seem to argue any right of supremacy or exclusivity for this version: its significance reflects the moral standing of its creator(s), rather than being measured by the effect it has on its audience. While the Master's novel, like the Biblical texts themselves, springs from and perhaps seeks to inspire what we might loosely term spirituality, it must be remembered that there is never the slightest suggestion that the Master is in a conventional sense a devout Christian, any more than Bulgakov was himself in his adult life. The Master's novel is not primarily a polemic with the Canon; first and foremost it is an act of justification for the Master as an artist.

Bulgakov had lost his religious faith as a teenager, at the time when he was applying to enter University as a medical student and planning a scientific career.[31] As Ellendea Proffer has observed, his fictional works contain a series of portrayals of religious leaders which without exception reveal his contempt for the cynicism and hypocrisy of representatives of the Church as an institution, ranging from Archbishop Afrikan in *Flight* and the Catholic Cardinal Charron in his Molière play, right up to Caiaphas in *The Master and Margarita*.[32] This was a sceptical stance towards established religion that he would maintain for some years. But the Bolshevik seizure of power in 1917 was accompanied by a shockingly ferocious attack on religion, in line with Marxist ideology which condemned religion as "the opiate of the people." Churches were closed and the buildings used as warehouses or destroyed, priests were arrested or even executed, and religious instruction all but banned. Bulgakov was appalled by this crass and violent assault on the value and belief system which had done so much to shape his upbringing and the lives of his own family and milieu in Russian society. As Erykalova observes, "Even in the first draft of *The White Guard* two characteristic features of Bulgakov's fiction had been established: the evaluation of social processes through Biblical imagery and in terms of the categories of Christian morality, and the appearance of the unclean powers as a means of opening up a chink between historical boundaries, and penetrating into the world of the eternal".[33] After his horrified visit with a Jewish friend in January 1925 to the newly established Bezbozhnik ("Godless") publishing house, he had written in his diary: "This crime is beyond price."[34] A reflection on the shifting of attitudes towards Christianity in the new state, also coloured by his fond recollections of his pious but tolerant father, was therefore an essential stimulus to this project. He clearly wished for people not to be cut off by the atheist philistinism of the modern age from one of the paradigmatic narratives of European civilisation. Erykalova reminds us that Bulgakov affirmed in his March 28, 1930 letter to the Soviet government that he was "a mystical writer," and she concludes that he was one of the last writers of his age to draw upon Christian morality and upon a philosophy of the immortality of the soul.[35] In this regard, Bulgakov's determination to resurrect for his readers the Passion story formed part of his general feeling of revulsion about the Bolsheviks' cultural iconoclasm, whether directed against literature or religion.

CHAPTER 8

Political Satire in *The Master and Margarita*

T he interpretation of Biblical themes in *The Master and Margarita* is ultimately so ambiguous that the reader is left wondering whether Bulgakov's
novel really is a fictional treatment of religious issues at all. Broader questions
about good and evil are certainly raised, largely in relation to Moscow's cultural
institutions, represented, on the one hand, by Berlioz, Ivan, and Massolit, and
on the other, by the luckless administrators of the Variety Theatre. However,
Woland and his retinue wreak havoc not only amongst the literary and theatrical elite of the Soviet capital, mocking their shallow, philistine values; they also
seize the opportunity during their visit to expose and upbraid ordinary citizens
for succumbing to all sorts of common human failings and foibles such as greed,
lying, hypocrisy, and lust. These episodes provide some of the most entertaining
and comical pages of the novel. But beyond these satirical attacks on cultural
values, policies and organisations, and depictions of petty universal weaknesses,
The Master and Margarita also contains a further, rather more discreet level of
satire—that of political satire—which conjures up the trauma and strains of living under Stalinist repression.

Andrew Barratt is perhaps mistaken when he asserts that "very little of
the satire has a specifically 'Stalinist' target."[1] He is nevertheless surely right to
express considerable reservations about certain interpretations of the novel
which have tried to argue that the entire work is essentially a political satire.
He is thus not persuaded by D. G. B. Piper's "brilliantly inventive" reading
"identifying" members of Woland's retinue with leading Bolsheviks of the day,
such as Molotov, Voroshilov, and Kaganovich. Piper interprets Sempleyarov
and Bengal'sky's fates as alluding to that of other notable political figures such
as Zinov'ev and Enukidze; and he sees Likhodeev's disappearance to Yalta as
being comparable to Trotsky's forcible removal to Alma-Ata in Kazakhstan in

January 1928, a mark of Stalin's triumph in the power struggle which followed upon Lenin's death in 1924.[2] Barratt also refers with considerable scepticism to a similar sort of 'cryptographic' deciphering of the novel's political allusions in Elena Mahlow's work, which "has been generally acknowledged as an example of careful textual scrutiny being harnessed to a thoroughly misguided purpose." He rightly concludes that "If cryptography really was Bulgakov's purpose, the critical reception of his novel would suggest that he was singularly incompetent at the task." In other words, if the text was ever intended to be read as an allegory of the political infighting amongst the Communist Party elite of the day, it ultimately fails to convey any kind of coherent message to its readers about what has been taking place.[3] Nevertheless, if the novel does not in fact provide an allegory of Party rivalries, it has to be acknowledged that allusions to life under the repressive Communist regime do pervade the text, sometimes in a cautiously disguised fashion, but more explicitly in other instances. Varlamov goes so far as to argue that, although the novel was being written from 1928 onwards, and much of it appears to be set in the 1920s rather than the 1930s, ultimately the work is dominated by the worst phases of the Terror: "*The Master and Margarita* is a novel about the year 1937 in Russia."[4]

The text is certainly full of passing references to the police state. In Chapter 1, for example, Ivan is bemused by the erudite discussion between Woland and Berlioz about the German philosopher Immanuel Kant's proofs for the existence of God, and he boorishly interrupts the two men to exclaim that this Kant fellow deserves to be sent off to Solovki (a notoriously harsh Soviet-era labour camp situated on islands in the White Sea, close to the Arctic Circle). In chapter 7, Likhodeev and Berlioz are described as living in a communal apartment—no. 50, Sadovaya Street—from which people have been "inexplicably" disappearing over the previous two years, invariably after being summoned by police officers. Contemporary readers would have recognised the allusion here to the wave of arrests which took place during the years of the Terror. Likhodeev, suffering from a terrible hangover during his early morning encounter with Woland, glances at Berlioz's door in the apartment that they share, and sees that it has been locked with an official seal—a sure indication that an investigation has been instigated by the secret police. He feels certain that his friend Berlioz cannot have done anything wrong, although the presence of the seal immediately prompts a slight doubt to enter his mind: as for so many Soviet citizens, it was difficult not to become suspicious of anyone who had been arrested by the authorities. And at the same time Likhodeev nervously recalls a "foolish" article he himself had written for Berlioz, and a "dubious" conversation he had had with him on an "unnecessary" topic: politically rash actions which he realises he may come to regret. As the story continues, others will be arrested from 50, Sadovaya Street, including most of the housing committee. The committee's Chairman Nikanor Bosoy has a nightmarish dream, in which he becomes the subject of a theatrically-staged shaming session where those who speculate in foreign currency are encouraged to confess. This episode seems to be depicting a somewhat softened version of a political show trial (chapter 15). In chapter 18 there is an aggressive discussion between the cat Begemot and Berlioz's terrified relative from Kyiv about the latter's passport. These passports had been introduced by a decree in December 1932, and obliged people to apply for one by filling in a form with a whole lot of potentially awkward questions about their social origins and any foreign relatives.[5] When Azazello approaches Margarita in the gardens outside the walls of the Kremlin, she immediately assumes that he is from the secret police, provoking his offended indignation: "What is all this? You only have to open your mouth here for people to assume they're being arrested!" (chapter 19).

The pervasive presence of the OGPU (later NKVD) in Soviet society is frequently alluded to through all sorts of cautious circumlocutions. As Likhodeev's story of his magical teleportation to Yalta becomes more and more incomprehensible, Rimsky tells Varenukha to take away the confusing telegrams from Likhodeev, for the authorities to deal with: "Let them sort it out over there" (chapter 10). Varenukha needs no further explanation as to where he should go; and then, when he fails to return, Rimsky simply wonders to himself "But what on earth for?" (that is, "why have they arrested him too?") (chapter 12). The NKVD headquarters are frequently referred to with elliptical phrases such as "there" or "another place" (evoking for Russian speakers the familiar euphemism «туда, куда надо», that is, "to the place where this needs to go"). There is also one much more explicit reference to "the entire floor of a certain Moscow organisation, with windows overlooking a large square" (that is, Lubyanka Square, where the headquarters of the secret police were situated). By the Saturday morning in Moscow nobody has been asleep in that building, as the police attempt in vain to make sense of the baffling events of the previous few days.

The atmosphere of the police state also occasionally penetrates the otherwise relatively neutral, omniscient voice which narrates the Moscow chapters: from time to time this storytelling voice is overlaid with the officialese of the police report which is apparently being compiled: "It is impossible to say . . . and nobody knows either . . . we are also unable to say, although we do know that . . ." (chapter 28). In a slippage characteristic of the novel's underlying and unifying poetics, such phrases are also echoed in the Ershalaim chapters: "No one knows . . . although we do know . . ." (chapter 26). For in the ancient world there is also an authoritarian police regime, with officials such as Afranius constantly monitoring and reporting on the thoughts and actions of the inhabitants of Ershalaim. Indeed, as Proffer notes:

> One favorite device of Bulgakov's is displacement. There is an important interrogation scene in the Pilate novel, but none in the Moscow strand, where one would expect it; the tyrant of Rome makes his power felt in every decision. All of what we have come to think of as typical of Soviet life in the 1930s under Stalin is shown most clearly in the Pilate chapters.[6]

Nevertheless, it would be difficult to agree with Varlamov, when he argues that Bulgakov disguised Stalin not as Woland, as some have argued, but as Pontius Pilate in his novel.[7] Both Woland and Pilate have far more complex and autonomous roles to play in the text than this reading would suggest.

The Master's fate is alluded to in equally circumspect terms. Even though his novel is rejected for publication, rumours about it circulate, and he begins to be attacked in the press by literary critics, who whip up accusations against him to suggest that he is politically suspect for promoting "Pilatism" (an imprecise neologism typical of the language of Soviet anti-religious propaganda). His sly neighbour Aloizy Mogarych seizes upon this opportunity in order to send the authorities a denunciation of the Master, accusing him of keeping banned literature in his home: but he does this simply because he wishes to take over his apartment. The Master suffers from terrifying presentiments, which are fulfilled by a tapping on the window one October evening. As he is telling Ivan in the psychiatric hospital what happened next, they hear people moving about outside the room, and the reader is excluded from the actual story of what transpired because the Master discreetly whispers the continuation in Ivan's ear. We are left to infer the truth about his having been arrested from the detail he reveals when it becomes safe to speak out loud again: that he was released three months later, in mid-January, with no buttons left on his coat. When the Master is magically restored to Margarita, the traumatic nature of his experiences under arrest is confirmed in Woland's observation that "They did a thorough job on him" and in the Master's own comment "They have broken me" (both chapter 24), as well as Margarita's weeping complaint that "they" have laid waste to his soul and crippled him (chapter 30).

Without operating strictly as allegory, the Ershalaim chapters do echo the Moscow chapters in their preoccupation with tyranny, with the moral and physical courage required to withstand the forces of repression, and with the destruction of innocence. These Biblical paradigms of ethical dilemmas have belonged to the whole of European culture since the time of Christ. But Pilate's shuddering vision of the suppurating ulcers on the face of Emperor Tiberius, his fearfulness about the professional and personal consequences for himself of allowing Ieshua's words about the transience of earthly power to go unpunished, and his own remorse about his moment of cowardice: these are all moments which speak to us in their own right, as well as carrying resonances for modern totalitarianism.

The repressions of the Stalin era thus form a backdrop to the main action of the novel, colouring the atmosphere of Moscow without becoming explicitly the principal focus of the novel. There is one episode, however, which is more directly rooted in a specific, historically real event than any of the rest of the story. Somewhat unexpectedly, the section with the greatest number of unambiguous links to a real event—and to real people—is constituted by the chapters describing what appears to be an utterly fantastical occasion, Satan's spring ball. The inspiration for this, one of the most colourful episodes in the fictional world of *The Master and Margarita*, was actually a real—and spectacular—party held at the American Embassy in Moscow on April 23, 1935.

Relations between the USA and the new Soviet state had remained tense and hostile ever since the Bolshevik Revolution of 1917. No formal diplomatic channels were established until the early 1930s, when Franklin Roosevelt decided to review the situation because of the need to build alliances in the face of the growing Nazi threat in Germany and the apparently imperialist aspirations of Japan. Towards the end of 1933 dialogue was resumed, and arrangements were at last made to open an American Embassy in Moscow. A very grand building on Spaso-Peskovskaya Square, known by the Americans as Spaso House, was allocated to the ambassador as his official residence: it had an imposing staircase, and an enormous two-storey-high domed ballroom with marble pillars and chandeliers.[8] William Bullitt, the first US Ambassador to the USSR, attended a performance of Bulgakov's play *The Days of the Turbins* at the Moscow Art Theatre in December 1933, shortly after his arrival, and was very impressed: "A wonderful play, wonderfully performed."[9] In March 1934 he requested that Bulgakov should send him a copy of the text, and the Bulgakovs were introduced to him in person at a reception in September that year, by which time, as Bullitt told them, he had been to see the play five times and still greatly admired it (his reactions were not unlike Stalin's, in fact).

The Bulgakovs also got to know some of the other Embassy staff, including Bullitt's interpreter and assistant, the flamboyant young diplomat Charles Thayer. During 1934 and 1935, in their role as representatives of Moscow's intellectual elite, the couple were driven to and from the US Embassy in American cars to attend elegant receptions, cocktail parties and film screenings. There was an agreeable day in October 1934 spent discussing theatre out at Thayer's country *dacha*. And the Americans came on several occasions to visit the Bulgakovs at home in their apartment, bringing flowers and whiskey. Elena would treat them to pies, caviar, sturgeon, salmon or veal, fried mushrooms, radishes, cucumbers, and sweetmeats. They conversed in a mixture of Russian, English, French, and German.[10] Always present on these occasions were official Soviet "interpreters," who were patently there in order to file reports on everything that was said.[11] George Kennan, himself a future ambassador, dropped by one day in 1936 to talk about the biography of Chekhov he planned to write; and Chip Bohlen—at that point, like Kennan, a Third Secretary—discussed his plan for translating Bulgakov's play *Zoyka's Apartment* into English. In September 1934 they spent an evening entertaining the youthful American cast who had staged *The Days of the Turbins* at Yale University the previous spring. The Americans showed Bulgakov a programme for their Yale production, which had been inscribed in English by the Soviet Ambassador to the United States with the comment that "Your production of Mikhail Bulgakov's 'Days of the Turbins' will be, I am sure, a landmark in the cultural and artistic approach [presumably he meant 'rapprochement'] of our two countries."[12]

It is difficult to overestimate what all this must have meant to Bulgakov in the mid-1930s. As Stalin's Terror was unleashed in Moscow he remained trapped in a country where his every artistic endeavour had been denigrated and frustrated: there was a very real prospect that his voice would be completely silenced, and indeed that his physical survival could come under threat. And yet here was a delegation of foreigners appearing in Moscow from glamorously distant parts, which quite frankly might just as well have formed part of another world. Led by a charismatic and authoritative figure, these foreigners singled him out for their praise and celebrated his writing, welcoming him into a realm of international cultural and intellectual exchanges. The parallels between Bulgakov's own relationship with these powerful Americans and the Master's relationship with Woland and his retinue must have seemed like a remarkable coincidence. He was probably quite aware at the same time, of course, that the friendly relations he was enjoying with the Americans could serve a useful Soviet propaganda purpose as well. As Varlamov puts it:

> His role was to demonstrate that writers and dramatists like himself could be found in the USSR, that plays like *The Days of the Turbins* were being staged [. . .] and that a talented author had the opportunity to mix freely with foreigners. This was the role of our hero in a performance which was being staged by the Lubyanka, and he could not fail to guess what his role was and who had in fact commissioned it.[13]

It was Charles Thayer whom Ambassador Bullitt entrusted with the task of organising the party at Spaso House in April 1935, the explicit purpose of which was to make a spectacular impression on the Soviet establishment through its ostentatious luxury and liveliness: it was intended to be the social event of the decade. Thayer arranged for there to be a Czech jazz band, a Gypsy orchestra, and Georgian sword dancing. There was lavish food and drink, served on tables which were carpeted with fresh chicory; the rooms were decorated with birch saplings which had been brought into leaf unseasonably early after being kept for a week or so in the Embassy bathrooms. Images of roses and camellias were projected on to the walls of the ballroom. Thayer organised a miniature farmyard in one room, with baby goats, roosters, and a baby bear, as well as golden pheasants, parakeets, and a hundred zebra finches in a gilded net (which escaped at the end of the party, much to Ambassador Bullitt's irritation).

The invitation to this midnight ball caused a great stir in the Bulgakov household: for one thing, Bulgakov didn't own a suitable evening suit, and so they had to visit the Torgsin store (which would later figure so entertainingly in *The Master and Margarita*) to buy some good English cloth for it, together with black shoes and black silk socks.[14] Elena left an ecstatic account of the event itself in her diary:

> My evening dress was a rippling dark blue with pale pink flowers; it came out very well. Misha [Mikhail] was in a very smart dark suit. At 11.30 pm we set off. [. . .] Never in my life have I seen such a ball. The ambassador stood at the top of the stairs to greet his guests. [. . .] Bohlen and another American, who turned out to be the military attaché, [. . .] came down the stairs to meet us and received us very cordially. There were people dancing in a ballroom with columns, floodlights shining down from the gallery, and behind a net that separated the orchestra from the dancers there were

live pheasants and other birds. [...] There were masses of tulips and roses. Of course there was an exceptional abundance of food and champagne. [...] And we left at 5.30 am in one of the Embassy cars, having first invited some of the Americans from the Embassy to call upon us.[15]

Six days after the party Thayer and Bohlen and some other Americans came round to spend the evening with the Bulgakovs, and doubtless there was much hilarity as they recounted the fraught preparations for the elaborate festivities, and the occasional mishaps during the party itself. Later on there were further visits and film shows and parties, where the Bulgakovs were introduced to the French, Turkish, and Romanian ambassadors, and to the French writer and pilot Antoine de St Exupéry. They also experienced American-style hospitality—an "*à la fourchette* buffet supper"—where they were served sausages with beans, spaghetti, and fruit. Some of the Americans suggested to the Bulgakovs that they should join them on a vacation trip to Turkey.[16]

It is quite obvious from Thayer's own very entertaining memoirs, in which he describes his time in Moscow (*Bears in the Caviar*, 1952), as well as from Elena's account in her diary, that the ambassador's ball contributed many of the *realia* which characterise Satan's midnight ball in *The Master and Margarita*, including the improbably spacious venue, the elegant clothes worn, the jazz band, the flora and fauna, and the escaping birds. Perhaps there is indeed something of the buccaneer Charles Thayer in the cat Begemot, at least for the duration of this episode? In earlier versions of the novel the occasion of Satan's ball had been envisaged somewhat less as a stylish society occasion, but rather as a full-blown witches' Sabbath, with scandalous erotic scenes. Chudakova describes as "Rabelaisian" a moment in the 1933 version of the novel, when a vase in the form of a golden phallus grows erect, to Margarita's laughter, at the touch of her hand.[17]

If Charles Thayer has some features in common with the irrepressible and impudent cat Begemot, then the figure of Ambassador Bullitt lends something of his charisma to Woland during this episode, not least in the respectful attentions he pays to the Master, the writer who shares so many autobiographical traits with Bulgakov himself. Early in 1936, Elena recorded proudly in her diary that "Bullitt spoke extremely favourably about the [Molière] play and about Mikhail Afanas'evich in general, and called him a master."[18] This was shortly before the catastrophe which saw the production of Bulgakov's play about Molière cancelled by the Moscow Art Theatre, after the excoriating attack on the pages of *Pravda*. The friendly contacts between the Bulgakovs and the

Americans had continued since the April 1935 ball, but they became more intermittent after this disaster, as the Bulgakovs felt awkward about the expressions of sympathy they might receive ("as always, the Americans are astonishingly kind to us," remarked Elena on April 12, 1936).[19] After Bullitt left his post in Moscow at the end of 1936, and as 1937 (the worst year of the Terror) began, the Bulgakovs' connections with the Americans soon ceased.

And what of the guests at Satan's ball? Korov'ev explains to Margarita that:

> We shall see people who commanded enormous authority in their time. But really, when you reflect on how infinitesimal their powers were by contrast with the powers of the one in whose retinue I have the honour to serve [that is, Woland, the devil], then they come to seem laughable, even pathetic. (chapter 22)

Margarita endures the exhausting task of receiving and welcoming Woland's guests, until "she felt as little interest in the Emperor Caligula and Messalina as she did in any of the rest of the kings, dukes, knights, suicides, poisoners, gallows-birds, procuresses, gaolers, card-sharps, hangmen, informers, traitors, madmen, detectives and seducers". (chapter 23) This parade of monstrous individuals—by analogy—is the equivalent to the gathering of five hundred guests who graced Bullitt's Embassy ball, including many members of the Communist Party leadership such as Litvinov, Voroshilov, Kaganovich, Bukharin, Egorov, Tukhachevsky, and Radek—in other words, almost all the Soviet élite of the day, with the exception of Stalin himself. But Korov'ev is notably "unable" to name the two very last guests who bring up the rear of the fictional procession, a pair of men who have evidently died recently and are attending the ball for the first time. As Piper and Lamperini have shown, their story, which involves one of them compelling the other to spray the walls of his successor's office with poison, is an anecdote that would immediately have been recognised by a contemporary audience. That same charge had been levelled against Genrikh Yagoda, the head of the NKVD, after his arrest in March 1937, when he was accused of instructing his subordinate to spray mercury around the office of his successor Nikolay Ezhov. His trial, widely reported in the press, took place in the first half of March 1938, just around the time when Bulgakov was starting to write the chapters about the ball.[20] This is a rare moment in *The Master and Margarita*, where Bulgakov risks going so far as to allude satirically to a topical scandal involving some of the most sinister and dangerous men in the land.

A final guest, who arrives at Satan's ball as it reaches its climax, is the ill-fated Baron Maigel', an official "guide for foreign visitors," notorious as an eavesdropper and spy. His death by shooting forms part of the ceremony conducted by Woland to crown the occasion (chapter 23). Maigel''s character, too, can easily find a specific real-life prototype in a man well known to Charles Thayer, a certain Baron Steiger, who was extremely well connected in the Soviet establishment. Every week Thayer used to deliver to him a tin of Edgeworth tobacco, which was then passed on to Stalin himself. Thayer recalls in his memoirs having a conversation with Steiger shortly before he too was arrested and shot in December 1937.[21] That he would have been associated in the Bulgakovs' minds with the American ball is indicated by Elena's first draft of her account of their drive home afterwards, in an Embassy car: "We were joined in the car by a man we hadn't met, but who is known throughout Moscow, and who is always to be found where foreigners are – I think he's called Steiger. He sat in the front with the driver, and we sat in the back."[22]

All in all, Bulgakov's experience of being recognised for his talent and lionised by the Americans during a span of about eighteen months between 1934 and 1936 represented an astonishing contrast with the fears and oppression of his everyday life in Moscow. The ball at the US Embassy figured as the high point of a glittering and surreal phase in Bulgakov's otherwise increasingly grim life. The Americans brought with them an incredible, almost magical glimpse of intellectual freedom, of luxury, and of a power that was not in the least cowed by the Soviet authorities. Bulgakov cherished this recognition, afforded him at a time when he could expect nothing but vilification from his fellow-countrymen. However, it would not be appropriate to extend the interpretation of Woland as having elements of Bullitt—and Begemot as having some of the traits of Charles Thayer—beyond the confines of the 2–3 chapters depicting Satan's springtime ball. Woland has other, more significant roles to play in the rest of the novel than that of the American plenipotentiary. Bulgakov's narrative of the ball scene also remains consistent with the wider themes of *The Master and Margarita*, especially where it is a question of the passing of judgement on the non-believer Berlioz, and the restoring of the Master to his lover Margarita. The discreetly concealed topical references to the American event thus have something of the private joke about them, as a subtext which would be picked up only by a few perspicacious readers. For his own amusement, and that of his family and closest friends, Bulgakov here recalls the splendid party thrown by Bullitt and Thayer for Stalin's henchmen by inserting into the text elements of a satirical political allegory which he dares not risk elsewhere in *The Master and Margarita*.

There are obvious reasons why it becomes unthinkable to attempt to publish an explicit political satire under a brutal totalitarian regime which doesn't even admit the possibility of a legal opposition. To the extent that Bulgakov does address political issues in his works, it tends to be in the context of the relationship between the free-spirited individual, often a writer, and the ruler. One pattern which does seem to emerge across Bulgakov's works involves a fascination with the man of power, who is often presented in a relatively sympathetic light. In his play about Molière the playwright is, at least for a time, favoured and protected by Louis XIV in recognition of his talent. It is the sinister Cabale des Dévots, a Catholic secret society implacable in its hostility to Molière, which is determined to bring about his downfall after his satirical exposé of religious hypocrisy in *Tartuffe*. In Bulgakov's play about Pushkin it is his fellow-writers and the secret police who together contrive his ruin, rather more than the Tsar Nicholas I himself. In the Ershalaim chapters of *The Master and Margarita* the Roman Hegemon Pontius Pilate is sympathetic to the radical philosopher Ieshua Ga-Notsri, and it is the local religious authorities led by Caiaphas who insist upon his death. In the Moscow setting, the Master is destroyed by the ideologically-driven members of MASSOLIT, the literary establishment. As in Bulgakov's own life, the head of state seems to be occasionally capable of benign interventions, such as when Stalin telephoned him at home in 1930, or casually brought about the return of *The Days of the Turbins* to the Moscow Art Theatre stage in 1932. If there is a consistent force for evil in society, Bulgakov seems to find it above all in the Establishment, in the collective actions of any grouping of people who combine to impose and regulate ideology and religion. While the head of state may prove fickle to the artist, or fail to attend to what is really going on, or may be swayed by the arguments of ideologues, the individual is left to fight his own battles with the authorities, drawing upon whatever moral or spiritual courage he can muster. Bulgakov's preoccupation throughout his works with the dilemmas of action and of conscience is in itself a political concern, especially in the Soviet state under Stalin, which was committed to an unprecedented degree to suppressing freedom of conscience, of thought, and of speech.

CHAPTER 9

Literature and the Writer in *The Master and Margarita*

The idea of writing as a calling, as a vocation, is one which has been deeply embedded in Russian culture since the age of the national poet Aleksandr Pushkin, who established the perception early in the nineteenth century of the writer as a man set apart from the common herd. The writer was seen—or saw himself—as the figure whose privilege and duty was to speak out about social or political issues, ethics, and personal morality. But the role also acquired a spiritual aura, with the writer becoming identified in some instances with the voice of the nation's conscience.

This concept of the central significance of literature, along with the cult of the individual and of genius, was one which continued to be strongly promoted during the era of European and Russian Romanticism in the first half of the nineteenth century. In Russia, the Realist movement which held sway in the later part of the nineteenth century then began to focus more on the content and the message of the work than on the role of the writer. But subsequently the emphasis switched back again, and a particular view of authorship and inspiration as having quasi-divine properties formed part of the aesthetic vision of Symbolist poets in Russia at the turn of the century. Bulgakov grew up in a cultural sphere shaped by these various traditions, and he would have imbibed their values just as he absorbed the values of the Russian Orthodox Church, in which so many of his family members had found their spiritual vocation. Everything in his upbringing and social circle would have served to validate the Russian cult of literature and the writer.

The advent of the Soviet regime saw the beginnings of a vigorous drive, especially from the later 1920s, to establish monopolistic state control over ideology and culture. The state came to see literary culture as a convenient popular substitute for religious worship in an atheistic society, with writers, their texts, and even their homes and their biographies commandeered for ideological purposes, encouraged and celebrated so long as they could be identified with socialist ideals. All this forced writers like Bulgakov into an embattled position. After having established himself as an outspoken satirist of the Soviet regime in the mid-1920s, especially with works such as his unpublished novella *Heart of a Dog* and his play *The Crimson Island*, he then saw all his plays banned early in 1929 as cultural politics became more repressive. As we have seen, in his notorious letter to the Soviet Government of March 28, 1930 Bulgakov had described how he had become a satirist "precisely at that moment when any true satire (of the kind that penetrates into forbidden territory) had become utterly unthinkable in the USSR." He went on to cite the views of a Communist literary critic who was one of his own most ardent opponents, Vladimir Blyum, who had recently argued that all satirical writing simply represented an attack on the USSR itself; and he ended this section of his letter with a grand rhetorical flourish—"Am I even thinkable in the USSR?"[1] After the banning of his plays Bulgakov had already made one futile attempt to present his thoughts and ideas in what he hoped would prove a less controversial framework, with his historical play of 1929 about Molière, which explored the various personal, ideological and political pressures which tainted the French playwright's final years. At the same time, nevertheless, he had embarked in secret upon the writing of the subversive novel that was to become *The Master and Margarita*. And as the constraints upon literary freedoms became increasingly oppressive during the 1930s, so the theme of literature and the writer came to occupy a more and more central significance in this novel.

The opening chapters of *The Master and Margarita* are focused around the topical issue of ideological conformism in literature. The discussion between the two writers at Patriarchs' Ponds involves the younger, relatively naïve and uneducated Ivan being taught a lesson in literary politics by the experienced Berlioz. As Chairman of the sardonically-named MASSOLIT organization, he represents Soviet Socialist Realism in action. This doctrine, promulgated in 1934 at the First Congress of the Union of Soviet Writers, encapsulated tendencies which had been taking shape for several years, as rival factions had competed during the later 1920s to seize the ascendant in literature. Exasperated by this in-fighting, Stalin had concluded in discussions with the father figure of Soviet literature, Maksim Gor'ky, together with other leading figures of the literary establishment, that the only solution was to set up a monolithic writers' organisation which would control literary production across the USSR. Access to publishing outlets, writing bursaries, and even supplies of typing paper would be dependent on membership of the newly created Writers' Union. In November 1938, for example, Elena was told that Bulgakov had exceeded his quota of four kilogrammes of paper per year, and that she was not allowed to buy any more. "What is he going to write on now?" she wondered.[2] Henceforth there was to be no alternative way of thriving as a writer in Soviet society, and it was these very practical and pragmatic reasons which prompted Bulgakov to fill out the forms and apply to join the Union as soon as applications first opened in the spring of 1934. This came at a time when he was already feeling very low and weary, anxious about his professional isolation, and fearful of death. He was in such a bad way that he was spending as much time lying down as possible.[3] Nevertheless, according to the poet Anna Akhmatova, Bulgakov had little genuine enthusiasm for the new organization, mockingly calling it the "Union of Professional Assassins."[4]

Socialist Realism was proclaimed at the inaugural 1934 Congress of the Writers' Union to be the official method of Soviet literature and of literary criticism, with the stated goal of reflecting contemporary reality while simultaneously highlighting those features of society which would lead to the creation of a Communist paradise. In order to belong to the literary establishment and gain the privileges associated with membership of the Union, you had to subscribe in your literary work and practices to the tenets of Socialist Realism. While we often think of Socialist Realism as a category of literature, typified by texts such as the new genre of "production novels" which described the heroic achievements of Soviet factory workers in building the new state, it can also be regarded as a set of processes, or as a mechanism. Socialist Realism was essentially created not so much by writers themselves, as by the literary bureaucracy, journal editors, and censors. Berlioz exemplifies this regulatory role when he patronizingly explains to Ivan that his new poem cannot be published because it "erroneously" presents Jesus Christ as someone who, however flawed, did actually exist. In order to feed into the Soviet state's militant atheism and its campaign to eradicate religious belief from the popular mind, everything that is described in the Bible had instead to be presented as a made-up story, as being no better than a fairytale.

This first episode of the novel concludes with Berlioz suffering an unexpectedly brutal death, which is surely to be read as a punishment for his unbelief and for his corrupting influence on Ivan. This event will provide the starting-point for one of the novel's gradually unfolding plotlines, which charts the ways in which Ivan becomes aware of the hollowness of his previously held, officially approved literary values, and starts to pursue his path towards a truer knowledge and understanding. The budding working-class writer Ivan has been writing under the pseudonym Ivan Bezdomny ("Ivan Homeless"), a pseudonym Bulgakov himself had adopted for some of the early comic sketches which he wrote for a newspaper published by the railway workers' union, shortly after his arrival in Moscow to embark on a literary career in September 1921.[5] In his horror and panic at the death of Berlioz, Ivan's first instinct is to pursue the mysterious stranger Woland, who appears to be complicit in the death, and have him arrested. After a confused and frustrating chase across Moscow, he turns up that evening at Griboedov House, the luxurious writers' club and restaurant which houses the MASSOLIT administration. Bulgakov gloatingly mocks the backbiting of the MASSOLIT committee members, and the greed and vanity of the diners enjoying their sumptuous meals on the verandah. This is not in fact a temple of art, but a monument to materialism.

Much later in the novel, the cat Begemot will visit Griboedov House with Korov'ev and exchange sardonic comments about the astonishing talents which must be developing under this roof, "like pineapples in a glasshouse," as Begemot puts it. They decide to enter and enjoy a meal at the writers' club themselves, but are stopped by a young woman who asks to see their membership cards. Korov'ev responds in mock astonishment: "In order to be convinced that Dostoevsky is a writer, would you need to ask him for his membership card?" The hapless young woman retorts—but not entirely confidently—that Dostoevsky is dead, to which Begemot protests that Dostoevsky is "immortal."[6] The visit of the mischievous pair ends, with a certain inevitability, in a conflagration: Griboedov House goes up in smoke. As they prepare to leave Moscow Woland and his retinue discuss the fire, and venture to hope that when it is rebuilt, Griboedov House will become an improvement on the previous place—and the reader is left with the tentative hope that this will therefore prove to have been a cleansing fire for Soviet literature (chapter 28). And indeed, as Lesley Milne observes, the very existence of Bulgakov's own project epitomized an act of protest against all that MASSOLIT—and official Soviet literature—stood for: "Against this background *The Master and Margarita* begins to look like a defiant peacock display of all the old, discredited, discarded, outmoded literary styles, themes and genres."[7] Varlamov agrees that Bulgakov's novel, while being wonderfully free and powerful and completely unlike anything else, is nevertheless at the same time linked to the inspirational pre-Soviet traditions of the likes of Dante, Goethe, Hoffmann, Pushkin, Gogol', and Dostoevsky, rather than having derived any of its qualities from the model of Socialist Realism which was being forced upon him and his contemporaries in the 1930s.[8]

After his visit to Griboedov House Ivan, who has become distressed and obstreperous, has been removed to the sanatorium run by the enigmatic Dr Stravinsky. Here he will undergo a splitting of his personality—essentially an epiphany—partly as a result of Stravinsky's calming treatment, and partly as a result of his encounter with the Master. On the one hand, he realizes that, rather than arresting Woland, what he actually wants most of all is simply to hear the continuation of that story Woland was telling him and Berlioz at Patriarchs' Ponds, about the encounter between Ieshua and Pilate. This is a token of the captivating storytelling skill of Woland; but it also demonstrates that Ivan has become immune to Berlioz's atheistic scepticism, that he has allowed himself to become spontaneously open towards the spiritual realm. And it only takes the Master to express some doubt about Ivan's literary talents—without ever having read anything he has ever written—for Ivan to acknowledge that his state-endorsed poetry is actually dreadful, and for him to undertake never to write poetry again. As an apparent reward, he dreams the continuation of the story of Ieshua—his crucifixion—when he next falls asleep. At the end of the novel we meet Ivan again some years later, when he has indeed abandoned his poetry and become instead a lecturer at an Institute of History and Philosophy. But he becomes troubled at every spring full moon, revisits Patriarchs' Ponds, and in his dreams not only sees again the end of the crucifixion, but is also granted a new vision, this time about the final outcome of Pilate's story, the true ending of the narrative, when Pilate is released to continue his conversation with Ieshua as they walk away up the moonbeam. He also glimpses again the figure of the Master, who pronounces him to be his disciple, and is soothed by a kiss from the beautiful Margarita. The ill-educated young man, whose instinctive spirituality prompted him in the first place to write a poem depicting a Jesus Christ who really existed, has followed a path which is quite at odds with the rest of Soviet society, and he is subsequently permitted to find occasional solace and peace only in the realm of dreams. A step into madness has liberated him, just as it does the main protagonist of Evgeny Zamyatin's dystopian novel *We* (1920), into venturing outside the safe world of regulated culture and into a bewildering but entrancing realm of freedom.

Nor is Ivan the only young writer who comes to reject the prevailing political ideology that has shaped his work. The poet Ryukhin helps to escort Ivan from Griboedov House to the sanatorium, and is rewarded for his pains by being accused by Ivan of complete hypocrisy, and of writing bombastic verses celebrating the proletariat when in fact his origins, like his attitudes, are those of the lower middle-class. As he returns to Moscow, Ryukhin is forced to admit that Ivan was telling the truth: "I don't believe in any of the things that I write!.." They drive past a monument to Pushkin, and Ryukhin shakes his fist resentfully at Russia's greatest writer, complaining that his poetry never had any especial merit and that his immortality was achieved only because he was shot in a duel. As day dawns, merciless and irrevocable, Ryukhin drowns his sorrows in drink (chapter 6).[9]

The writer who is of central importance to *The Master and Margarita* is, of course, the Master. In the first drafts of the novel he figured as the learned scholar "Fesya," although subsequently he loses any name and simply becomes an anonymous—and therefore more universal—figure. Inspiration for his character may have derived in part from Bulgakov's father, the theologian Afanasy, whom Bulgakov referred to as having provided the original inspiration for this novel, and also from one of his most devoted friends and closest confidants, the philosopher and literary historian Pavel Popov. Both of these men had a command of several ancient and modern languages, a detail which survives into the characterization of the Master. In February 1930 the devout Christian Pavel Popov was arrested on a charge of espionage, and although he was released after two months of detention and interrogation, he was given a sentence of internal exile, meaning that he was not permitted to live in the capital cities (Moscow and Leningrad), although these penalties were soon commuted. It is possible that his connections with the distinguished Tolstoy family—his wife was Lev Tolstoy's grand-daughter—afforded him some protection. Popov was interrogated again in March 1931, and suffered an episode when his wife tried to get him admitted to a psychiatric hospital because of his increasing paranoia. He and his wife certainly claimed to recognize their Moscow home in the basement apartment where the two lovers meet in *The Master and Margarita*.[10] Like Popov, the Master, in recounting his story to Ivan, makes it clear that he was not a professional writer originally; in fact, the Master's career has been that of a museum specialist. It is only accidental wealth (a lottery win) that prompts him to give up his job at the museum and start to write instead.

In the encounter with Ivan at the sanatorium, the Master establishes himself as an uncompromising figure with some intellectual authority as well as erudition—he immediately grasps who Woland is, for example, by spotting the connections between the character's name and appearance and Goethe's *Faust*. But his claim of the title of "Master" rather than mere "writer" is simultaneously impressive and also faintly comical (perhaps an autobiographical moment of self-ironization on Bulgakov's part?):

"Are you a writer?" the poet asked with interest.

His guest's face darkened, and he shook his fist at Ivan, before saying: "I am a Master". He took on a stern look, and drew out of the pocket of his dressing-gown a completely greasy black cap, with the letter "M" sewn on to it in yellow silk. He placed this cap on his head and showed himself to Ivan in profile and face forward, to demonstrate that he was a Master. (chapter 13)[11]

And indeed, he reveals himself in his personal life, and particularly in his contacts with the literary establishment, to have been a somewhat weak figure. As his narrative of his previous life is unfolded to Ivan, it becomes apparent that he has become increasingly dependent on Margarita's courage and strength of character. She it was who urged him to try to get the novel he had written about Pilate published, but when it is rejected and attacked in the press he becomes increasingly fearful and intimidated, and she has to start taking care of his mental and physical health. Margarita undertakes a bold, not to say reckless commitment when she enters into a pact with Woland in the hope of bringing the Master back from wherever he has vanished to, and it is she, not the Master, who negotiates with the devil. Even when the Master is magically restored to Margarita after his arrest and the time he has spent taking refuge in the psychiatric hospital, he still leaves it to her to make decisions about their future and clings to her for his sanity. It is not difficult to read a grateful tribute to his fiercely protective wife Elena into Bulgakov's depiction of the Master's feisty companion.

It is notable that we never learn anything about what prompts the Master to write his novel, why he chose to write about Pilate, nor about how the writing process actually proceeded. One of the reasons for this is of course related to the discreet aligning of portions of the Master's actual text (chapters 25 and 26 in *The Master and Margarita*) with Woland's narrative and Ivan's dream, for purposes that we have explored elsewhere. It is also consistent, to some extent, with the way that Bulgakov writes about writers in other contexts. In his biographical plays about Molière and Pushkin, for example, he was determined to do everything in his powers to avoid showing "the genius at work," this despite the director Konstantin Stanislavsky's insistence—to Bulgakov's intense irritation—that Molière should appear on stage in Bulgakov's play at the Moscow Art Theatre, quill in hand, composing immortal works of art. In what we might recognise as an explicit nod in these works in the direction of Romanticism, writing of integrity in Bulgakov's world is created as the direct product of inspiration and of genius, and should not be subjected to either explanation or analysis. We are left with a degree of uncertainty about the Master's writing of the Ershalaim narrative, however: has it in fact involved any creative inventiveness on his part, and is he a truly original artist, or has he merely served as a vehicle for transmitting a vision that he has received from on high?

The Master's sole literary work nevertheless has a significance which elevates it beyond that of a mere novel. As Chudakova puts it: "The Master's novel takes on the status of some sort of 'fore-text,' which has existed since primordial times and has only been drawn from the darkness of oblivion into the 'bright field' of modern consciousness by the genius of the artist."[12] In her view, the Master has had a transcendental vision, apparently in some sort of neo-Platonic Romantic fashion, an adumbration of the world beyond, and he has more or less "transcribed" this eternal narrative in order to offer it to a contemporary readership. Furthermore, as we have seen, this narrative is presented as being the absolute truth of the events which took place in Ershalaim. In the sixth draft of the novel there was an exchange that Bulgakov eventually crossed out, where Woland confirms this directly to the Master: "Listen to me, Master, [. . .] in your novel you guessed / wrote the truth. Everything happened precisely as you described it."[13] And indeed, when Ivan's retelling in the sanatorium of Woland's narrative about Pontius Pilate draws to a close, the Master clasps his hands together "reverently" and whispers: "Oh, how I guessed it! Oh, how I guessed it all!" (chapter 13).

Both Woland and Ieshua evidently appreciate the true importance of the Master's achievement: Woland understands the significance of the Master's novel the moment the manuscript appears in his hands, and Ieshua subsequently requests that the Master should be granted peace as his reward. And the ultimate reason for this benevolence towards the Master, fallible as he is, becomes apparent in the final chapter of *The Master and Margarita*, chapter 32. The Master and Margarita are brought to a place where they discover the figure of Pilate, still tormented after two thousand years by remorse for his actions. Woland explains to the Master that his novel is not, as he had imagined, completely finished. The Master immediately grasps that it is up to him to step forward to complete the story, by freeing Pilate to stride up the moonbeam with his faithful dog Banga, to rejoin Ieshua and continue their absorbing conversation. He cries out: "Free! You are free! He is waiting for you!" (chapter 32). In other words, having served the cause of good by writing the novel in the first place, the Master is now empowered to become an active agent within the story itself, bringing Pilate's torments to a close. Thus the widest temporal parameters of *The Master and Margarita* turn out to be defined by the period which stretches from the day Pilate commits an appalling deed in Ershalaim by failing to save Ieshua, until the moment two thousand years later when his act of cowardice is at last forgiven.

The Master remains an elusive figure throughout the text, however, as do most of the writer protagonists in Bulgakov's works. He only appears fleetingly for the first time in chapter 11, and the two eponymous characters who give Bulgakov's novel its title only begin to be delineated for the first time in the course of chapter 13, nearly halfway through the book. The Master announces to Ivan that he has renounced his name, his lover and his entire past, as indeed he has renounced his novel by burning it in a moment of fearfulness. He figures relatively infrequently in the rest of the narrative, and does little to move the action forward. The one thing he clings to is his status as a Master, bestowed upon him by Margarita and represented by her gift of love, the cap with the letter "M" embroidered upon it which serves as his poet's crown of laurel leaves. Margarita is not only devoted to him as a man, but she also passionately supports his writing. However, she is not by any means his muse, for his has been an entirely solitary engagement with his own inspiration, and the novel is something he has already nearly completed by the time he meets her. And given the hostile reception his novel then receives at the hands of the Soviet critical establishment, it becomes apparent that what lends his creation worth cannot be its popular reception, but the qualities of the original inspiration which gave birth to it. This too is a neo-Romantic conception of art; it had previously been well encapsulated in the Symbolist poet Aleksandr Blok's poem entitled "The Artist" (1913), in which the poet is described as a figure set apart from the crowd, who exists for the exquisite experience of inspiration, and scorns the actual poem which he writes, comparing that to a captive bird in a steel cage, whose song merely pleases the common man.

The press attacks on the Master's work—even though it had remained unpublished—are all too reminiscent of the abusive and denunciatory language which Bulgakov himself had had hurled at him by Vladimir Blyum and other Soviet establishment critics, and which he detailed at length in his letter to Stalin and the Soviet government of March 28, 1930. Bulgakov told Stalin and his colleagues that he had assembled a scrapbook of 301 comments made about him in the press, of which only 3 had been favourable. In the others, which he quotes in part, his "stinking" play *The Days of the Turbins* is described as the creation of someone who has picked leftovers out of a heap of vomit; and his hero Aleksey Turbin is described more than once as a "son of a bitch." Bulgakov himself is described as the idol of the bourgeoisie, whose "satire" amounts to mere slander. The destruction of his works is therefore something only to be celebrated, as a great achievement.[14] The critic Latunsky, whose flat Margarita wrecks in the novel, was based on a certain Osaf Litovsky, another of Bulgakov's most persistent and outspoken opponents in this vein. Elena referred to Litovsky as a "scoundrel" on February 6, 1936, noting that a review he had written of the production of the Molière play "exuded malice."[15]

The Master begins to suffer from depression after these attacks, which builds into a paranoiac fear of a sinister octopus, clearly representing the threat of persecution by the authorities. He burns his manuscript in a gesture of fear and despair shortly before he is indeed arrested. The fact of his arrest is indicated by a detail which contemporary readers would instantly have understood, merely because of the image of his being released a few months later on to the street with all his buttons missing (these were always removed from prisoners' clothes). In his living existence, he will never again be reconciled to his art, even when Woland restores the work to him with that great affirmation of the power of art to outlive the contingencies of political persecution, enunciated in one of the most celebrated phrases in *The Master and Margarita*: "Manuscripts don't burn" (chapter 24). Only after the Master's death, achieved at Woland's behest with poetic aptness by poisoning with "the same Falernian wine" which Pilate had drunk with Afranius two millennia earlier, does the Master regain his faith in his novel.[16] Margarita frets that they should carry the text of the work away with them to their immortal destiny, but the Master insists that he will never forget any of it now.

There is perhaps a degree of criticism implied in Ieshua's final judgement on the Master, as conveyed to Woland by Matvey: "He has not earned the light, he has earned peace" (chapter 29). As Bulgakov contemplated the ruin of his own literary ambitions during the 1930s, and reflected upon moments of doubt, hesitation and regret which had coloured his own life, he too had come to long for nothing more grandiose than to be left in peace. Woland had stated that "All theories are equally valid. There is amongst them one, according to which each shall be rewarded according to his faith. So be it!" (chapter 23). The Master's destiny is shaped by the limitations of his character: he has doubted Margarita's love and he abandoned his artistic creation as well. He has never sought the supreme reward of "light" (which perhaps stands here for religious faith, as well as the achievement of glory), lacking as he does both perseverance and courage. When he speaks the words which release Pilate, he is acting specifically in his capacity as an artist. Margarita, upon seeing Pilate's distress, had at first sought to release him herself from his torments, prompted by compassion, as she had absolved Frieda at Satan's ball. But here it is the artist who must act, crowning his labours with the concluding words to his novel. These turn out to be not at all the ones which he and Margarita had so long anticipated, about the fifth Procurator of Judaea. The Master's novel had offered an unusually sympathetic portrayal of the figure of Pilate, normally a detested figure in Christian culture. As so often in his writing, Bulgakov commends the forgiveness of sins, of cowardice, and of moral weakness. He also offers a promise that the memory of wrongdoing and failure—whether by Pilate or by the Master—will be allowed to fade and be erased.

The ultimate destiny granted to the "thrice Romantic Master," as Woland describes him (chapter 32), is indeed invested with the trappings of nineteenth-century Romanticism: a domestic idyll alongside his beloved, reached by walking across a moss-covered stone bridge, in a quiet house adorned with a curling vine and surrounded by cherry trees, where the music of Schubert will be played and sung in a candlelit room, and where he can carry on his writing with a goose quill.[17] And he too will be freed from his distressing recollections: "The Master's memory [...] began to fade. Someone had released the Master into freedom, just as he himself, a moment earlier, had released the hero he had created" (chapter 32).

The Master may have achieved personal fulfilment, but it remains far from certain whether the atheistic materialism of Soviet society has been affected in any way by what he has written. The manuscript of the novel has in fact now been destroyed for a second time, in a further conflagration as the Master's semi-basement apartment catches fire at their deaths. Although the story it told turned out, as Woland prophesied, to have some surprises still in store for the Master, nothing of it remains behind in the real, physical world of Moscow. The Master's narrative of the supreme story of the Gospels has been rejected and ignored in the atheist USSR, where people have remained indifferent and deaf to the messages he has offered them. Overall, then, *The Master and Margarita* ends on a note of subdued pessimism. The writer may be identified with the highest ideals of the human spirit, but he has been defeated and silenced in the secular world. Bulgakov opens the final chapter of his novel (chapter 32) with the following lyrical reflection:

> My gods, my gods! How sad the earth is at evening! And how mysterious the mists are over the marshes. Anyone who has lost his way in such mists, anyone who has suffered a great deal before death, anyone who has winged

his way over this earth, bearing an impossible burden on his back – that man knows this. The weary man also knows it. And he will quit without regret the earth's mists, its marshes and its rivers, and he will deliver himself with an easy heart into the arms of death, knowing that death alone [can soothe him].[18]

Perhaps we can detect the author's own longing here for oblivion in the final months of his life, as the terrors of the Stalinist age gave way to the sufferings he endured in his painful illness. But nothing would shake his belief in the integrity of great art and the vocation of the writer, as was confirmed in one of the final letters written to him in loving tribute in December 1939 by his close friend Pavel Popov:

Reading the lines that you have written, I know that a genuine literary culture still exists: transported by fantasy to the places you describe, I understand that the creative imagination has not run dry, that the lamp lit by the Romantics, by [E. T. A.] Hoffmann and others, burns and gleams, and that altogether the art of words has not forsaken mankind. . . .[19]

As Popov shrewdly observed, Bulgakov, in positioning himself in the lineage of the nineteenth-century European Romantics, was asserting the durability of eternal literary values and the supreme role of authorship. Prime amongst these values were those of subjectivity, and of creative freedom. Another characteristic device of Romantic writing which Bulgakov frequently adopted was the practice of blurring the boundaries between author and fictional hero, so that *The Master and Margarita* becomes yet another example of a Bulgakov work where a quasi-autobiographical hero (often sketchily delineated) shares the dilemmas and torments that Bulgakov himself endured in real life. The genius may simultaneously reveal himself to be a weak man or a persecuted victim, in the tradition of Romantic heroes as "noble failures." Bulgakov's highly original plots and ingenious dramatic structures showed no concern whatsoever for prevailing trends or for extrinsic criteria such as morality, utility or conformity to predetermined aesthetic standards. If Romanticism had originally in the nineteenth century represented the rejection of a neo-Classical past, for Bulgakov the assumption of Romantic attitudes in the twentieth century indicated the rejection of the "bright future" promised to him and his contemporaries by the Communist Party, and above all a rejection of what was envisaged by the doctrine of Soviet Socialist Realism.

"So who are you, then?" Narrative Voices in *The Master and Margarita*, Followed by a Stylistic Analysis of Extracts from the Text

This question, which is raised in the epigraph to the novel in the form of the quotation from Goethe's *Faust*, is one which has wide resonances for the novel as a whole. It does of course refer primarily to the issue of how the reader—and the characters within the novel—should evaluate the identity and actions of the mysterious Woland, and in particular the question of whether he serves the forces of good or evil. But it is a question which we as readers will find ourselves asking of the text in other respects as well. Who is Ieshua Ga-Notsri? He is at once Christ and not-Christ. Pontius Pilate is recognisably the Biblical Pilate, and at the same time he is portrayed as a character with far more psychological complexity—and is Levy Matvey simply the evangelist Matthew? As the chapters of the novel succeed one another during our first reading of it, we will also find ourselves wondering about the very title of the novel we picked up to read: who is the Master, and who is Margarita? Neither of them even figures in the first third of the text, and the eponymous hero will forever remain anonymous, referred to only by his honorific title of "Master." His beloved is described—but not named—in that same chapter 13, and it is only in chapter 19 that the narrator will provide us with her actual name and patronymic: Margarita Nikolaevna.

What's more, the complexity of the novel's plot, as it shifts back and forth between Moscow and Ershalaim, throws up vital questions about the identity of the narrator—or narrators—as well.[1] When Woland first tells Berlioz and Ivan the story of Pilate and Ieshua in chapter 2, he claims to do so, however improbably, in his capacity as a witness: he was there, he saw these events unfold. But his Ershalaim narration is offered as a self-contained text, and it is articulated in a voice entirely different from that which he has hitherto used in chapter 1. Up until now his voice has been insecure, puzzling: his appearance causes Berlioz and Ivan to assume that he is a foreigner, possibly a German or an Englishman—or perhaps a Frenchman, or Pole? In any case he speaks to them with a heavy foreign accent, although his conversational Russian is otherwise correct: so perhaps he is a Russian émigré, come to Moscow as a spy? But as soon as he starts to tell them about Ershalaim his accent entirely disappears. The descriptive language he uses in Russian becomes nuanced and sonorous, relatively formal in register and full of historically specific detail. But subsequently, after the shocking death of Berlioz, Woland starts to pretend in chapter 4 that he barely speaks or understands Russian any more. Ivan is left absolutely bemused about his true identity.

One characteristic feature of Bulgakov's devices for individualising the protagonists of his works is his acute attention to their voices: in this novel Woland speaks in a bass register, while his assistant (and supposed former choral conductor) Korov'ev speaks in a comical, cracked tenor; meanwhile the traitor Judas has a strikingly thin and high voice. To some extent this reflects Bulgakov's heightened sensitivity to music, and his great familiarity with operatic libretti in particular, where different roles tend to be identified with different voices (the rich *basso profundo* for men who command power, for example). His extensive experience as a playwright further enriches the ways in which spoken dialogue comes to occupy a central significance in his prose, where it is never casual or merely instrumental. We should bear in mind as well the number of occasions when he transformed his own prose works into plays: there is always a piece of theatre poised to burst out of Bulgakov's short stories and novels, and *The Master and Margarita* is no exception. Several of Bulgakov's friends and relations have testified to the fact that one of his gifts was that he could always "act out" his prose works, just as well as he could his dramas. As the writer Konstantin Paustovsky put it: "He was capable of representing any character from his stories and novels with unusual expressiveness. He had seen them, he had *heard* them [my italics], he knew them through and through."[2] The literary consultant of the Moscow Art Theatre, Pavel Markov, with his enormously wide experience of the theatre, also recognised in him an unusual dramatic gift:

> In actual fact Bulgakov was himself a wonderful actor. [. . .] But there was one paradoxical thing: his appetite as an actor and author could not be satisfied by any single role in a play: what he needed was not just one character, but many characters, not one image, but many images. If you had asked him to perform any play he had written, he would have performed it in its entirety, role after role, and he would have done it with perfect skill. And so it was with *The Days of the Turbins*: he demonstrated almost all the parts during rehearsals, helping the actors very willingly and generously.[3]

The boundaries between real life and the dramatic were far from rigid for him: not only did he pour his lived experiences into theatre, but he also theatricalised all his prose writings, as well as his past and present lives.

As we have already suggested, the "identity" of the voice in which Woland tells Berlioz and Ivan the Pilate story becomes far more problematic when we realise that the continuation of the story (chapter 16, dreamt by Ivan; and chapters 25 and 26, read by Margarita) exactly follows on from and matches Woland's account in chapter 1, as much in narrative style as in content. The "voices" of Woland, of Ivan's dream, and of the Master's fiction are apparently identical: but how can any rational explanation be found for this being the case? This tension between identification and discrepancy amongst the narrators of the Ershalaim chapters is very blatant and has implications, as we have seen, for the structure and the metaphysics of Bulgakov's novel as a whole.

What is less often observed, however, is the way in which the rest of *The Master and Margarita*—in other words the Moscow chapters—is also narrated to the reader in a variety of different voices. In 1926 Bulgakov had told his friend Pavel Popov that "My favourite writer is Gogol': in my opinion nobody can compare with him. I read *Dead Souls* at the age of nine."[4] Bulgakov might in any case have felt a natural sense of identity with Nikolay Gogol', who like himself was a Russian writer brought up in Ukraine, and then moved to Russia to achieve success as a writer. It is with Gogol', too, that we associate the paradigmatic act of burning his manuscripts, something Gogol' performed more than once as he struggled with his writing, and which colours our sense of what this same traumatic act meant both to the Master in the novel, and to Bulgakov in his own life. Gogol' was also a passionate enthusiast of the theatre, and in his works, whether prose works or drama, dialogue always has an enhanced significance. The range of narrative voices which appear and disappear during the course of *The Master and Margarita* is certainly comparable to those which figure in Gogol''s great but unfinished comic novel, *Dead Souls*, the first volume of which was published in 1842. Bulgakov had occasion to reflect specifically upon the voices and the narration of Gogol''s *Dead Souls* during his own writing of *The Master and Margarita*, since he made a stage adaptation of the work for the Moscow Art Theatre in 1932, which did (for once) get staged, even though Bulgakov's most inventive ideas—precisely concerning the role of the narrator—were, as so often, rejected by the theatre's directors.[5]

Chapter 1 of *The Master and Margarita* is recounted by an omniscient narrator who shares certain characteristics with some of Gogol''s narrators, whom the Russian Formalist critics have categorised as *skaz* narrators.[6] What is meant by this is that they are chatty, sometimes excessively casual and colloquial storytellers, who seem to belong in the same time and place as the protagonists by virtue of their apparent familiarity and intimacy with all aspects of their world, and in the way that they use a similar style of language to that of the protagonists. Their story-telling is exclamatory and sometimes rather disconnected, occasionally verging on the irksomely intrusive. Thus we are told by the narrator of chapter 1 of *The Master and Margarita* that the first man to visit Patriarchs' Ponds that evening was "none other than" Mikhail Aleksandrovich Berlioz—a phrase which implies the narrator's pre-existing awareness that Berlioz is a significant figure on the Moscow literary scene. The phrase also seems to presume—again in the style of a *skaz* narration—that the reader similarly belongs within this same fictional world, and will be equally impressed to encounter this literary bigwig. The *skaz* narrator is intensely self-aware, recounting his tale like an oral anecdote, in such a way as to orchestrate and interact with the listener/reader's reactions: "Yes," the narrator continues, "it is important to note the first strange aspect of that terrifying evening in May." If we look through the rest of this first chapter, similarly colloquial, chatty tones shape the narrative:

> "I'll ask you please to note . . ."
> "But, alas, it was so . . ."
> "Their conversation, as was subsequently established, was about Jesus Christ."
> "It should be noted that . . ."
> "Subsequently, when to be frank it was already too late, various organisations submitted short reports describing this man. . . ."
> "It has to be admitted that not one of these short reports was of any use at all."

Not only is the reader constantly being asked to make an evaluative assessment of what is being described, but the narrator also introduces another perspective, which will reappear intermittently throughout the Moscow chapters: that of the authorities, and in particular that of the police forces attempting to draw up reports of the events after they occur, and to make sense of them. This humorous reflection of their ongoing bewilderment will find its fullest development in the Epilogue, in which their absurd and helpless attempts to explain away all that has happened—essentially by reference to a purported criminal abuse of mass hypnotism—clearly founder. Bulgakov invokes this further narrative perspective largely to entertain, although it also serves to remind the reader of the sinister nature of the secret police who discreetly manage the city, arresting people and making them vanish when this is deemed necessary, thus providing another understated hint in the novel of the nervous atmosphere which prevailed in Moscow during Stalin's Terror in the 1930s.

The omniscient narration very occasionally anticipates the action, to create an intriguing effect of suspense, as in the description of the evening light cast on to the windows by "a sun that was departing from Mikhail Aleksandrovich forever"—this comes in chapter 1, well before it has even been suggested that Berlioz is going to die. The omniscient narrator here thrusts himself forward, becomes conspicuous, as though to emphasise that omniscience too can have subjective dimensions. This chapter is otherwise dominated, as is so much of the novel, by direct speech in the form of dialogue, a feature again reflecting the "dramatic" nature of so much of Bulgakov's prose writing. By the time he embarked upon *The Master and Margarita* he had indeed become a thoroughly confident playwright, and his awareness of the power of well-written dialogue to carry the action—and indeed on occasions to reveal far more than what is actually being said—was a dramatic talent matched only by his illustrious predecessor at the Moscow Art Theatre, Anton Chekhov. As in his first novel *The White Guard*, characters are essentially defined through their words, and also through their actions: very rarely is comment or psychological analysis provided by the narrator. Direct speech in the novel is occasionally varied with unspoken thoughts, also rendered as speech: "Berlioz was speaking, yet at the same time he was thinking to himself: 'But all the same, who on earth is he? And why does he speak Russian so well?'" (chapter 1). Elsewhere, the narrator occasionally pretends ignorance, as in chapter 4, where a distraught Ivan is trying to pursue Woland and unexpectedly finds himself inside an apartment where he bursts in on a naked woman taking her bath. Before leaving the apartment again through the back entrance, he steals a candle and a small paper icon: "Nobody knows what thought had suddenly seized Ivan . . ." Here supposed ignorance is deployed for ironic purposes: in other words, the narrator doesn't like to acknowledge explicitly that Ivan is superstitious—or even religious—enough to believe that Christian symbols might protect him from Satan.

A further reinforcement of the notion that the narrator belongs to the same world as Berlioz and Ivan comes in chapter 5, set in the MASSOLIT writers' club, Griboedov House. Here "the author of these most truthful lines" reports a conversation which he himself once supposedly overheard by the railings outside the club's tempting restaurant. He goes on to describe all the delicious dishes served there before exclaiming: "But enough of this, reader, you are getting distracted! Follow me!.." This introduces a new dimension of the story-telling voice, in which the author/narrator proclaims not only his authority, but also his intention to pursue some pre-conceived plan, along a narrative route which the reader is going to be obliged to follow as well. Here is an echo of one of the other narrative voices deployed in Gogol"s *Dead Souls*, in which the author addresses the reader directly in order to defend and justify his choice of plot and hero, and to assure the reader who is dissatisfied with the lowly subject-matter apparently chosen by Gogol' that the novel (in its later, never-to-be-completed second and third volumes) will rise to greater heights and nobility in due course—in other words, that here, too, there is a plan, and a path which the reader must follow.

In *The Master and Margarita* this "authorial" authority is reinforced for us in a curious detail, where the repellent vulgarity of the gluttonous diners at Griboedov House is emphasised, followed by the exclamation: "O gods, my gods, bring me poison, poison!.." This phrase is another example of the breaching of boundaries between the different worlds of the novel, for it is directly drawn from Pilate's unspoken thoughts in chapter 2, the first portion of the Ershalaim narrative. It can therefore only be known to Mikhail Bulgakov, the author of the entire novel *The Master and Margarita* (or conceivably to the Master, whose novel is identical with Woland's narrative) rather than to the mostly comical narrator of the events which have preceded this moment. It affirms, in other words, the existence of an overarching authorial project which will bind the seemingly distinct Moscow and Ershalaim chapters together.

The different narrative voices established in the opening chapters—several varieties of omniscience for a Gogolian *skaz*-style narrator, a consistent, sober voice for the Ershalaim chapters, and much of the narrative actually carried through the direct speech of the enormous number of protagonists crowding the text – all continue to make themselves heard for many pages to come. A new voice appears, however, at the end of chapter 18, which marks the transition from Part I of the novel to Part II. As so often, the transition involves repetition across the chapter-break: but a hitherto unheard intonation also emerges for the first time:

> (*end of Part I. Chapter 18: "Some Unfortunate Visitors"*):
> What further extraordinary events occurred in Moscow that night we do not know, and nor, of course, will we seek to discover them—especially since it is now time for us to pass on to the second part of this truthful narrative. Follow me, reader!
> (*Part II. Chapter 19: "Margarita"*):
> Follow me, reader! Who told you that there is no such thing in the world as true, faithful, eternal love! May they cut out the filthy tongue of that liar! Follow me, my reader, follow me alone, and I will show you such a love! No! the Master was mistaken when he said with bitterness to Ivanushka in the hospital, at the hour when night was tipping past midnight, that she had forgotten him. This could not be. Of course she had not forgotten him. First of all, let us reveal the secret which the Master did not choose to reveal to Ivanushka. His beloved was called Margarita Nikolaevna.

This passage contains many of the chatty and playful *skaz* narrative characteristics we have encountered hitherto, as well as a reiteration of the speaker's claims about the veracity of his story. However, the voice which we first heard outside Griboedov House, teasingly summoning the reader to follow him, has here acquired a new colouring. The writing has become more poetic, and its rhythmical qualities in the Russian original are quite emphatically marked. A striking and fresh lyrical perspective is introduced for the first time, to celebrate with earnest passion a loving devotion between the Master and Margarita which surely also reflects the deep love felt by Bulgakov for Elena. Once again, we can recognize something of Gogol"s more melancholy and self-reflective intonations from *Dead Souls*. This lyrical, authorial-sounding voice reemerges more poignantly towards the very end of the novel, in those opening lines of chapter 32 which we have quoted previously:

> My gods, my gods! How sad the earth is at evening! And how mysterious the mists are over the marshes. Anyone who has lost his way in such mists, anyone who has suffered a great deal before death, anyone who has winged

his way over this earth, bearing an impossible burden on his back—that man knows this. The weary man also knows it. And he will quit without regret the earth's mists, its marshes and its rivers, and he will deliver himself with an easy heart into the arms of death, knowing that death alone [can soothe him].[7]

It seems plausible to assume that these lines were inserted into the text by Bulgakov at a late point in the writing, when he had become aware that to complete the novel was going to be a race against time, as he succumbed to severe illness. There is a new, tragic appropriateness therefore, in the way that the opening words once again seem to echo Pilate's unspoken thoughts invoking the Roman gods as he contemplates suicide in chapter 2.

This insistent presence of the subjective in Bulgakov's novel is equally one of the most striking features of his dramatic writing, where he was always seeking ways to include subjective perspectives, whether through extensive, "novelistic" stage directions or through the presence on stage of a "narrator" figure, even though drama is a genre in which the subjective authorial voice is usually presumed to be absent. In addition, Erykalova has commented on Bulgakov's frequent use of dreams as a device both in his drama and his prose works, to create "free zones" in the texts in which subjectivity can manifest itself. This is used to most original effect in his play *Flight*, the entirety of which is couched not in the usual "scenes" but in a sequence of eight "dreams," suggesting the perspective of some dreamer's overarching consciousness. In *The Master and Margarita*, dreams offer oblivion and an escape from the everyday into the eternal, just as much for Pilate as for the Master and Margarita themselves: "The protagonists' dreams in Bulgakov's works offer not only a temporary liberation from the shackles of everyday reality, but also the continuation, and occasionally even the completion of the action."[8] One example of this would be Ivan's recurrent annual dreaming of the true culmination of the Pilate story, at the very end of the Epilogue.

Yet another device commonly used by Bulgakov to complicate our perception of his works and assert the subjective consciousness which has created them is through his frequent insertion of texts within texts. The "novel within the novel" in *The Master and Margarita* echoes as a device the inclusion of plays within plays in works such as *The Crimson Island* or his Molière play. Justin Weir has observed that: "Through the *mise en abyme* of the Master's novel, *The Master and Margarita* smuggles a literary historical past into the present."[9] We could add, however, that for Bulgakov the use of this device of inserting texts within texts also becomes a means for him to reclaim his own, subjective voice as an artist, a voice which the Soviet authorities were doing their best to silence.

Many attempts have been made to identify a genre category to which Bulgakov's *Master and Margarita* can be assigned. One such category, which for a certain period proved rather popular amongst Bulgakov scholars, was that of "Menippean satire," a term derived from the influence of the Greek satirist Menippus (third century BC). Erykalova quotes Mikhail Bakhtin's account of the genre in his book *Problems of Dostoevsky's Poetics*, which became enormously influential in the years after its publication in 1972 (more or less contemporaneously with that of the full text of *The Master and Margarita*):

> It is in Menippean satire that depictions first appear of various types of madnesses, the splitting of the personality, unbounded dreaminess, and unusual dreams . . . Visions, dreams and madness break down man's epic and tragic essence, as well as his fate: the possibilities of another being and another life are revealed in him, he loses his completeness and unique significance, and he ceases to coincide with the outlines of his own selfhood.[10]

This aspect of Menippean satire certainly helps us to reconcile the paradox of the Master's human weakness and vulnerability with the visionary nature of his literary undertakings, a paradox which characterizes the role of Ivan in the novel as well. Abram Vulis was one of the first to identify Menippean satire as a helpful way of understanding the novel in his "Afterword" to the very first partial publication of the novel in *Moskva* in 1966. Ellendea Proffer in her 1971 PhD at Indiana State University also explored the question of the extent to which *The Master and Margarita* could be matched to the full fourteen-point definition of the genre offered by Bakhtin.[11] A whole raft of other commentators, however, have since argued that the attempt fails to cover all the complexities and originality of the novel. In more recent years, the work has more commonly been assigned— retrospectively and therefore anachronistically—to the somewhat nebulous category of "magic[al] realism," to which the works of Jorge Luis Borges, Gabriel García Márquez, and Salman Rushdie, have also been attributed. Most of the discussions of the novel's genre have proved largely inconclusive, however, and scarcely illuminating. Ultimately, Bulgakov emerges as a writer who is as unique and original as his beloved Nikolay Gogol', who succeeded in inventing European Modernism (with its fractured narrative constructs, portrayals of the unreal city, and explorations of alienation troubled by sexual anxieties) a full sixty years before its time. Bulgakov's *Master and Margarita* matches Gogol''s inventiveness, inasmuch as both authors wrote works which were quite unlike anything that had come before them, and which have inspired few imitators to match them.

STYLISTIC ANALYSIS OF BULGAKOV'S THE MASTER AND MARGARITA

If, following the example of Roman Jakobson and the Formalist School of criticism, we are to draw a distinction between ordinary and poetic language, then there is no doubt that Bulgakov's use of language is distinctly "poetic."[12] The words he chooses to use fulfil a function which goes beyond the merely communicative, calling attention to the medium itself and adding layers of further meaning, thereby achieving complex aesthetic purposes as well as straightforward communication. His text repays close analysis, in order for us to be able to appreciate the subtlety and variety of devices he employs in the writing of prose. Two passages from the novel have therefore been selected for close analysis in this section, the first from one of the episodes set in Moscow, the other from one of the Ershalaim chapters. These passages are provided in Russian for those familiar with the original, followed by a translation into English with numbered lines for ease of reference.

In order fully to appreciate what Bulgakov is seeking to achieve, we need to imagine ourselves back into the position of a first-time reader of the text, someone who is as yet unaware of how the plot will develop subsequently. By the time the reader reaches the passage from chapter 13 of Part I selected below as a first example, s/he will be fully aware of the presence of a Satan figure in Moscow and of the havoc being wrought upon the worlds of literature and of theatre, which together have brought the young poet Ivan Bezdomny to Doctor Stravinsky's sanatorium. In this chapter, however, Ivan gets to know an entirely new protagonist, the mysterious man who slips into his room at night from the sanatorium balcony at the very end of chapter 11, and immediately implores him not to make any noise. This is promptly succeeded by the very entertaining and amusing chapter 12, describing Woland's "black magic" show in the Variety Theatre, but which tells us nothing further about Ivan's visitor, thus creating a tremendous effect of suspense. So far in chapter 13 we have learnt that his visitor is a fellow-patient of nervous disposition, who is somewhat dismayed to learn that Ivan is a poet and promptly urges him to stop writing. Upon discovering that the diabolical Woland's story about Pontius Pilate is what has brought Ivan to the sanatorium, the intriguing visitor exclaims in apparent astonishment that this is a great coincidence, and Ivan at last finds a thoroughly attentive listener to hear the extraordinary tale he has to tell of his day's adventures. This includes a retelling of Woland's account of the encounter between Pilate and Ieshua

Ga-Notsri. At this point we are entirely unable to understand the true significance of the visitor's exclamation "Oh, how I guessed it! Oh, how I guessed it all!" The visitor, evidently, grasps immediately who Woland is, and explains to Ivan that he too finds himself in the sanatorium because of Pontius Pilate, about whom he has written a novel. He denies, however, that he is a writer, claiming instead the title of "Master," and refusing to reveal his actual name. The visitor tells Ivan how he used to work in a Moscow museum, but moved into a cozy basement apartment and started writing his novel after winning a lottery ticket. But one day he goes out and encounters a woman in the street carrying yellow flowers.[13] He admits to her that he dislikes her flowers (he loves roses instead), but nevertheless realizes that he has loved her "all his life":

Extract from Part I, Chapter 13

Так вот, она говорила, что с желтыми цветами в руках она вышла в тот день, чтобы я наконец ее нашел, и что, если бы этого не произошло, она отравилась бы, потому что жизнь ее пуста.

Да, любовь поразила нас мгновенно. Я это знал в тот же день уже через час, когда мы оказались, не замечая города, у Кремлевской стены на набережной. [...]

— А кто она такая? – спросил Иван, в высшей степени заинтересованный любовной историей.

Гость сделал жест, означавший, что он никогда и никому этого не скажет, и продолжал свой рассказ.

Ивану стало известным, что мастер и незнакомка полюбили друг друга так крепко, что стали совершенно неразлучны. Иван представлял себе ясно уже и две комнаты в подвале особнячка, в которых были всегда сумерки из-за сирени и забора. Красную потертую мебель, бюро, на нем часы, звеневшие каждые полчаса, и книги, книги от крашеного пола до закопченного потолка, и печку.

Иван узнал, что гость его и тайная жена уже в первые дни своей связи пришли к заключению, что столкнула их на углу Тверской и переулка сама судьба и что созданы они друг для друга навек.

Иван узнал из рассказа гостя, как проводили день возлюбленные. Она приходила, и первым долгом надевала фартук, и в узкой передней, где находилась та самая раковина, которой гордился почему-то бедный больной, на деревянном столе зажигала керосинку, и готовила завтрак, и накрывала его в первой комнате на овальном столе. Когда шли майские грозы и мимо подслеповатых окон шумно катилась в подворотню вода, угрожая залить последний приют, влюбленные растапливали печку и пекли в ней картофель. От картофеля валил пар, черная картофельная шелуха пачкала пальцы. В подвальчике слышался смех, деревья в саду сбрасывали с себя после дождя обломанные веточки, белые кисти. Когда кончились грозы и пришло душное лето, в вазе появились долгожданные и обоими любимые розы.

Тот, кто называл себя мастером, работал лихорадочно над своим романом, и этот роман поглотил и незнакомку.

— Право, временами я начинал ревновать ее к нему, — шептал пришедший с лунного балкона ночной гость Ивану.

Запустив в волосы тонкие с остро отточенными ногтями пальцы, она без конца перечитывала написанное, а перечитав, шила вот эту самую шапочку. Иногда она сидела на корточках у нижних полок или стояла на стуле у верхних и тряпкой вытирала сотни пыльных корешков. Она сулила славу, она подгоняла его и вот тут-то стала называть мастером. Она нетерпеливо дожидалась обещанных уже последних слов о пятом прокураторе Иудеи, нараспев и громко повторяла отдельные фразы, которые ей нравились, и говорила, что в этом романе — ее жизнь.

Literal translation of the same passage by JAEC

And so she told me that she had gone out that day with the yellow flowers in her hands so that I should at last find her, and that if this had not occurred, she would have poisoned herself, because her life was empty.

Yes, love struck us instantaneously. I already knew this on that same day,
5   within an hour, when we found ourselves, oblivious to the city, on the embankment by the wall of the Kremlin. [. . .]
"But who is she then?" asked Ivan, fascinated to the highest degree by the love story.
His guest made a gesture which signified that he would never tell that to
10 anyone, and continued his tale.
Ivan came to learn that the Master and the unknown woman fell in love with each other so strongly that they became utterly inseparable. Ivan could even already clearly imagine to himself the two rooms in the basement of the little house, in which there was always a half-light
15 because of the lilac and the fence. The worn red furniture, the desk, on it a clock which chimed every half hour, and books, books from the painted

floor up to the soot-covered ceiling, and the stove.

Ivan discovered that his guest and his secret wife, already in the first days of their liaison, had come to the conclusion that fate itself had brought

20   them up against one another on the corner of Tverskaya Street and the alleyway, and that they had been created for one another for eternity. Ivan discovered from his guest's tale how the enamoured pair spent their day. She would arrive, and her first task would be to put on an apron, and in the narrow hallway where that same sink was, which the poor invalid

25   was for some reason proud of, she would light the kerosene stove on the wooden table and make lunch, and she would lay it out on the oval table in the first room. When the thunderstorms occurred in May, and water noisily streamed past the half-blind windows, threatening to flood their final refuge, the lovers would stoke the stove and bake potatoes in it. Steam poured

30   from the potatoes and the blackened potato skins stained their fingers. Laughter could be heard in the little basement, and the trees in the garden stripped themselves of their snapped-off twigs and white flower clusters after the rain. When the thunderstorms ceased and stifling summer came, there

35   appeared in the vase the long-awaited roses loved by them both. The man who called himself the Master worked feverishly on his novel, and this novel consumed the unknown woman as well.

"Truly, at times I began to be jealous of her and of it," whispered the nocturnal guest who had come from the moonlit balcony to Ivan.

40   Plunging into her hair her slender fingers with their sharply filed nails, she would endlessly read over what had been written, and when she had read it again, she sewed this same cap here. Sometimes she would sit on her heels by the lower shelves or stand on a chair next to the upper ones, and she would wipe the hundreds of dusty spines with a cloth. She

45   anticipated fame, she drove him on, and it was then that she began to call him Master. She was waiting with impatience for the final words which had already been promised, about the fifth Procurator of Judaea, she would repeat in a chant, out loud, certain phrases which she liked, and she would say that in this novel was her life.

One of the many notable features to observe about this passage is the subtle way the narrative perspective is handled. The section is introduced as the Master's direct speech, and certain colloquialisms serve as markers to confirm that "oral" perspective ("And so . . ." [line 1]; "Yes . . ." [4]). Ivan responds with a direct question "But who is she then?" [7], a question which of course echoes the epigraph from Goethe's *Faust* with its probing of the true nature of Mephistopheles, and extends still further the exploration of the issue of uncertain personal identity which pervades Bulgakov's entire novel. Ivan's question receives no adequate answer as yet. However, the phrase in line 10 observing that the visitor "continued his tale" marks a transition to a more distanced, third-person perspective.

The following three paragraphs are introduced with a highly charged echoing pattern: "Ivan came to learn . . ."; "Ivan discovered . . ."; "Ivan discovered . . ." [11, 18, 22]. This is further reinforced by the second and third sentences of the first paragraph, shaped by the semantically similar construction "Ivan could [. . .] clearly imagine to himself" [12–13], which is followed by a list of direct objects which extend all the way from that sentence to the following one: the third sentence does not in fact contain a main verb and functions in apposition to the previous one, a grammatical construction made much more apparent in the original Russian through its string of accusative noun and adjectival endings [13–17]. This slightly incantatory pattern, to which intensity is added by the switch from semantically similar phrases ("came to learn"/ "could clearly imagine" / "discovered") to exact repetition ("discovered"/ "discovered"), is one of the many features which marks this passage out as being highly structured and aesthetically complex, even though the subject matter being described (their daily domestic routine) appears somewhat banal. And indeed, if we read the text in Russian another highly poetic feature of Bulgakov's prose style becomes apparent, namely his musicality, his awareness of the harmonies of vowel and consonant, and rhythmical patterning as a means of delivering a compelling narrative.

The Master's description to Ivan of the early weeks of their love affair could scarcely be more mundane. Margarita comes regularly to see him, puts on an apron, makes lunch using a kerosene stove; occasionally they bake potatoes; she dusts his books. The very banality of what the Master chooses to recount to Ivan serves to give us a glimpse of his true personality: what he essentially values is intimacy, domesticity, tranquility. This jars for us already with the information that Margarita "anticipated fame, she drove him on" [45], and prefigures the crisis that will befall them when he leaves his haven of creativity and love, to submit his novel for publication and confront the external world of Soviet culture represented by MASSOLIT. The Master is a man who has hitherto appeared to Ivan as an authority figure: he has the run of the sanatorium, he knows Berlioz and other literary critics, he judges Ivan's poetry to be worthless without even reading it and insists he should abandon literature, he is fully confident of his own literary worth, and he has the erudition to recognize who Woland is from the cultural sources (Goethe, Gounod) that have shaped the enigmatic visitor's physical appearance and role. And yet as a private individual he values very modest joys, and domestic harmony. We should note, too, the nuance offered by the third-person narrator's reference to him as a "poor invalid" [24], suggesting a better-informed estimation of the Master's character than the one Ivan has gained so far. Although the relationship is presented as a great passion, there is no explicit physicality, and little emphasis is placed upon the woman's beauty. There is just a delicate hint of transferred eroticism in lines 31–3, with the couple's shared laughter juxtaposed with the trees stripping off their twigs and scented lilac clusters after the storm, like lovers undressing.

In other words, this passage, for a first-time reader at least, seems largely to fill in background, providing merely contextual information. It does not seem to invite a reading requiring heightened attentiveness. If you return to this passage on a subsequent reading, however, when you are familiar with the rest of Bulgakov's novel, you will start to notice a remarkable number of images and phrases here which correlate—often unexpectedly—to other moments in the text. We can enumerate these as follows:

- "at last" [2], "already knew" [4], "fate itself" [19]: these phrases underpin the theme of predestination which runs through much of the text, confirming Woland's dictum that "All will be as it should be. That is how the world is made." (chapter 32)
- "she would have poisoned herself, because her life was empty" [3]. In another breaching of the boundaries between the two worlds of the novel, Margarita's intentions echo Pilate's repeated longing for poison in order to commit suicide, which is first introduced as early as chapter 2. The perspicacious Ieshua Ga-Notsri makes it clear that he is aware of what Pilate wants, and he comments with a smile that Pilate's life is an impoverished one. Margarita's life is not a miserable existence, but she has intimations of other possibilities and hopes, which make her present life intolerable.
- "oblivious to the city" [5], "the Kremlin" [6]: the settings of *The Master and Margarita* are shaped by two great cities, both central to the history of Christianity: Ershalaim (Jerusalem) and Moscow. In both parts of the novel, the seats of power and oppression—Herod's palace and

the Kremlin—dominate the cities. Becoming "oblivious" to the city is an indication that the lovers have escaped the constraints of their circumstances—and yet, their walk takes them alongside the Kremlin itself, a reminder that the real world will soon press in on them again.

- "But who is she then?" [7]: we have already seen that Ivan's question echoes the lines from Goethe's *Faust* which serve as the epigraph to *The Master and Margarita*. She continues to be referred to as "the unknown woman" [11] and his "secret wife" [18], and will not be identified by name and given a biography until chapter 19.

- "they had been created for one another for eternity" [21]: at this point in the novel this seems like a somewhat insignificant, clichéd phrase, which is simply being used to support the theme of predestination. The first-time reader at this stage cannot yet imagine that the plot of *The Master and Margarita* will indeed conclude with the lovers being grant-ed eternal life together in the afterworld.

- "May thunderstorms" [27]; "stifling summer" [34]: the issue of how the Hebrew date of 14 Nisan (the date of Christ's crucifixion) in chapter 2, describing events in Ershalaim, correlates exactly to the calendar in modern Moscow is considered elsewhere in this study.[14] Nevertheless, it is striking that the beginning of their love affair takes place in the springtime, like everything else that happens later in the novel, and that the climatic conditions are dominated in that year by the imminence of—or experience of—thunderstorms, together with stifling heat, just as events will be in Ershalaim and in the present day of the narrative in Moscow.

- "final refuge" [28–9]: it is absolutely not clear why the lovers' cosy home should be referred to in these terms at this juncture. This fore-shadows the plot development which will see them parted in due course, with the Master being swindled out of his apartment. Howev-er, it also anticipates the heading of the final full chapter of *The Master and Margarita*, chapter 32: "Forgiveness and Eternal Refuge," where a shared home they could never have imagined will indeed be provided for them in the afterlife.

- "the long-awaited roses loved by them both" [35]: in chapter 2, by con-trast, we have learned that Pilate detests roses and the scent of roses.

- "nocturnal guest . . . moonlit balcony" [39]: these images describe the present situation of the Master and Ivan, but they also prefigure the events in Ershalaim described (in an extract from the Master's novel read by Margarita) at the end of chapter 26, when Afranius approaches Pilate from the moonlit balcony to report on the death of Judas.

- "sharply filed nails" [40]: this seemingly unimportant little detail in fact prefigures Margarita's later transformation into a witch, something which the Master cannot possibly have anticipated at this juncture.
- "the final words . . . about the fifth Procurator of Judaea" [46, 47]: both the Master and Margarita believe that they know exactly how his novel about Pilate will end. In the event, they will discover that his text has yet to be completed, and that the liberating of Pilate from his two thousand years of torment will constitute the true ending of the Master's novel—and also of Bulgakov's *The Master and Margarita*.
- "she would say that in this novel was her life" [48–9]: this phrase recalls an entry in Elena's diary for December 20–1, 1938: "For me, when he is not working, not writing his own things, life loses all meaning."[15]

What is so unusual about this set of phrases, so many of which set up echoes and reverberations across the entire novel, is the way in which they bridge different sections of the text. This narrative of a love affair in modern-day Moscow reveals itself to be verbally, not to say poetically, interwoven with the narrative of events in Biblical Ershalaim, irrespective of whether those events purport to have been narrated by Woland, dreamt by Ivan or written by the Master. This linguistic cohesiveness across different sections of *The Master and Margarita* also extends further, to encompass plot events of which neither we nor the protagonists can have any awareness as yet. Neither the Master, whose words are supposedly being reported to us indirectly by a narrator, nor Ivan the listener, nor we as readers, have any means whatsoever at this stage of anticipating the significance of Margarita's sharpened nails: this device can only therefore be an authorial choice. Bulgakov, in other words, scatters his text with allusions well before their meaning becomes fully apparent: when Margarita is subsequently transformed into a witch we may not even as first-time readers recall this earlier mention of her nails. But we will be more powerfully convinced of this development because we have been subconsciously prepared for it: the linguistic fabric of the text has served to achieve a poetic cohesiveness across the novel, which overrides even rational explanations. Margarita's suicidal thoughts are couched in the same terms as Pilate's are in the Master's novel, even before she has come to know about the existence of the Master's text. Roses carry a marked, if diametrically opposite, significance for the protagonists in Ershalaim and Moscow, but the very echoing of the image establishes a poetically associative—but semantically irrelevant—bridge between the two worlds of *The Master and Margarita*. This wonderfully rich poetic tapestry of Bulgakov's prose writing, incorporating vivid threads of colour, some of which are used only very sparingly, creates a system of leitmotifs and constitutes one of his unique contributions to Russian literature.

The second passage selected for analysis comes from one of the Ershalaim chapters, read by Margarita once the Master and his manuscript have been restored to her after Satan's ball (chapter 25). The very title of the chapter is ironic: "How the Procurator attempted to save Judas of Karioth." In actual fact, what is described in the chapter is the encounter between Pilate and his chief of secret police Afranius, in which Pilate, devastated by the events which have led to Ieshua's death, and tormented by a dream in which he has yearned to continue his conversation with the fascinating "philosopher," essentially instructs Afranius to kill Judas as retribution for his betrayal of Ieshua. David Bethea has described this dialogue as "a bravura performance of Aesopian language."[16]

Afranius has been summoned to this meeting, and arrives soaking wet after the ominous thunderstorm which breaks over Ershalaim as the crucifixion reaches its end. He is described as a man with a pleasant face and a benevolent expression, with hooded eyes which suggest a sly sense of humour. But occasionally he gives his interlocutor a brief, piercing, and direct glance, which suggests a different character to their relations. Pilate courteously treats his visitor to food and wine, and the first part of their conversation concerns the mood in the city; then Pilate asks for a report on the execution of Ieshua, Dismas, and Barabbas. We get a first sense of the power dynamic between the two men when Afranius describes how the three victims were offered a drink before they were crucified: "'But he', and here Pilate's guest closed his eyes, 'refused to drink.' 'Which one of them precisely?' asked Pilate. 'Forgive me, Hegemon!' exclaimed his guest. 'Did I not say? Ga-Notsri.'"

This exchange is fascinating in two respects. Firstly, it is apparent that Afranius is perfectly aware of the fact that Pilate is extremely interested—indeed, perhaps culpably interested—in Ieshua. His pretence not to have thought to name him here is, in fact, a mark of his superior knowledge, and of the hold this knowledge has afforded him over Pilate's emotions. Secondly, we simply haven't been told whether Ieshua turned down an opportunity to drink *before* he was tied to the cross, but the account of the crucifixion in chapter 16 (Ivan's dream) describes in full how in fact Ieshua greedily drinks from the sponge raised to his lips by the executioner just before his torments are ended.

Not only that, but the executioner makes it clear that this gesture of mercy is accorded to Ieshua on Pilate's particular instructions, and Ieshua actually dies whispering (gratefully?) the word "Hegemon." Afranius must know that Pilate would be desperately pleased and relieved to know about this—but he deliberately decides not to tell Pilate about it, instead leaving him with the impression that Ieshua spurned his kindness. Afranius, in other words, is the man who is entirely in control of this conversation, and of this situation.

In the section which follows after this exchange, Pilate claims to Afranius that he has received information from an unknown source about a threat to the life of Judas from Karioth, who lured Ieshua into the compromising conversation which led to his arrest:

Extract from Part II, Chapter 25

— [. . .] Сведения же заключаются в том, что кто-то из тайных друзей Га-Ноцри, возмущенный чудовищным предательством этого менялы, сговаривается со своими сообщниками убить его сегодня ночью, а деньги, полученные за предательство, подбросить первосвященнику с запиской: «Возвращаю проклятые деньги».

Больше своих неожиданных взглядов начальник тайной службы на игемона не бросал и продолжал слушать его, прищурившись, а Пилат продолжал:

— Вообразите, приятно ли будет первосвященнику в праздничную ночь получить подобный подарок?

— Не только не приятно, — улыбнувшись, ответил гость, — но я полагаю, прокуратор, что это вызовет очень большой скандал.

— И я сам того же мнения. Вот поэтому я прошу вас заняться этим делом, то есть принять все меры к охране Иуды из Кириафа.

— Приказание игемона будет исполнено, — заговорил Афраний, — но я должен успокоить игемона: замысел злодеев чрезвычайно трудно выполним. Ведь подумать только, — гость, говоря, обернулся и продолжал: — выследить человека, зарезать, да еще узнать, сколько получил, да ухитриться вернуть деньги Каифе, и все это в одну ночь? Сегодня?

— И тем не менее его зарежут сегодня, — упрямо повторил Пилат, — у меня предчувствие, говорю я вам! Не было случая, чтобы оно меня обмануло, — тут судорога прошла по лицу прокуратора, и он коротко потер руки.

— Слушаю, — покорно отозвался гость, поднялся, выпрямился и вдруг спросил сурово: — Так зарежут, игемон?

— Да, — ответил Пилат, — и вся надежда только на вашу изумляющую всех исполнительность.

Гость поправил тяжелый пояс под плащом и сказал:

— Имею честь, желаю здравствовать и радоваться.

— Ах да, — негромко вскричал Пилат, — я ведь совсем и забыл! Ведь я вам должен!...

Гость изумился.

— Право, прокуратор, вы мне ничего не должны.

— Ну как же нет! При въезде моем в Ершалаим, помните, толпа нищих... я еще хотел швырнуть им деньги, а у меня не было, и я взял у вас.

— О прокуратор, это какая-нибудь безделица!

— И о безделице надлежит помнить.

Тут Пилат обернулся, поднял плащ, лежащий на кресле сзади него, вынул из-под него кожаный мешок и протянул его гостю. Тот поклонился, принимая его, и спрятал под плащ.

Literal translation by JAEC

"The information amounts to the fact that one of the secret friends of Ga-Notsri, outraged by the monstrous treachery of the money changer, has conspired with his fellows to murder him tonight; and the money that he received for his treachery will be tossed back over the wall to the High

5   Priest with a note saying 'I am returning the accursed money.'"

The head of the secret service did not cast any more of his unexpected glances at the Hegemon, but continued to listen to him with narrowed eyes, while Pilate went on:

"You can imagine whether it will be pleasant for the High Priest to receive

10   a gift like that on a festive night..."

"Not only will it not be pleasant," answered the guest, smiling, "but I reckon, Procurator, that it will provoke a huge scandal."

"And I am of the same opinion myself. And it is for this reason that I am asking you to take charge of this business, that is to take all the steps

15   necessary for the protection of Judas from Karioth."

"The Hegemon's instructions will be carried out," Afranius spoke, "but I can reassure the Hegemon that the evildoers' plan will be extremely hard

to carry out. Just think, after all," and here the guest turned away as he
spoke, and continued: "to track a man down, stab him to death, and then
20   also find out how much he received, and contrive to return the money to
Caiaphas, and all this in one night? Tonight?"
"And nevertheless he will be stabbed tonight," repeated Pilate stubbornly,
"I have a premonition, I tell you! There has never been an instance when
my premonitions have deceived me." A shudder passed across the
25   Procurator's face at that moment, and he briefly wrung his hands.
"I hear you and obey," responded the guest meekly, and he stood, drew
himself up, and suddenly asked in a stern voice: "And so he will be
stabbed to death, Hegemon?"
"Yes, replied Pilate," and all my hopes rest on your remarkable
30   competence."
His guest adjusted his heavy belt under his cloak and said:
"My respects, and I wish you health and joy."
"Ah, yes," exclaimed Pilate softly, "I had almost forgotten! I owe you
money, of course!.."
35   His guest looked astonished.
"Truly, Procurator, you don't owe me anything."
"What do you mean, not anything! When I was entering Ershalaim, don't
you recall, there was a crowd of poor people . . . I wanted to fling some
coins to them, but I didn't have any, and I borrowed some from you."
40   "Oh, Procurator, that was just a trifle!"
"One shouldn't forget trifles."
Here Pilate turned, picked up the cloak that was lying on the seat behind
him, took a leather pouch out from beneath it and handed it to his guest. The
latter bowed as he took it, and concealed it beneath his cloak.

This passage demonstrates Bulgakov's skill at portraying the subtleties
of a complex psychological interaction, the true nature of which is not represented at all accurately or fully by the actual words uttered by the two speakers. The "information" Pilate has supposedly received is in fact laying out for
Afranius the detailed script of what Pilate wishes to happen to Judas. Afranius
in lines 6 and 7 weighs up the veiled instructions he is being given: this is not
the occasion for one of his penetrating glances, but instead for a moment of
evaluation, conveyed to us simply by the narrowing of his eyes. Pilate shares
with him the plan not only to punish Judas, but also to embarrass Caiaphas,
in retaliation for the latter's refusal to save Ieshua when Pilate asked for him to

be pardoned. In lines 16–21 Afranius purports to be reassuring Pilate that the sequence of events he supposedly fears is unlikely to come to pass, not least because it will be so complicated for all this to occur in the space of one single night. In reality what Afranius is doing is pointing out to Pilate that the cost of this rather complex set of tasks with which he is being entrusted will be very high. In line 18 Afranius is even described (somewhat unexpectedly) turning his face away from Pilate as he lists all the things that will need to be done: in other words, Afranius conceals his expression from Pilate, to leave him on tenterhooks as to whether he will agree to take the mission on. Pilate's "stubborn" response (line 22) indicates that he will accept whatever terms Afranius demands from him.

In lines 23–4 Pilate speaks of having confidence in his own premonitions—superficially to reinforce the idea that his information is reliable, but also almost as a way of convincing Afranius that Judas's death is predestined. We, however, will eventually come to understand that Pilate's premonitions truly do never deceive him—at least as far as his premonition of a universal catastrophe associated with the death of Ieshua is concerned, and also possibly his hopeful premonition of ultimate forgiveness for himself. Nevertheless, Pilate cannot stop himself from shuddering, and even wringing his hands, thereby exposing fully to Afranius his raw emotional state, which of course is an indication of vulnerability which places him even more firmly in his interlocutor's power. The "wringing" of his hands is an image which indirectly recalls the image of him "washing" his hands in the Gospels (Matthew 27:24), and in all subsequent representations of him in European culture, as a gesture denying his guilt for what has happened. It also foreshadows the gesture which will characterise him for the remainder of *The Master and Margarita*, as remorse torments him in his long period of purgatory.

In lines 26 and 27 Afranius responds firstly with apparent meekness ("I hear you and obey"), but he also allows a flash of 'sternness' to come into his voice (and he adopts a more challenging physical stance at the same time): he is confirming that he has understood his instructions correctly, and that what has been required of him is now irrevocable. He makes to leave, and Pilate, who knows what is expected of him in this dangerously compromising bargain, suddenly "remembers" that he owes Afranius some money (lines 33–4). He hands over a full pouch of money, which is clearly far more than the few coins he supposedly borrowed, and which in fact has been prepared in advance for this anticipated transaction. Pilate had, however, discreetly placed the pouch on the seat, hidden under his cloak and out of the sight of prying eyes, until it was needed: and Afranius responds with equal discretion, swiftly tucking the pouch away under his own cloak before he leaves.

A close reading of these two passages has revealed Bulgakov to be a true craftsman of the Russian language, and helps us to understand why the writing and rewriting of the novel became such a protracted business over twelve years when he often could only find time to work on *The Master and Margarita* very late at night, and into the small hours. This was not just because of all the unremitting constraints in his life, obliging him to devote his time to other tasks and projects in his professional life as a writer. With this novel he became a perfectionist, "polishing it until it gleamed," as he said of his *Don Quixote* play in the summer of 1938.[17]

CHAPTER 11

English Translations of
The Master and Margarita

The 1966/1967 publication in Moscow of large portions of Bulgakov's novel in the journal *Moskva* was one of the literary sensations of the decade, comparable in its impact in Russia and abroad only with the 1962 appearance of Aleksandr Solzhenitsyn's *One Day in the Life of Ivan Denisovich*. The Solzhenitsyn book had opened up for the first time the taboo subject of Stalin's labour camps, marking a true Thaw in the repressive totalitarian culture which had dominated the previous forty years. The publication of *The Master and Margarita* offered a less bleak, more exuberant look at the earlier decades of Soviet power, and of the Stalin era. Its combination of inventiveness, beauty and comedy won it an instant success. The striking story of its composition in secret and the survival of the novel's typescript through nearly three decades of turbulent events in the USSR only aroused even more curiosity. Not surprisingly, there was an immediate rush to translate the work into English, so that Anglo-Saxon readers could discover for themselves this hitherto unknown treasure of early twentieth-century Russian literature.

One of the first to publish a translation was the publisher Collins and Harvill Press, based in London. Two impressions of that first edition came out in the same month, November 1967, less than a year after the *Moskva* publication was completed. The translator, Michael Glenny, was one of the most respected British translators of Russian literature, with an exceptionally long and distinguished list of publications of canonical twentieth-century Russian texts in English. His version has tremendous verve. But the haste with which the task had to be completed does unfortunately show, and although it remains one of the most readable versions available in English, it would be good if a few really unfortunate slips and omissions could be remedied. Glenny's publishers had evidently negotiated and paid for the right to work from the 'uncensored' version of the Russian text which Elena Sergeevna had managed to deliver to the Italian publishers Einaudi, so that the Collins and Harvill Press edition is essentially a publication of the complete text.

The American Grove Press also published a translation before the end of 1967, by Mirra Ginsburg, but despite its undoubted stylistic merits it was based solely on the truncated 1966–7 *Moskva* publications, so as an incomplete text with significant omissions it really cannot be recommended to the reader. Andrew Barratt has pointed out that there are, unexpectedly, quite a few significant discrepancies between Glenny's version and the Possev edition in Russian published in Germany in 1969, which also purported to be made up of the combined *Moskva* publications, plus the omitted passages. It would appear that Glenny and Possev were supplied with slightly different typescripts of the novel, and since both original typescripts have now apparently been lost it has become impossible to reconstruct the exact nature of their source texts.[1] I myself once asked Michael Glenny what had happened to the Russian typescript of *The Master and Margarita* which he had been working from, and he claimed to have passed it on to Sir Isaiah Berlin in Oxford. However, enquiries to Sir Isaiah, and a check through his archives after the latter's death, have not revealed any such typescript to have remained in his hands.

As we have seen, the first full publication of the novel in Russian in the Soviet Union, edited by Anna Saakyants in 1973, became for a long time the definitive version for Russian readers. Later scholarship has established, however, that Saakyants made some controversial editorial decisions, which have been challenged in the Yanovskaya and Kolysheva editions of 1989 and 2014 respectively. In the West, readers of Bulgakov in English simply had to choose between the influential versions by Glenny and Ginsburg, which dominated the scene for many years. But the American publisher Ardis, co-founded by the first major American Bulgakov scholar, Ellendea Proffer, then commissioned a new translation of the novel in 1995. Ellendea Proffer selected as the basis for this translation the Russian edition published by Yanovskaya in 1989, with some "cross-checking" against the 1973 Saakyants version. As she puts it, "Where line readings differ in meaningful ways between these two texts, I have chosen the one most consistent with Bulgakov's general usage."[2] In other words, the Ardis translation is based on a new scholarly interpretation of the available Russian sources, which established a new, slightly different version again of the Russian text. Ellendea Proffer also appended some very helpful commentaries on cultural references that a non-Russian speaker might struggle to catch, as well as a biographical note and an afterword briefly discussing the novel's history, meaning and significance. This translation into English was completed not by Proffer herself, but by two translators working as a team, Diana Burgin and Katherine O'Connor.

As Burgin and O'Connor announced in the introductory pages to the book, "all aspects of the work on this translation were done equally by the two of us." They explained their approach as follows:

> In realizing this translation, we strove, first of all, to produce what has been lacking so far: a translation of the complete text of Bulgakov's masterpiece into contemporary standard American English. At the same time, our translation aims to be as literal a rendering of the original Russian as possible. [...] We have made every effort to retain the rhythm, syntactic structure, and verbal texture of Bulgakov's prose. We have often eschewed synonyms in favour of repeating the words that Bulgakov repeats, and we have tried, as far as possible without sacrificing clarity, not to break up Bulgakov's long sentences and to adhere to his word order. In sum, we strove for an accurate, readable American English translation of *The Master and Margarita* that would convey the specifically Bulgakovian flavour of the original Russian text.[3]

This ambition to prioritise the literal over the literary, and to retain such elements as syntactic structure, sentence length and word order is certainly an unusual one amongst translators from Russian, given the very different ways sentences are constructed in the two languages, and the far greater number of words usually needed in English to translate a typical Russian sentence. But their aspiration to combine accuracy with readability reassures us that this was not a project undertaken mechanically.

In 1997, another pair of translators, Richard Pevear and Larissa Volokhonsky, produced a new translation for Penguin Books / Random House. As Richard Pevear puts it in his introduction, commenting on the immediate popularity of the work when it first appeared, "Certain sentences from the novel immediately became proverbial. The very language of the novel was a contradiction of everything wooden, official, imposed. It was a joy to speak."[4] This edition also comes with an introduction to the text and notes to explain obscure points in the text. The account of the choice of source text used here acknowledges the Bulgakov scholar Marietta Chudakova's advice on the different options, and is described as follows: "The present translation has been made from the text of the original magazine publication, based on Elena Sergeevna's 1963 typescript, with all cuts restored as in the Possev and YMCA-Press editions. It is complete and unabridged."[5] Richard Pevear is not a fluent Russian speaker, and relies on his native-speaker wife to explicate the original for him before they produce their final version. Their translations of a number of classics of Russian literature have provoked heated discussions as to their merits and failings.

More recently the well-known translator Hugh Aplin produced a new translation for Oneworld Classics in Britain, which was published in 2008. It also offers notes, a biographical introduction to Bulgakov, and relevant diary extracts, as well as a brief account of adaptations of the work. Aplin explains that the text he has based his version on is one approved by the Bulgakov estate, and was published in a three-volume edition of his works in Moscow in 1996, as well as being reproduced in a two-volume edition published by RIPOL Klassik in 2004.

In order to compare and contrast these different versions in English, I have selected a sample passage from the opening chapter of the novel, as the enigmatic stranger insists on involving himself in the conversation between Berlioz and Ivan, declaring himself to be fascinated by their bold affirmations of atheism. He asks them what they think of the arguments that have been put forward for the existence of God, and when Berlioz declares that there can be no rational proof of his existence, Woland congratulates him on his echoing of "the thinking of that restless old man Immanuel." This is a reference to the work of Immanuel Kant, who had offered a systematic critique of a number of rational ways of justifying the existence of God. Woland goes on to point out that Kant, nevertheless, almost seems to contradict himself, and ultimately appears to endorse the existence of God in his later writings. This is a reference to Kant's investigation of moral faith, involving the moral efforts we can make as individuals to achieve the Highest Good and the Ethical Community. Individual actions, in other words, can and should have a moral value.[6] There has been much scholarly discussion about the numbering of the various proofs offered by Kant for the existence of God; but Bulgakov makes clear where he stands on the question by giving the title "The Seventh Proof" to chapter 3 of *The Master and Margarita*, in which the death of Berlioz, foretold by Woland, comes to pass exactly as predicted. The existence of God, seemingly, is confirmed by evidence of the existence of the Devil.

In this selected extract Berlioz responds to Woland's remarks and elegantly dismisses Kant's apparent concessions to the truth of the Christian faith, after which an irritated Ivan interrupts their erudite exchange with some blunt remarks, much to Woland's amusement. One of the challenges for translators, therefore, is to capture the very different intonations of all of the three speakers.

The Russian is provided first of all here, followed by the versions offered by different translators. Line references provided in the commentaries refer to each individual translation, rather than to the Russian original.

EXTRACT FROM PART I, CHAPTER 1

Russian original (the trickiest phrases to translate are highlighted in **bold**):

— Доказательство Канта, – **тонко** улыбнувшись, возразил образованный редактор, — также неубедительно. И **недаром** Шиллер говорил, что кантовские рассуждения по этому вопросу могут удовлетворить только рабов, а Штраус просто смеялся над этим доказательством.

Берлиоз говорил, а сам в это время думал: «Но, все-таки, кто же он такой? И почему так хорошо говорит по-русски?»

— Взять бы этого Канта, да за такие доказательства **года на три в Соловки!** — совершенно неожиданно **бухнул** Иван Николаевич.

— Иван! — сконфузившись, шепнул Берлиоз.

Но предложение отправить Канта в Соловки не только не поразило иностранца, но даже привело в восторг.

— **Именно, именно**, — закричал он, и левый зеленый глаз его, **обращенный** к Берлиозу, **засверкал**, — ему там самое место! Ведь говорил я ему **тогда** за завтраком: «Вы, профессор, **воля ваша**, что-то нескладное придумали! Оно, может, и умно, но **больно непонятно**. Над вами потешаться будут».

Берлиоз **выпучил глаза**. «За завтраком. . . Канту?.. Что это он **плетет**?» – подумал он.

— Но, — продолжал **иноземец, не смущаясь** изумлением Берлиоза и **обращаясь** к поэту, — отправить его в Соловки невозможно по той причине, что он уже с лишком сто лет **пребывает** в местах значительно более отдаленных, чем Соловки, и **извлечь его оттуда** никоим образом нельзя, уверяю вас!

— **А жаль!** — отозвался **задира**-поэт.

Glenny

"Kant's proof," objected the learned editor with a thin smile, 'is also unconvincing. Not for nothing did Schiller say that Kant's reasoning on this question would only satisfy slaves, and Strauss simply laughed at his proof."

5   As Berlioz spoke he thought to himself: "But who on earth *is* he? And how does he speak such good Russian?"

"Kant ought to be arrested and given three years in Solovki asylum for
that 'proof' of his!" Ivan Nikolayich burst out completely unexpectedly.
"Ivan!" whispered Berlioz, embarrassed.

10   But the suggestion to pack Kant off to an asylum not only did not surprise
the stranger but actually delighted him. "Exactly, exactly!" he cried and his
green left eye, turned on Berlioz, glittered. "That's exactly the place for
him! I said to him myself that morning at breakfast: 'If you'll forgive me,
professor, your theory is no good. It may be clever, but it's horribly

15   incomprehensible. People will think you're mad.'"
Berlioz's eyes bulged. "At breakfast . . . to Kant? What is he rambling about?"
he thought.
"But," went on the foreigner, unperturbed by Berlioz's amazement and
turning to the poet, "sending him to Solovki is out of the question, because

20   for over a hundred years now he has been somewhere far away from
Solovki and I assure you that it is totally impossible to bring him back."
"What a pity!" said the impetuous poet.

Glenny's version has many merits. These include the natural-sounding fluency of certain phrases: "who on earth *is* he?" [5]; "Kant ought to be arrested
and given three years in Solovki" [7]; the colloquial abbreviation of the patronymic Nikolayevich to "Nikolayich" [8]; "his green left eye, turned on Berlioz, glittered" [11–12]; "that morning at breakfast" [13]; "unperturbed" [18].
In other words, a highly experienced translator such as Glenny is not afraid to
insert additional details necessary to clarify the meaning in English. But unfortunately, his haste shows elsewhere. In line 1 Berlioz's smile is surely not "thin,"
which would suggest surly contempt; it is subtle, knowing, a smile that indicates his readiness to engage with his learned interlocutor on equal terms. There
is a really regrettable howler in line 7. Since Glenny's skilful insertion of the
phrase about an arrest makes it clear that he does in fact know what the notorious Solovki prison camp on the White Sea denoted, it is probably an aberration
that he goes on to describe it as an "asylum" [7, 10] (perhaps he was subconsciously conflating this moment with the Master's experience of arrest followed
by a period in an asylum?). In lines 11 and 12 it is also perhaps unfortunate
that he uses the word "exactly" three times, when the Russian uses an entirely
different phrase on the first occasion. Glenny has also perhaps not been very
enterprising with some of the more colloquial turns of phrase which, rather
unexpectedly, characterize Woland's Russian at this stage. "No good" [14] is
adequate, but doesn't quite convey the richness of the original, which would

be more like "doesn't make sense" / "doesn't add up"; "will think you're mad" [15] is similarly a little thin for a phrase which suggests "mock you" / "pull your leg." His choice of the word "impetuous" for Ivan in line 22 doesn't quite hit the mark, either: the original word suggests something more of a hot-tempered, irascible man who is not afraid to pick quarrels.

Burgin and O'Connor

"Kant's proof," retorted the educated editor with a faint smile, "is also unconvincing. No wonder Schiller said that only slaves could be satisfied with Kant's arguments on this subject, while Strauss simply laughed at his proof."

5   As Berlioz was speaking, he thought, "But, who is he anyway? And how come his Russian is so good?"
"This guy Kant ought to get three years in Solovki for proofs like that," blurted out Ivan Nikolayevich, completely unexpectedly.
"Ivan!" whispered Berlioz in consternation.

10   But the suggestion that Kant be sent to Solovki not only failed to shock the foreigner, it positively delighted him.
"Precisely so, precisely so," he cried, and his green left eye, which was focused on Berlioz, sparkled. "That's the very place for him! As I told him that time at breakfast, 'As you please, professor, but you've contrived

15   something totally absurd! True, it may be clever, but it's totally incomprehensible. People will laugh at you.'"
Berlioz's eyes popped. "At breakfast . . . with Kant? What kind of nonsense is this?" he thought.
"However," continued the foreigner, unflustered by Berlioz's

20   astonishment and turning to the poet, "he can't be sent to Solovki for the simple reason that for more than a hundred years now he's been somewhere far more remote than Solovki, and there's no way of getting him out of there, I assure you!"
"Too bad!" responded the poet-bully.

Burgin and O'Connor do rather a good job with the hidden intricacies of this passage, and come up with several very pleasing solutions: "faint" smile [1]; "As Berlioz was speaking" [5]; "blurted out" [8]; "in consternation" [9]; "not only failed to shock" [10]; "Precisely so [. . .] the very place" [12, 13]; "far more remote" [22]. But possibly, a reader in English would welcome an elucidation of the first reference to "Solovki" [7], perhaps as "the prison camp at Solovki." There are just a couple more slight awkwardnesses, for example with "As you please" [14], and "responded the poet-bully" [24] which fails to conjure the hot-headed social clumsiness of Ivan's intervention. Despite the aspirations that Burgin and O'Connor proclaim in their introduction, the syntactic structure and word order of the Russian text have had to be adjusted fairly frequently, but their version remains faithful to the nuances and style of the original and is also very readable.

Pevear and Volokhonsky

"Kant's proof," the learned editor objected with a subtle smile, "is equally
unconvincing. Not for nothing did Schiller say that the Kantian reasoning on
this question can satisfy only slaves, and Strauss simply laughed at this proof."
Berlioz spoke, thinking all the while: "But, anyhow, who is he? And why
5   does he speak Russian so well?"
"They ought to take this Kant and give him a three-year stretch in Solovki for
such proofs!" Ivan plumped quite unexpectedly.
"Ivan!" Berlioz whispered, embarrassed.
But the suggestion of sending Kant to Solovki not only did not shock the
10   foreigner, but even sent him into raptures.
"Precisely, precisely," he cried, and his green eye, turned to Berlioz,
flashed. "Just the place for him! Didn't I tell him that time at breakfast: 'As
you will, Professor, but what you've thought up doesn't hang together. It's
clever, maybe, but mighty unclear. You'll be laughed at.'"
15   Berlioz goggled his eyes. "At breakfast . . . to Kant? . . . What is this drivel?" he
thought.
"But," the outlander went on, unembarrassed by Berlioz's amazement and
addressing the poet, "sending him to Solovki is unfeasible, for the simple
reason that he has been abiding for over a hundred years now in places
20   considerably more remote than Solovki, and to extract him from there is
in no way possible, I assure you."
'Too bad!' the feisty poet responded.

Pevear and Volokhonsky also come up with a couple of good ideas for rendering certain phrases, such as "equally unconvincing" [1–2]; "three–year stretch" [6]; "Too bad!," and "feisty poet" [22]. However, what jars so much in their translation of Bulgakov, as it does in so many of their other translations of the classics of Russian literature, is their choice of a lexicon which seems completely inappropriate for the period and context of the original phrase. Elsewhere they introduce obscurities or heaviness to an expression which in the original was relatively neutral; and sometimes their translations even offer locutions in English which are never normally used, and which grate horribly on the ear. The result is that an elegant, rhythmically subtle, and verbally poised piece of writing by Bulgakov is sometimes rendered overliterally, occasionally becoming awkward and even—as several commentators have observed— simply weird. In this passage this is exemplified in peculiar phrases, such as "Ivan plumped" [7]; Berlioz, who "goggled his eyes" [15]; the inappropriately dismissive reference to "drivel" [15]; the completely bizarre choice of "outlander" [17] to render a word which, while admittedly a little less common in Russian than the standard term used in line 10, simply means "foreigner" or "stranger"; and syntactical or stylistic clumsinesses such as "unembarrassed by Berlioz's amazement" [17]; "unfeasible" [18] to render a simple word meaning "impossible"; the unnatural-sounding phrase "he has been abiding for over a hundred years" [19]; and the literalistic plural of "places" [19] for an idiomatic phrase meaning "place." All the musicality and poetry of Bulgakov's writing is lost, and he is presented instead in this translation as a writer with a very peculiar and inconsistent style, where the fluency of our reading is constantly interrupted by discordant notes. Pevear claimed that the language of the novel was "a joy to speak," but their English version of it is by no means a joy to read.

Aplin

"Kant's proof," objected the educated editor with a thin smile, "is also unconvincing. And not for nothing did Schiller say that the Kantian arguments on the question could satisfy only slaves, while Strauss simply laughed at that proof."

5 Berlioz spoke, yet at the same time he was thinking: "But all the same, who on earth is he? And why does he speak Russian so well?"

"This Kant should be taken and sent to Solovki for two or three years for such proofs!" Ivan Nikolayevich blurted out quite unexpectedly.

"Ivan!" whispered Berlioz, embarrassed.

10 But not only did the proposal to send Kant to Solovki not shock the foreigner, it even sent him into raptures.

"Precisely, precisely," he shouted, and a twinkle appeared in his green left

eye, which was turned towards Berlioz, "that's the very place for him! I
said to him then over breakfast, you know: 'As you please, Professor, but
15   you've come up with something incoherent! It may indeed be clever, but
it's dreadfully unintelligible. They're going to make fun of you.'"
Berlioz opened his eyes wide. "Over breakfast . . . to Kant? . . . What nonsense
is this he's talking?" he thought.
"But," the foreigner continued, with no embarrassment at Berlioz's
20   astonishment and turning to the poet, "sending him to Solovki is
impossible for the reason that he's already been in parts considerably
more distant than Solovki for over a hundred years, and there's no
possible way of extracting him from there, I can assure you!"
'That's a pity!" responded the quarrelsome poet.

Aplin's version offers a straightforward and accurate rendering of the Russian.
He is prepared to insert conjunctions or adapt word order so as to make the
English read more naturally, as with "yet at the same time" [5]; "who on earth"
[6]; "a twinkle appeared in his green left eye, which was turned" [12–13]; and
"What nonsense is this he's talking?" [17–18]. Elsewhere there are slight awkwardnesses or less fluent turns of phrase, as with "should be taken and sent" [7];
"he shouted" [12]; "As you please" [14], which everyone struggles with, and
might perhaps be rendered more naturally as "Forgive me"; and like the other
translators, he also doesn't come up with a very natural phrase in "dreadfully
unintelligible" [16], which would sound more authentically colloquial simply
as "impossibly hard to understand." In the penultimate paragraph, "parts" [21]
is a pleasing equivalent, although it appears as part of a rather heavy-footed version of Woland's witty final remark.

To conclude: the Burgin and O'Connor version and Hugh Aplin's translation both offer very readable versions of the text, though neither has quite the
paciness of Glenny's interpretation. If the actual inaccuracies of that version
could just be tidied up in a revised republication, the Glenny would offer the
most enjoyable read and is truest in spirit to the exuberant original. The Pevear
and Volokhonsky translation should be avoided at all costs.

Afterword—A Personal Reflection

It was simply a matter of fortunate timing for me that Bulgakov's novel *The Master and Margarita* was published for the first time while I had already embarked upon the study of the Russian language at school. I was lucky enough to have five full years of Russian teaching at that point, so that before I started my undergraduate studies in Russian I had already progressed to reading texts like Lermontov's novel *A Hero of Our Time*, Pushkin's poem *The Bronze Horseman*, and Chekhov's *The Cherry Orchard* in the original Russian. *The Master and Margarita* I had read only in English, so tackling this novel in Russian as an undergraduate at university was a prospect I looked forward to with eagerness. And when it came to selecting a subject for doctoral research towards the end of the 1970s, Bulgakov became the obvious choice. The full text of *The Master and Margarita* had appeared in the Soviet Union in 1973, but because Bulgakov's name had been neglected and suppressed during the later decades of Stalin's rule, little scholarly investigation into his life and works had as yet been undertaken.[1]

At the time the USSR was still under the leadership of Leonid Brezhnev, who from 1964 onwards came to preside over what is now known as the "era of stagnation": Soviet Communism became more and more bureaucratic at home, while its foreign policy came to be defined by the suspicious and aggressive attitudes of the Cold War. In 1962 the publication of Solzhenitsyn's *One Day in the Life of Ivan Denisovich* under Nikita Khrushchev had for the first time lifted the veil of silence which had, up until that moment, concealed the history of the Gulag from public view. But this brief glimpse of life in Siberian labour camps did not mark the opening of the floodgates, and was not followed by a rush of other such publications. On the contrary, literary censorship seemed to regroup and reassert itself, and further controversial works by Solzhenitsyn and others failed to be granted permission to be published. And as often as a relatively outspoken or liberal work of literature did get past the censors, so equally often were intellectuals harassed or put on trial for spurious offences: and so the dissident movement was born, with liberally-inclined intellectuals banding loosely together to outwit the authorities where possible, often with the connivance—or at least the tacit encouragement—of westerners interested in Soviet culture.

There were many courageous Soviet literary scholars such as Marietta Chudakova, who did their best to circumvent the restrictions the authorities placed upon the free circulation of information. As an archivist at the Manuscript Department of the Lenin Library in Moscow, it was she who was charged with cataloguing Bulgakov's archive, which they acquired from his widow Elena in the late 1960s. She has written very entertainingly about how long it took her to get her first major article describing Bulgakov's life and works past the censors in 1976. For example, she was determined to allude to the presence in the archive of the manuscript of Bulgakov's satirical tale *The Heart of a Dog*, but that text had not yet been licensed for publication in the USSR (it had appeared in the West in 1968), and so she was not allowed to mention its title. In the kind of discreet game-playing so characteristic of the enterprising scholarship of Soviet academics at that time, she simply decided to smuggle a description of this archival item into her article by inconspicuously starting to talk about it as "Bulgakov's third tale," without ever mentioning it by name—and although on this occasion the censor did notice what she had been up to, he eventually conceded that this reference could stay in. The same paranoid official attitudes were apparent when it came to providing specific references to catalogue numbers of the archive: Chudakova and others went to enormous lengths in a series of publications during those difficult years, to smuggle in the occasional specific mention to a catalogue reference, so that other scholars could have some hope of tracking down the relevant item.

It was my privilege to benefit from this kind of generosity on the part of Chudakova and other Bulgakov scholars when I made two 4-month visits to the USSR in 1979 and 1980, as a very green postgraduate student, to do research on Mikhail Bulgakov for my Oxford University D.Phil. dissertation. My visit, like those of other British postgraduates in those years, was arranged under the terms of a cultural exchange agreement between the British and Soviet governments. British students, who like most westerners had a tendency to want to pry into controversial subjects, were not entirely welcome, but had to be tolerated if the Soviet side were to be able to send its own students abroad. And so we were allowed to go there, and even to go to archives in some cases (though it took a full twelve years before I was finally allowed to use the main Bulgakov archive, in the Lenin Library). If you did get inside an archive building, it turned out that there were various unwritten rules. First and foremost amongst these was that foreigners could not be granted permission to view any of the catalogues. This meant that if you were to have any hope of doing any useful work, you had to be very thoroughly prepared: you needed to have read every available publication on your subject, and thanks to the generosity of scholars like Chudakova, you could assemble a few crumbs of information from these, on which to base your archival requests. Other kindnesses, from a number of scholars, included allowing me to copy out notes they themselves had previously taken in archives from which I myself was banned; and even on one occasion being lent some documents as I left Moscow to take a train to Leningrad, with the strict instruction that I must post the documents back to Moscow even before I reached my Leningrad hotel, where there might be hidden cameras.

Another hindrance placed in our way by the Soviet authorities could emerge as you were leaving the country: there were several instances of western postgraduates having all their research materials simply confiscated at the border. This threat was alleviated by the staff of the Cultural Section at the British Embassy, who looked after us during our stay: they allowed us very kindly (and quite illegally) to use the diplomatic bag, and towards the end of our stay we were allowed to go along there and stuff up to 2 kg of papers and microfilms into a plastic bag. After our return we then had to go along to King Charles Street in London, to the Foreign and Commonwealth Office, to collect our research materials and take them back to our universities.

Many Soviet scholars went out of their way to talk to us, entertained us in the evenings to delicious meals and much vodka, educated us so that we should have a reasonable understanding of the world we were trying to describe, and sometimes even copied out portions of the archive catalogues for us, to try and fill the gaps we were struggling with thanks to the Soviet authorities' obstructiveness. When I did finally complete my doctorate on Bulgakov in 1982, a significant proportion of the footnotes purporting to contain archival references simply had to be faked; and my examiners, who included Lesley Milne, agreed that this was of course the only honorable option. Spelling out just where I had got my information from could have compromised colleagues back in the Soviet Union, and caused them much unpleasantness.

During the 1970s and the 1980s the main priority for most western scholars was therefore to unearth and disseminate nuggets of information that the Soviet authorities were sedulously concealing or withholding. Early studies of Bulgakov squeezed every last drop of information out of their sources, and scholars such as Lesley Milne, A. C. Wright, and Ellendea Proffer in the West, or Chudakova and Grigory Faiman within Soviet Russia, pieced together a remarkable amount of information against considerable odds. Chudakova and Faiman undertook an extraordinary piece of detective work, for example, on the basis of one small scrap of paper in Bulgakov's archive which contained just part of one word from the title of a newspaper. After years of searching through ephemeral newspaper publications, they managed to identify it as coming from a newspaper published in Grozny in the North Caucasus, and eventually to track down the relevant copy. There they found an entirely unknown and inflammatory early publication by Bulgakov, his anti-Bolshevik diatribe of late 1919 published as "Prospects for the Future." Bulgakov had deliberately assembled his papers in such a way as to leave tiny clues for posterity such as this one, about publications he certainly did not want the Soviet authorities to know about.

After Mikhail Gorbachev came to power in 1985, he inaugurated a new cultural policy of *glasnost'*, a term which suggests bringing hidden information into the light, and of giving a voice to that which has been silenced. This opened the way to a flood of publications by authors from the entire Soviet era whose works had been banned, and which had only become available in some cases in émigré publications: this is when Akhmatova and Zamyatin, Solzhenitsyn and Pasternak and many other authors had their most controversial works published at last in their native land. For Bulgakov this meant the publication of *A Heart of a Dog* and of his play about Stalin, *Batum*. The culmination of this process was the startling moment in 1990 when the KGB's archivists revealed that they still held a typed copy they had made of a diary Bulgakov had had confiscated in 1926. When he finally had these diaries restored to him some years later, he promptly burned them, appalled at the thought that anything so intimate and private could fall into the hands of others. He of course never knew that a copy had been made while they were in KGB hands, so that their reemergence in the final year of the Soviet Union's existence became yet another testimonial to the truth of his dictum that "manuscripts don't burn."

1991 saw the proclamation of the end of Soviet power and the emergence of a new world order. It also happened to be the year of the centenary of Bulgakov's birth, and so a wave of literary events and academic conferences ushered in a new, freer post-Soviet approach to the study of his life and works. By that time, it has been calculated, about forty separate editions of *The Master and Margarita* had been published over a period of twenty years—and during the centenary year of 1991 itself it was reckoned that every tenth book published in Russia was written by Mikhail Bulgakov. For a while at least archives opened up (although the KGB ones closed down again before long); publications which could command commercial success became entirely unrestricted, and readers could at last freely purchase copies of his works, while schools and universities increasingly placed him at the center of twentieth-century Russian literature *curricula*.

The course which Bulgakov scholarship has taken in the post-Soviet era closely reflects developments in the political culture of the country over the same period.[2] It was notable that when the early 1920s diaries from the KGB archives were first published in 1990, the well-meaning editors simply decided to excise a number of comments Bulgakov made about Jewish people, without even indicating that they had made any cuts. Given Bulgakov's upbringing as a Russian Orthodox Christian in Kyiv, there was nothing particularly remarkable or untypical in his constant awareness of Jewishness amongst his acquaintances, and a couple of his remarks are indeed uncomfortably disparaging. On the other hand, we could mention the repeated expressions of outrage in his fiction about violence perpetrated against the Jewish population of Kyiv by Petlyura's Ukrainian nationalists, and we could point to the Jewish people in his circle of friends. In any case, the diary editors' misguided discretion on Bulgakov's behalf spectacularly backfired, and figures such as Viktor Losev used the ensuing scandal enthusiastically to claim Bulgakov for the emerging trend towards Russian nationalistic triumphalism, which dismissed the entire Bolshevik phase of Russia's history as a Jewish-led aberration. This was an early glimpse of the new social trends emerging in post-Soviet society. At the same time, none of this prevented Bulgakov's works gathering a larger and larger following, with ever-growing numbers of adaptations being made for the stage, TV, and the cinema, not to mention a massive online presence for his fans. Alongside this surge of popularity, museums have opened up and tourist attractions have been developed, including city tours to show people around Bulgakov's Moscow, and a thriving trade in trinkets and souvenirs.[3] All of this emerged in parallel with other transformations of the Russian cultural scene during the 1990s, due to rapid commercialisation.

In more recent times, as Vladimir Putin has steered the country back towards Russian Orthodoxy, Bulgakov has come under attack from certain quarters for the supposedly "demonic" aspects of his writing in *The Master and Margarita*, and in particular for his quasi-blasphemous presumption in writing a fifth Gospel, as well as for the supposedly evil actions undertaken by Satan and his minions in the guise of Woland and his retinue. The huge popularity of Bulgakov's novel amongst young people has raised just the same kinds of concerns amongst conservative Orthodox Christians in Russia as J. K. Rowling's equally successful Harry Potter books have done in certain quarters in the West, provoking very similar debates about the role of demons and black magic in fiction, and their possible harmful consequences for the morality of the naïve and the young. In 2005 there was an extremely popular TV adaptation in Russia of *The Master and Margarita* by Vladimir Bortko, who had already had a great success in 1988 with his film adaptation of Bulgakov's *Heart of a Dog*. Jeffrey Brassard has argued that the adaptation skilfully soft-pedalled the sinister role of the NKVD in the Soviet Union, while placing far more emphasis on the economic hardships people suffered under Soviet rule, in order to "mute the critiques of Soviet authoritarianism that might also be applied to Putin and his regime while supporting his state-led economic policy by highlighting how far Russia has progressed economically since 1999."[4] Since 2014, Bulgakov has equally come under strong attack in his home town, where Ukrainian patriots have reproached him for his sarcastic and negative portrayals of Ukrainian nationalism in *The White Guard*. After the Russian occupation of the Crimea in that year, these critics have not hesitated to identify him with attitudes of Russian nationalist hostility towards Ukraine. Things became so tense that in Kyiv the museum staff based in the building on Andreevsky Hill, where the family used to live, felt obliged to put up a defensive notice stating that any visitors who supported the Russian actions in Crimea in 2014 were simply not welcome in the museum.

In other words Mikhail Bulgakov's biography, and his most famous writings, have become during the twenty-first century an arena for hotly contended debates. These closely mirror the directions in which post-Soviet society in the age of Vladimir Putin has moved, especially towards new redefinitions of Russian national identity, both in relation to its Slav neighbors and in relation to its spiritual role as a Christian nation, as well as in comparison to its Soviet past. In some Russian intellectual circles it has become fashionable to profess unenthusiastic and blasé attitudes towards a novel such as *The Master and Margarita*. But its ongoing wide popularity amongst Russian readers and foreign audiences has incontestably secured the work the status of a Russian classic. Living through the years of Stalin's Terror, Bulgakov could scarcely have hoped that his "sunset novel" would ever attain such a status.

Acknowledgements

In a number of ways that will have become apparent from this book, the scholarly study of the works of Mikhail Bulgakov has been something of a collaborative effort over the years, with researchers in the Soviet Union and in the post-Soviet era in Russia generously sharing their information and their expertise with western scholars as well as with the wider public. It is therefore a pleasure to acknowledge the contributions, inspiration and help of the major Bulgakov specialists whose work has preceded mine. As far as the study of *The Master and Margarita* is concerned these have particularly included Marietta Chudakova, Lidiya Yanovskaya, Viktor Losev, Grigory Faiman, Irina Erykalova, Irina Belobrovtseva and Svetlana Kul'yus, Aleksey Varlamov, and Elena Kolysheva, as well as A. C. Wright, Ellendea Proffer, Lesley Milne, Andrew Barratt, Riitta Pittman, Laura Weeks, David Bethea, Justin Weir, and many others.

It is also a pleasure to acknowledge my gratitude to Professor Thomas Seifrid, Oleh Kotsyuba, and Kate Yanduganova at Academic Studies Press for their suggestion that I should undertake this book, and for their prompt and very helpful editorial contributions. I am grateful to the anonymous readers of my manuscript for their suggestions, and owe especial thanks to Rosemary Nixon, a friend and experienced literary editor who gave very generously of her wisdom and expertise. I would also like to thank my talented undergraduates who have studied Bulgakov at Oxford University, who also kindly volunteered to provide comments and suggestions on my first draft.

As ever my thanks go to my family, and especially to Ray, whose support and patience have been unstinting as ever, through so many Bulgakov projects.

Notes

FOREWORD

1   See Stephen Lovell, "Bulgakov as Soviet Culture," *Slavonic and East European Review* 76, no. 1 (January 1998): 28–48.

2   See J. A. E. Curtis, *Manuscripts Don't Burn. Mikhail Bulgakov: A Life in Letters and Diaries* (London: Bloomsbury, 1991), 79 and 133. The links between Gogol' and Bulgakov will be explored in greater detail later in this book. One of the best accounts of the overall importance of Gogol' for Bulgakov is to be found in Marianne Gourg, "Gogol et *Le Maître et Marguerite*," *Revue De Littérature Comparée* 331 (July–September 2009): 359–70.

3   Lesley Milne, *Mikhail Bulgakov. A Critical Biography* (Cambridge: Cambridge UP, 1990), 230–4. For a further reflection on the links between *The Master and Margarita* and Pasternak's *Dr Zhivago*, specifically in respect of the relationship between author and addressee, see Carol Avins, "Reaching a Reader: The Master's Audience in *The Master and Margarita*," *Slavic Review* 45, no. 2 (Summer 1986): 272–85. The two authors' use of *mise en abyme* in relation to their sense of selfhood and literary tradition is the subject of Justin Weir's fascinating study *The Author as Hero. Self and Tradition in Bulgakov, Pasternak and Nabokov* (Evanston, IL: Northwestern UP, 2002).

4   *Salman Rushdie. Critical Essays*, vol. 2, ed. Mohit Kumar Ray and Rama Kundu (New Delhi: Atlantic Publishers and Distributors, 2006), 189.

5   http://www.masterandmargarita.eu/en/05media/stones.html, accessed February 25, 2018.

6   http://www.oprah.com/book/the-master-and-margarita-by-mikhail-bulgakov#ixzz57ww5yi7V and https://www.talesofsuccess.com/daniel-radcliffe-favourite-books-17885/, accessed February 24, 2018.

7   See http://www.toptenbooks.net/authors/annie-proulx, accessed February 24, 2018.

8   Interview in *The Guardian*, February 10, 2018.

9   http://www.beatdom.com/happy-birthday-to-mikhail-bulgakov-from-patti-smith-and-beatdom/, accessed February 24, 2018.

10 The essential volumes of critical writing in English specifically devoted to this novel include: Lesley Milne's *'The Master and Margarita': A Comedy of Victory*, (Birmingham: Birmingham UP, 1977); Andrew Barratt's *Between Two Worlds. A Critical Introduction to 'The Master and Margarita'* (Oxford: Clarendon Press, 1987), which provides a particularly helpful survey of the critical debates in its first half; and the collection of essays edited by Laura Weeks, *'The Master and Margarita'. A Critical Companion* (Evanston, IL: Northwestern UP, 1996), including her own introductory essay, "What I Have Written, I Have Written," 3–67. A fuller list of recommended reading on the novel can be found in the Bibliography.

CHAPTER 1

1 In writing the first two chapters of this book I have drawn partially on research I undertook for my two biographies of Bulgakov, *Manuscripts Don't Burn. Mikhail Bulgakov: A Life in Letters and Diaries* (London: Bloomsbury, 1991), and *Mikhail Bulgakov* (London: Reaktion Books, 2017), as well as important studies such as Aleksey Varlamov's *Mikhail Bulgakov* (Moscow: Molodaya Gvardiya, 2008).

2 For further consideration of the specific significance of Gounod's opera for Bulgakov's creative imagination, see Boris Gasparov, "Iz nablyudeniy nad motivnoy strukturoy romana M. A. Bulgakova *Master i Margarita*," *Slavica Hierosolymitana* 3 (1978): 198–251; and also David Lowe, "Gounod's *Faust* and Bulgakov's *The Master and Margarita*," *Russian Review* 55, no. 2 (1996): 279–86.

3 Varlamov, *Mikhail Bulgakov*, 36–40.

4 From the story *The City of Kyiv* (1923), I, 296. The most complete and authoritative Russian edition of Mikhail Bulgakov's works is the eight-volume annotated edition edited by Viktor Losev and published by Azbuka (2011–13). The eight volumes are unnumbered, so for ease of reference I have given them Roman numerals (see Bibliography for further details). References to Bulgakov's works and other documents given in my text will be to this edition, unless otherwise indicated. Translations from the Russian are all my own.

5 The best account of these formative years in Bulgakov's writing career is to be found in Edythe Haber's book *Mikhail Bulgakov. The Early Years* (Cambridge, MA: Harvard UP, 1998).

6 Varlamov, *Mikhail Bulgakov*, 333–6.

7 Letter to the Soviet Government, March 28, 1930, quoted in *Bulgakovy Mikhail i Elena—Dnevnik Mastera i Margarity*, ed. V. I. Losev (Moscow: PROZAiK, 2012), 104.

8 For further reflections on the psychological impulses prompting Bulgakov to turn to these themes at this moment in his life, see Alexandra Nicewicz Carroll,

"Reimagining Woland: The Shadow Archetype and the Paradox of Evil in *The Master and Margarita*," *Russian Review* 74, no. 3 (July 2015): 419–34.

CHAPTER 2

1   From Bulgakov's autobiographical piece *To a Secret Friend*, Azbuka, I, 375.
2   Subsequent quotations from *The Master and Margarita* will be followed in my text by a reference to the relevant chapter of the novel.
3   Letter from Elena Sergeevna to A. S. Nyurenberg, February 13, 1961, in Pavel Fokin, *Bulgakov bez glyantsa* (St. Petersburg: Amfora, 2010), 281–2.
4   For a good survey of Gor'ky's role in Soviet culture see Tova Yedlin's *Maxim Gorky: A Political Biography* (Westport, CT: Praeger Publishers, 1999).
5   Letter of July 1929 to I. V. Stalin, M. I. Kalinin, A. I. Svidersky and A. M. Gor'ky, *Dnevnik Mastera i Margarity*, 92–4.
6   Letter to A. I. Svidersky, *Dnevnik Mastera i Margarity*, 95.
7   Letter of August 24, 1929 to N. A. Bulgakov, Azbuka, VIII, 261–3.
8   Letter of January 16, 1930 to N. A. Bulgakov, *Dnevnik Mastera i Margarity*, 99.
9   Bulgakov, Mikhail, *Pis'ma. Zhizneopisanie v dokumentakh*, ed. V. I. Losev and V. V. Petelin (Moscow: Sovremennik, 1989), 279–90.
10 Aleksey Varlamov points out that this event took place on the afternoon of Good Friday, a fact Bulgakov can scarcely have failed to notice. Varlamov, *Mikhail Bulgakov*, 478.
11 Letter to Pavel Popov, April 14–20, 1932, quoted in Losev, *Dnevnik Mastera i Margarity*, 128.
12 Diary of Elena Sergeevna, September 1, 1933, quoted in Losev, *Dnevnik Mastera i Margarity*, 159.
13 *Dnevnik Mastera i Margarity*, 240.
14 Nadezhda Mandelstam, *Hope Against Hope. A Memoir* (London: Collins & Harvill Press, 1971), 39.
15 *Dnevnik Mastera i Margarity*, 293.
16 *Dnevnik Mastera i Margarity*, 240.
17 September 6, 1937, *Dnevnik Mastera i Margarity*, 384.
18 May 19, 1937, *Dnevnik Mastera i Margarity*, 359.
19 Letter to S. A. Ermolinsky, June 18, 1937, *Dnevnik Mastera i Margarity*, 368.
20 Letter to V. V. Veresaev, *Dnevnik Mastera i Margarity*, 393.
21 Letter to Pavel Popov, April 28, 1934, *Dnevnik Mastera i Margarity*, 197.
22 February 12, 1937, *Dnevnik Mastera i Margarity*, 333.
23 Losev in *Dnevnik Mastera i Margarity*, note to p. 309, 657.
24 Losev in *Dnevnik Mastera i Margarity*, note to p. 311, 657–8.
25 October 23, 1938, *Dnevnik Mastera i Margarity*, 480.

CHAPTER 3

1 Milne, *Critical Biography*, 247.

2 See M. A. Bulgakov, *Master i Margarita. Polnoe sobranie chernovikov romana. Osnovnoy tekst*, ed. Elena Yu. Kolysheva, 2 vols (Moscow: Pashkov Dom, 2014), II, 15 for an illustration of the significant differences between the two, even as regards the opening sentence of the novel.

3 Kolysheva I, 7; II, 16; and see Lidiya Yanovskaya, *Poslednyaya kniga, ili Treugol'nik Volanda*, (Moscow: PROZAiK, 2013), 56–63 for her discussion of the supposedly missing notebook(s).

4 Marietta O. Chudakova, "Arkhiv M. A. Bulgakova: Materialy dlya tvorcheskoy biografii pisatelya," *Zapiski otdela rukopisey Gos. B-ki im. Lenina* 37 (1976): 25–151; and "Tvorcheskaya istoriya romana M. Bulgakova *Master i Margarita*," *Voprosy literatury* 1 (1976): 218–53.

5 Yanovskaya, *Poslednyaya kniga*, 17–127.

6 Kolysheva I, 8–9.

7 Kolysheva I, 9–28; II, 5–31, 84–6.

8 Bulgakov, *Pis'ma. Zhizneopisanie*, 279–90.

9 Irina Erykalova, *Fantastika Bulgakova. Tvorcheskaya istoriya. Tekstologiya. Literaturnyi kontekst* (St. Petersburg: Izd-vo SPbGUP, 2007), 18.

10 Bulgakov may well have been familiar with the vivid accounts of Gogol''s traumatic final days collected by his friend Vikenty Veresaev in the second volume of his documentary biography of Gogol', *Gogol' v zhizni*, (1933).

11 Marietta Chudakova, "Opyt rekonstruktsii teksta M. A. Bulgakova," *Pamyatniki kul'tury. Novye otkrytiya* (1977): 93–106; Yanovskaya, *Poslednyaya kniga*, 36–40.

12 Irina Belobrovtseva and Svetlana Kul'yus, *Roman M. Bulgakova "Master i Margarita." Kommentariy* (Moscow: Knizhnyi klub 36.6, 2007), 139.

13 Erykalova, *Fantastika Bulgakova*, 203 ff. She points out that this only serves to strengthen our sense of the close echoes between Pilate and the guilt-ridden General Khludov, from Bulgakov's recently-completed play *Flight*.

14 Ibid., 240.

15 Kolysheva, I, 12.

16 Yanovskaya, *Poslednyaya kniga*, 698.

17 Belobrovtseva and Kul'yus, *Roman M. Bulgakova*, 30.

18 Varlamov, *Mikhail Bulgakov*, footnote on p. 725.

19 Belobrovtseva and Kul'yus, *Roman M. Bulgakova*, 203.

20 Erykalova, *Fantastika Bulgakova*, 10, 36.

21 Losev, *Dnevnik Mastera i Margarity*, note to p. 111, 627.

22 Quoted by Belobrovtseva and Kul'yus, *Roman M. Bulgakova*, 16; and in *Dnevnik Mastera i Margarity*, 146.

23 Belobrovtseva and Kul'yus, *Roman M. Bulgakova*, 16.

24 Ibid., 17.

25 *Dnevnik Mastera i Margarity*, 165–70.

26 Yanovskaya, *Poslednyaya kniga*, 18.

27 *Dnevnik Mastera i Margarity*, 179.

28 Ibid., 212.

29 Ibid., note to p. 212, 646.

30 Ibid., note to p. 233, 648.

31 Yanovskaya, *Poslednyaya kniga*, 629.

32 Belobrovtseva and Kul'yus, *Roman M. Bulgakova*, 22.

33 Kolysheva, I, 15, 16.

34 Yanovskaya, *Poslednyaya kniga*, 52–3.

35 Ibid., 57–8.

36 *Dnevnik Mastera i Margarity*, 356.

37 Ibid., 371.

38 Ibid., 383, 399.

39 Ibid., 386.

40 Ibid., 418.

41 Yanovskaya, *Poslednyaya kniga*, 704–5. The functions of the OGPU were transferred to the NKVD in 1934.

42 *Dnevnik Mastera i Margarity*, 434.

43 Ibid., 440–2.

44 Ibid., 442.

45 Ibid., 521.

46 Ibid., 535.

47 Ibid., 538.

48 Milne, *Critical Biography*, 224.

49 Cited in Kolysheva II, 7.

50 Ibid., 9.

51 Kolysheva, II, 18, note 7.

52 *Dnevnik Mastera i Margarity*, note to p. 574, 678–9.

53 January 15, 1940, *Dnevnik Mastera i Margarity*, 580.

54 *Dnevnik Mastera i Margarity*, note to p. 582, 682.

55 M. A. Bulgakov, *Moi bednyi, bednyi master . . . Polnoe sobranie redaktsiy i variantov romana "Master i Margarita,"* ed. V. Losev, (Moscow: Vagrius, 2006).

56 Kolysheva, II, 18.

57 Ibid., II, 18–19.

58 Ibid., II, 19.

59 Ibid., II, 20–2.

60 Belobrovtseva and Kul'yus, *Roman M. Bulgakova*, 53.

61 Kolysheva II, 23.

62 Kolysheva II, 52; see also a discussion of this in Yanovskaya, *Poslednyaya kniga*, 112–16, 650–1.

63 Belobrovtseva and Kul'yus, *Roman Mikhaila Bulgakova*, 447–48, 457.
64 Kolysheva, II, 84–86.

CHAPTER 4

1   Viktor Losev, "K istorii voskresheniya 'Mastera,'" Azbuka VI, 5.
2   Cited in Kolysheva II, 11; also in *Dnevnik Mastera i Margarity*, note to p. 582, 684.
3   Letter from Pavel Popov to Elena, December 27, 1940, in Bulgakov, *Pis'ma. Zhizneopisanie*, 533.
4   Varlamov, *Mikhail Bulgakov*, 750.
5   Ibid., 753.
6   D. G. B. Piper, "An Approach to Bulgakov's *The Master and Margarita*," *Forum for Modern Language Studies* 7, no. 2 (1971): 136, 144–46.
7   Chudakova's views are reported and discussed by Varlamov, *Mikhail Bulgakov*, 594–604.
8   Ibid.
9   Ibid., 446.
10 Marietta Chudakova, *Zhizneopisanie Mikhaila Bulgakova* (Moscow: Kniga, 1988—second, fuller edition), 481.
11 *Dnevnik Mastera i Margarity*, 583.
12 Bulgakov, *Pis'ma. Zhizneopisanie*, 500–01.
13 Yanovskaya, *Poslednyaya kniga*, 574–75.
14 Bulgakov, *Pis'ma. Zhizneopisanie*, 545–47.
15 Losev, "K istorii voskresheniya 'Mastera,'" *Azbuka* VI, 6.
16 Letters of September 14, 1961 (*Dnevnik Mastera i Margarity*, note to p. 138, 633); and September 7, 1962 (in Azbuka VI, 6).
17 Mikhail Bulgakov, *Zhizn' gospodina de Mol'era*, (Moscow: Molodaya Gvardiya, 1962), 226–27.
18 Cited in Losev, "K istorii voskresheniya 'Mastera,'" *Azbuka* VI, 6–12.
19 Ibid., 14.
20 Ibid., 21.
21 G. Lesskis and K. Atarova, *Putevoditel' po romanu Mikhaila Bulgakova "Master i Margarita"* (Moscow: Raduga, 2007), 416–20.
22 Belobrovtseva and Kul'yus, 30; for more details on the nature of the cuts see Lesskis and Atarova, 225–28, as well as D. M. Fiene, "A Comparison of the Soviet and Possev Editions of *The Master and Margarita*, with a Note on the Interpretation of the Novel," *Canadian-American Slavic Studies* XV, nos. 2–3 (Summer/Fall 1981): 330–54.
23 Laura D. Weeks, "What I have written, I have written," in Laura D. Weeks, ed., *"The Master and Margarita." A Critical Companion* (Evanston, IL: Northwestern UP, 1996), 7.

24   Losev, "K istorii voskresheniya 'Mastera,'" *Azbuka* VI, 20.

25   Andrew Barratt, *Between Two Worlds. A Critical Introduction to "The Master and Margarita"* (Oxford: Clarendon Press, 1987), 14–33.

26   Stephen Lovell, "Bulgakov as Soviet Culture," *Slavonic and East European Review* 76, no. 1 (January 1998): 29.

27   Belobrovtseva and Kul'yus, *Roman M. Bulgakova*, 30.

28   Losev, "K istorii voskresheniya 'Mastera,'" 17–19, 21; Lesskis and Atarova, *Putevoditel' po romanu, Azbuka* VI, 179.

29   Yanovskaya, *Poslednyaya kniga*, 651–53.

30   Belobrovtseva and Kul'yus, *Roman M. Bulgakova*, 30.

31   Barratt, *Between Two Worlds*, 27.

32   Hedrick Smith, *The Russians* (1976), quoted in Barratt, *Between Two Worlds*, 38.

33   Belobrovtseva and Kul'yus, *Roman M. Bulgakova*, 30–31.

CHAPTER 5

1   I have shared my chapter title with Barbara Kejna Sharratt's article "The Tale of Two Cities: the Unifying Function of the Setting in Mikhail Bulgakov's *The Master and Margarita*," *Forum for Modern Language Studies* 16, vol. 4 (October 1980): 331–40: she argues that the thematic bonds between the two settings augment the wider symbolic opposition of "the home" and "the world outside," which is characteristic of many of Bulgakov's works.

2   Erykalova, *Fantastika Bulgakova*, 257.

3   G. A. Lesskis, "*Master i Margarita* Bulgakova (manera povestvovaniya, zhanr, mikrokompozitsiya)," *Izvestiya AN SSSR (seriya literatury i yazyka)* 38, no. I (1979): 52–59, and Boris Gasparov, "Iz nablyudeniy nad motivnoy strukturoy romana M. A. Bulgakova *Master i Margarita*," *Slavica Hierosolymitana* 3 (1978): 198–251 are but two examples among many.

4   Barratt, *Between Two Worlds*, 118.

5   See B. A. Beatie and P. W. Powell's exhaustive study, "Story and Symbol: Notes towards a Structural Analysis of Bulgakov's *The Master and Margarita*," *Russian Literature Triquarterly* 15 (1978): 219–51.

6   *Dnevnik Mastera i Margarity*, 371.

7   Nisan is the name of the month in the Hebrew calendar: the date of Christ's crucifixion, the fourteenth of Nisan, is referred to in Leviticus 23:5.

8   D. M. Bethea, "History as Hippodrome: the Apocalyptic Horse and Rider in *The Master and Margarita*," *Russian Review* 41, no. 4 (1982), 373–99.

9   Gasparov, "Iz nablyudeniy," 200–03.

10   Milne, "*The Master and Margarita*," 4–6.

11   E. N. Mahlow, *Bulgakov's "The Master and Margarita": the Text as Cipher* (New York: Vantage Press, 1975), 8, 63, 66–68.

12 Piper, "An Approach," 145–47; L. Rzhevsky, "Pilatov grekh: O tainopisi v romane Bulgakova *Master i Margarita*," *Novyi zhurnal* 90 (1968): 60–80.

13 Barratt, *Between Two Worlds*, 120.

14 Ellendea Proffer, *Bulgakov. Life and Work* (Ann Arbor: Ardis, 1984), 540.

15 Justin Weir, *The Author as Hero. Self and Tradition in Bulgakov, Pasternak and Nabokov* (Evanston, IL: Northwestern University Press, 2002), 31.

16 Ellendea Proffer, "Bulgakov's *The Master and Margarita*: Genre and Motif," *Canadian Slavic Studies* 3, no. 4 (Winter 1969): 628.

17 Weeks, "*The Master and Margarita*," 28–30.

18 Milne, "*The Master and Margarita*," 15.

19 L. Skorino, "Litsa bez karnaval'nykh masok (polemicheskie zametki)," *Voprosy literatury* 6 (1968): 33.

CHAPTER 6

1 *Dnevnik Mastera i Margarity*, 534.

2 Barratt, *Between Two Worlds*, 171.

3 Cited by Yanovskaya, *Poslednyaya kniga*, 728.

4 Varlamov, *Mikhail Bulgakov*, 747.

5 M. A. Orlov, *Istoriya snoshenii s d'yavolom*, (St. Petersburg: Izd. P. F. Panteleeva, 1904), 7–8. A different explanation of Woland's role is offered by Laura Weeks, who argues that in the Hebraic Old Testament tradition, too, Satan is not seen as the source of all evil, but metes out justice instead. See Laura D. Weeks, "Hebraic Antecedents in *The Master and Margarita*: Woland and Company Revisited," *Slavic Review* 43, no. 2 (Summer 1984), 224–41.

6 Erykalova, *Fantastika Bulgakova*, 10.

7 Kolysheva I, 12.

8 For an early investigation of this topic, see Elisabeth Stenbock-Fermor, "Bulgakov's *The Master and Margarita* and Goethe's *Faust*," *Slavic and East European Journal* 13 (1969): 309–25.

9 See, for example, the translations by N. Kholodkovsky (1878) and by Boris Pasternak (1949).

10 Yanovskaya, *Poslednyaya kniga*, 567–69.

11 Yanovskaya, *Tvorcheskii put'*, 224; Belobrovtseva and Kul'yus, 180–81.

12 Ibid., 560–64.

13 Losev, Notes, Azbuka VI, 564.

14 Belobrovtseva and Kul'yus, *Roman M. Bulgakova*, 141.

15 Milne, *Critical Biography*, 217.

16 See Michael Glenny, 'Existential Thought in Bulgakov's *The Master and Margarita*', *Canadian-American Slavic Studies*, XV, 2–3 (Summer-Fall, 1981), 238–49.

17   Chudakova, "Tvorcheskaya istoriya," 233.

18   See J. A. E. Curtis, "Down with the Foxtrot! Concepts of Satire in the Soviet The-atre of the 1920s," in *Russian Theatre in the Age of Modernism*, ed. R. Russell and A. Barratt (Basingstoke and London: Macmillan, 1990), 219–235.

19   Milne, *Master and Margarita*, 24.

20   Extensive research has concluded that there were not in actual fact any tram lines then running around Patriarchs' Ponds, as implied in *The Master and Margarita*. See S. Pirkovsky, "Virtual'naya real'nost', ili tramvai na Patriarshikh," *Voprosy literatury* 4 (2004): 267–82

CHAPTER 7

1   Donald Fanger, "Rehabilitated Experimentalist," *Nation*, January 22, 1968, 118.

2   "Introduction to the Synoptic Gospels," in *The Jerusalem Bible* (London: Double-day; Darton, Longman & Todd, 1966), 5–7.

3   Max Hayward, "Pushkin, Gogol and the Devil," *Times Literary Supplement*, May 28, 1976, 631.

4   See Marietta Chudakova, "Uslovie sushchestvovaniya," *V mire knig* 12 (1974): 80.

5   J. A. E. Curtis, *The Englishman from Lebedian'—A Life of Evgeny Zamiatin (1884–1937)* (Brighton, MA: Academic Studies Press, 2013), 137–39.

6   B. A. Beatie and P. W. Powell have argued that Florensky's theories are scientifi-cally absurd, if aesthetically appealing. See their "Bulgakov, Dante and Relativity," *Canadian-American Slavic Studies* XV, nos. 2–3 (Summer/Fall 1981): 253. For a more elaborate theory about how his reading of Florensky may have inspired Bul-gakov in *The Master and Margarita* see Milne, *Critical Biography*, 251–56.

7   Florensky, *Mnimosti v geometrii*, 7.

8   See Edward E. Ericson Jnr, "The Satanic Incarnation: Parody in Bulgakov's *The Master and Margarita*," *Russian Review* 33 (1974): 20–36.

9   The relevant chapter was first published by Bethea as "History as Hippodrome," 393.

10   Lidiya Yanovskaya, *Tvorcheskii put' Mikhaila Bulgakova* (Moscow: Sovetskiy Pisa-tel', 1983), 241–60. I have drawn on her investigations for some of what follows.

11   A. Zerkalov, *Evangelie Mikhaila Bulgakova* (Ann Arbor: Ardis, 1984), 213.

12   Belobrovtseva and Kul'yus, *Roman M. Bulgakova*, 45–46.

13   Varlamov, *Mikhail Bulgakov*, 794.

14   Diary entry for October 26, 1923, in J. A. E. Curtis, *Manuscripts Don't Burn. Mikhail Bulgakov—A Life in Letters and Diaries* (London: Bloomsbury, 1991), 53–54.

15   Belobrovtseva and Kul'yus, *Roman M. Bulgakova*, 63.

16   For an extended analysis of Bulgakov's reading of A. Drews, see Edythe C. Haber, "The Mythic Bulgakov: *The Master and Margarita* and Arthur Drews's *The Christ Myth*," *The Slavic and East European Journal* 43, no. 2 (1999), 347–60.

17 Yanovskaya, *Tvorcheskiy put'*, 249.

18 Ernest Renan, *Vie de Jésus* (Paris, 1870), 295.

19 Yanovskaya, *Tvorcheskiy put'*, 254–56.

20 Yanovskaya, *Poslednyaya kniga*, 444–45.

21 H. El'baum, *Analiz iudeiskikh glav "Mastera i Margarity" M. Bulgakova* (Ann Arbor: Ardis, 1981), 104, 116.

22 Milne, *Critical Biography*, 231.

23 El'baum, *Analiz iudeiskikh glav*, 46.

24 Weir, *The Author as Hero*, 18.

25 Quoted from the English original: F. W. Farrar, *The Life of Christ*, (London, no date—although first publication was 1874), 666.

26 Both quoted in Varlamov, *Mikhail Bulgakov*, 729–30.

27 Milne, *Critical Biography*, 234.

28 Ibid., 15, 151.

29 Varlamov, *Mikhail Bulgakov*, 726–29.

30 Ibid., 748–49.

31 Ibid., 35.

32 Proffer, *Bulgakov*, 541.

33 Erykalova, *Fantastika Bulgakova*, 34.

34 Azbuka VIII, 106; Yanovskaya, *Poslednyaya kniga*, 23.

35 Erykalova, *Fantastika Bulgakova*, 54–55.

CHAPTER 8

1 Barratt, *Between Two Worlds*, 88. Some of the material for this chapter is drawn from my article "Mikhail Bulgakov and the Red Army's Polo Instructor: Political Satire in *The Master and Margarita*," (in Weeks, "*The Master and Margarita*," 213–26).

2 Barratt, *Between Two Worlds*, 97; Piper, "An Approach," 136, 144–46. Varlamov provides an even fuller list of the various "improbable" prototypes that have been proposed for the fictional characters in *The Master and Margarita* (Varlamov, footnote on page 731).

3 Barratt, *Between Two Worlds*, 4, 98–99.

4 Varlamov, *Mikhail Bulgakov*, 725.

5 Belobrovtseva and Kul'yus, *Roman M. Bulgakova*, 329.

6 Proffer, *Bulgakov*, 539–40.

7 Varlamov, *Mikhail Bulgakov*, 441.

8 While it is obvious that Spaso House provided the most significant inspiration for the setting of Satan's ball in *The Master and Margarita*, Sidney Dement has pointed out that Bulgakov drew upon the interiors of Moscow's famous Sandunov Baths as well, especially its swimming pool surrounded by columns and statues, in order

to provide additional echoes of the Roman Empire in the Moscow chapters. See his "Architectural Details from Moscow's Sandunov Banyas in M. A. Bulgakov's *Master and Margarita*," *Slavic and East European Journal* 60, no. 1 (2016): 87–105.

9   From Elena's diary for December 19, 1933, *Dnevnik Mastera i Margarity*, 182.

10   *Dnevnik Mastera i Margarity*, 229.

11   Varlamov comments on the fact that when two of these "interpreters" (Emmanuil Zhukhovitsky and Kazimir Dobranitsky) were subsequently arrested in the course of the Terror, they neither of them in fact mentioned Bulgakov during their inter-rogations, and Varlamov wonders why not. "The most logical explanation is that they were aware in the NKVD that Bulgakov was under Stalin's protection, and for that reason they were afraid to touch him, turning him instead into a figure whose voice was silenced. Of course the full details in this matter can only be provided by the FSB [successor organization to the KGB]." (Varlamov, *Mikhail Bulgakov*, 603).

12   *Dnevnik Mastera i Margarity*, 224, 225.

13   Varlamov, *Mikhail Bulgakov*, 599.

14   *Dnevnik Mastera i Margarity*, 258. The Torgsin or "Trade with Foreigners" shops were set up in the summer of 1930 to allow the purchase of luxury goods for foreign currency, and Soviet citizens had been permitted to use them since the autumn of 1931 (Belobrovtseva and Kul'yus, *Roman M. Bulgakova*, 412).

15   Curtis, *Manuscripts Don't Burn*, 198–99. Variants of the text of this diary entry exist, for example, in *Dnevnik Mastera i Margarity*, 264–65: "We arrived there for midnight. [. . .] The orchestra had been brought in from Stockholm. M. A. was above all entranced by the conductor's tails—they were right down to his heels. [. . .] On the walls were cages with cockerels. At about 3 am the accordions struck up and the cockerels began to crow. *Style russe.* [. . .] At around 6 am we got into one of the Embassy Cadillacs and went home."

16   *Dnevnik Mastera i Margarity*, 266–67.

17   Chudakova, "Tvorcheskaya istoriya," 235–36.

18   Diary entry for February 21, 1936, *Dnevnik Mastera i Margarity*, 306.

19   *Dnevnik Mastera i Margarity*, 312.

20   D. G. B. Piper, 146; M. P. Lamperini, "Glosse al 23ismo capitol del *Maestro e Margherita* di M. A. Bulgakov," *Atti del Convegno 'Michail Bulgakov,'* (Milan: University of Milan, 1986), 281–85.

21   Thayer, *Bears in the Caviar*, 155–56.

22   First draft of diary entry for April 23, 1935, later revised; see *Dnevnik Mastera i Margarity*, note to p. 265, 652. See also Leonid Parshin, *Chertovshchina v Amerikanskom posol'stve v Moskve, ili 13 zagadok Mikhaila Bulgakova* (Moscow: Knizhnaya palata, 1991), 114–27. The subject of William Bullitt's importance for Bulgakov is also addressed in the chapter "The Ambassador and Satan," in Alexander Etkind's *Eros of the Impossible: The History of Psychoanalysis in Russia* (Boulder, CO: Westview Press, 1997).

CHAPTER 9

1   *Dnevnik Mastera i Margarity*, 104.

2   Ibid., 482.

3   Ibid., 204, 205.

4   Belobrovtseva and Kul'yus, *Roman M. Bulgakova*, 151, quoting the memoirs of Akhmatova's friend and confidante, Lidiya Chukovskaya.

5   Belobrovtseva and Kul'yus, *Roman M. Bulgakova*, 151. There is a thoughtful account of the role of Ivan Bezdomny to be found in Laura D. Weeks, "In Defense of the Homeless: On the Uses of History and the Role of Bezdomnyi in *The Master and Margarita*," *Russian Review* 48, no. 1 (1989): 45–65.

6   Erykalova reminds us that in the 1920s and 1930s Dostoevsky was pretty much banned in Soviet Russia, especially for his novel *The Demons*, which caricatured revolutionaries and the very idea of revolution. (Erykalova, *Fantastika Bulgakova*, 33).

7   Milne, *Critical Biography*, 257.

8   Varlamov, *Mikhail Bulgakov*, 751.

9   Various Soviet writers have been suggested as possible prototypes for the character of Ryukhin, including Vladimir Mayakovsky and Dem'ian Bedny. E. Kuznetsov reviews the evidence and makes an argument in favour of the poet Aleksandr Zharov in "Kto takoy Aleksandr Ryukhin? (Po stranitsam romana M. Bulgakova *Master i Margarita*)," *Voprosy literatury* 3 (2008): 321–35.

10 J. A. E. Curtis, *Mikhail Bulgakov* (London and Chicago: Reaktion Books, 2017), 125.

11 We need not go so far as Andrew Barratt, however, who is inclined to view the Master as an altogether ridiculous figure, mocked by Bulgakov for the "sheer pomposity of his diction and the crude theatricality of his gestures" when he declares himself a Master and puts on his cap for Ivan. Barratt views the Master as being "more comic than tragic," and is not moved by his account of his love affair: "his tale is replete with the sort of hackneyed clichés and melodramatic effects one associates with the very worst boulevard romances." Barratt also refers to his "dubious literary skills" even if he is a "persecuted genius. [. . .] Woland has come to open the Master's eyes not only to his success, but also to his *failure*. [. . .] The novel that the Master writes does not end in quite the way that his original inspiration had dictated that it should. His novel is flawed." (Barratt, *Between Two Worlds*, 250–62).

12 Chudakova, "Arkhiv," 130.

13 Ibid., "guessing" and "writing" are evidently alternatives in the draft.

14 *Dnevnik Mastera i Margarity*, 101–07.

15 Erykalova, *Fantastika Bulgakova*, 16–17; *Dnevnik Mastera i Margarity*, 299, 300.

16 The reference to the specific wine here is presumably an oversight on Bulgakov's part: in chapter 25 Pilate had told Afranius that it was not in fact Falernian, but came from Caecuba.

17 I have written more broadly about Bulgakov's aesthetic outlook in terms of a Romantic vision in chapter 5 of my monograph *Bulgakov's Last Decade. The Writer as Hero* (Cambridge: Cambridge UP, 1987).

18 The final sentence here was left unfinished in the original draft, and was evidently completed for publication by Elena. (Losev, Azbuka VI, note to p. 524, 592).

19 Letter of December 5, 1939, (Curtis, *Manuscripts Don't Burn*, 291). The sense of a connection with the German Romantic author of fantasy and Gothic horror E. T. A. Hoffmann was one which Bulgakov himself acknowledged in a letter to Elena on August 7, 1938: "By chance I came across an article on the fantastic in [E. T. A.] Hoffmann. I'm keeping it for you, knowing that it will strike you as much as it did me. I am right in *The Master and Margarita*! You will understand, how much this realization means to me—that I am right!" (*Dnevnik Mastera i Margarity*, 458).

CHAPTER 10

1 A good introduction to this topic is to be found in Barbara Kejna Sharratt, "Narrative Techniques in *The Master and Margarita*," *Canadian Slavonic Papers / Revue Canadienne des Slavistes* 16 (1974): 1–13. See also C. E. Pearce, "A Closer Look at Narrative Structure in Bulgakov's *The Master and Margarita*," *Canadian Slavonic Papers / Revue Canadienne des Slavistes* 22, no. 3 (1980): 358–71.

2 Quoted in Fokin, *Bulgakov bez glyantsa*, 39.

3 Ibid., 69.

4 Curtis, *Manuscripts Don't Burn*, 79.

5 He also made a film scenario of Gogol"s novel. See Curtis, *Bulgakov's Last Decade*, 115–21.

6 See, for example, Boris Eikhenbaum's seminal article in which he analyses *skaz*, his 1919 "How Gogol"s *Overcoat* is made." The word *skaz* can be translated into English as "tale," but the Formalist critics developed its use and application in specific contexts to describe a very particular type of narrative voice.

7 See Chapter 9, "Literature and the Writer," note 18.

8 Erykalova, *Fantastika Bulgakova*, 48, 50–52.

9 Weir, *The Author as Hero*, xxiv, xx–xxi.

10 Erykalova, *Fantastika Bulgakova*, 224.

11 See Proffer's 1969 article "Bulgakov's *The Master and Margarita*: Genre and Motif," reprinted in Weeks, "*The Master and Margarita*," where she argues that the category of Menippean satire provides a helpful way of accounting for the apparent inconsistencies in the text, and for showing that they are in fact deliberate (Proffer, "Bulgakov," in Weeks, "*The Master and Margarita*," 98–100).

12 See, for example, Roman Jakobson's essay "Linguistics and Poetics" (1960).

13 A remarkable recording has survived of Bulgakov's widow Elena reading this passage describing the first encounter of the Master and Margarita. It is held in the archive of the Vladimir Dahl State Museum of the History of Russian Literature in Moscow, and can be found here: https://drive.google.com/open?id=0B-As60QIqM-7jNlNvd0gyZFNhLTg.

14 For more information about calendars see http://www.rosettacalendar.com/.

15 *Dnevnik Mastera i Margarity*, 503.

16 Bethea, "History as Hippodrome," 379.

17 *Dnevnik Mastera i Margarity*, 449.

CHAPTER 11

1 Barratt, *Between Two Worlds*, 74–75.

2 Translation by Diana Burgin and Katherine Tiernan O'Connor (Ann Arbor: Ardis, 1995), 337.

3 Ibid., "Translators' Note," vii.

4 Translation by Richard Pevear and Larissa Volokhonsky (London: Penguin, 1997), vii.

5 Ibid., xix.

6 Viktor Losev comments that Bulgakov was fascinated by this question all his life. The writer derived some of his information about Kant and Schiller from the articles about Kant and about God in the Russian Brockhaus-Efron encyclopaedia, which was one of Bulgakov's most frequently used reference works. Commentaries, Azbuka VI, 569; Belobrovtseva and Kul'yus, *Roman M. Bulgakova*, 170–72.

AFTERWORD—A PERSONAL REFLECTION

1 The phenomenon of delayed publication, so common for subversive works of Russian literature in the twentieth century, raises countless fascinating issues for the study of literary history, especially when it comes to issues of "dating" a work or evaluating its literary influence on subsequent works. Another problematic issue arises when we try to understand what a work's intended audience might have been, and how that differs from subsequent "first readers." Maria Kisel suggests that in the 1930s Bulgakov's imagined reader might have been simultaneously "an object of ridicule and a desired interlocutor." See her article "Feuilletons Don't Burn: Bulgakov's *The Master and Margarita* and the Imagined 'Soviet Reader,'" *Slavic Review* 68, no. 3 (2009): 582–600 (587).

2 The best survey of the broad social impact of *The Master and Margarita*'s publication up until the end of the twentieth century is provided by Stephen Lovell in his

article "Bulgakov as Soviet Culture," *Slavonic and East European Review* 76, no. 1 (1998): 28–48.

3   For an account of the cult phenomenon of graffiti writing in the stairwell of the Moscow apartment where Bulgakov briefly lived from 1921, and which inspired the "accursed apartment" at 50 Sadovaya Street in *The Master and Margarita*, see John Bushnell, "A Popular Reading of Bulgakov: Explication des Graffiti," *Slavic Review* 47, no. 3 (1988): 502–11.

4   Jeffrey Brassard, "Bortko's *The Master and Margarita*: Adaptation in the Service of Vladimir Putin," *Journal of Popular Film and Television* XL, no. 3 (2012), 151–58 (152).

Bibliography

1) EDITIONS OF BULGAKOV'S WORKS AND LETTERS

Bulgakov, M. *Zhizn' gospodina de Mol'era*. Moscow: Molodaya Gvardiya, 1962.

———. *Master i Margarita*. *Moskva* 11 (1966): 6–130 and 1 (1967): 56–144.

———. *Master i Margarita*. Frankfurt am Main: Possev-Verlag, 1969.

———. *Tri romana*, edited by A Saakyants. Moscow: Khudozhestvennaya Literatura, 1973.

———. *Master i Margarita*, edited by L. Yanovskaya. Kyiv: Dnipro, 1989. Reprinted in volume 5 of *Sobranie sochinenii v pyati tomakh*. Moscow: Khudozhestvennaya Literatura, 1989–90.

———. *Pis'ma. Zhizneopisanie v dokumentakh*, edited by V. I. Losev and V. V. Petelin. Moscow: Sovremennik, 1989.

———. *Moy bednyi, bednyi master . . . Polnoe sobranie redaktsiy i variantov romana "Master i Margarita,"* edited by Viktor Losev. Moscow: Vagrius, 2006.

Bulgakovy Mikhail i Elena—Dnevnik Mastera i Margarity, edited by V. I. Losev. Moscow: PROZAiK, 2012.

The most complete Russian edition of Mikhail Bulgakov's works is the eight-volume annotated edition edited by Viktor Losev and published by Azbuka (St. Petersburg: Azbuka, 2011–13). The eight volumes are unnumbered, so for ease of reference I have given them Roman numerals, following for the most part the chronological sequence of their contents:

I   *Zapiski yunogo vracha. Morfiy. Zapiski na manzhetakh. Zapiski pokoinika. (Avtobiograficheskaya proza)*. St. Petersburg: Azbuka, 2011.

II   *Belaya gvardiya. Dni Turbinykh. Beg. (Roman, p'esy, stat'i, rasskazy)*. St. Petersburg: Azbuka, 2011.

III   *Sobach'e serdtse. D'yavoliada. Rokovye yaytsa*. St. Petersburg: Azbuka, 2011.

IV   *Ivan Vasil'evich. Zoykina kvartira. Adam i Eva. Aleksandr Pushkin. (P'esy i instsenirovki 20–30kh godov)*. St. Petersburg: Azbuka, 2011.

V   *Zhizn' gospodina de Mol'era. Kabala svyatosh. Poloumnyi Zhurden. Skryaga. (Roman-biografiya, p'esy)*. St. Petersburg: Azbuka, 2011.

VI   *Master i Margarita*. St. Petersburg: Azbuka, 2013.

VII   *Knyaz' t'my. (Redaktsii i varianty romana "Master i Margarita")*. St. Petersburg: Azbuka, 2011.

VIII *Pod pyatoy: Dnevnik (Pis'ma i dokumenty)*. St. Petersburg: Azbuka, 2011.

Bulgakov, M., *Master i Margarita. Polnoe sobranie chernovikov romana. Osnovnoy tekst*, edited by Elena Yu. Kolysheva, 2 volumes. Moscow: Pashkov Dom, 2014.

2) ENGLISH TRANSLATIONS OF *THE MASTER AND MARGARITA*

1) *The Master and Margarita.* Translated by Michael Glenny. London and New York: The Harvill Press and Harper & Row, 1967.

2) *The Master and Margarita.* Translated by Mirra Ginsburg. New York: Grove Press, 1967.

3) *The Master and Margarita.* Translated by Diana Burgin and Katherine Tiernan O'Connor. Ann Arbor: Ardis, 1995.

4) *The Master and Margarita.* Translated by Richard Pevear and Larissa Volokhonsky. London: Penguin, 1997.

5) *The Master and Margarita.* Translated by Hugh Aplin. Richmond, Surrey: Oneworld Classics, 2008.

3) SECONDARY LITERATURE—SELECTED WORKS

Avins, Carol. "Reaching a Reader: The Master's Audience in *The Master and Margarita.*" *Slavic Review* 45, no. 2 (Summer 1986), 272–85.

Barratt, Andrew. *Between Two Worlds. A Critical Introduction to "The Master and Margarita."* Oxford: Clarendon Press, 1987.

Beatie, B. A., and P. W. Powell. "Story and Symbol: Notes towards a Structural Analysis of Bulgakov's *The Master and Margarita.*" *Russian Literature Triquarterly* 15 (1978): 219–51.

——. "Bulgakov, Dante and Relativity." *Canadian-American Slavic Studies* XV, nos. 2–3 (Summer/Fall 1981): 250–70.

Belobrovtseva, Irina, and Svetlana Kul'yus. *Roman M. Bulgakova "Master i Margarita." Kommentariy.* Moscow: Knizhnyi klub 36.6, 2007.

Bethea, David M. "History as Hippodrome: the Apocalyptic Horse and Rider in *The Master and Margarita.*" *Russian Review* 41, no. 4 (1982): 373–99.

——. *The Shape of Apocalypse in Modern Russian Fiction.* Princeton: Princeton UP, 1989.

Brockhaus-Efron (Brokgauz-Efron, publ.). *Entsiklopedicheskiy slovar',* 82 +4 volumes (1890–1907), and 29 volumes of projected 48 (1911–16).

Bushnell, John. "A Popular Reading of Bulgakov: Explication des Graffiti." *Slavic Review* 47, no. 3 (1988): 502–11.

Carroll, Alexandra Nicewicz. "Reimagining Woland: The Shadow Archetype and the Paradox of Evil in *The Master and Margarita.*" *Russian Review* 74, no. 3 (July 2015): 419–34.

Chudakova, Marietta. "Uslovie sushchestvovaniya." *V mire knig* 12 (1974): 79–81.

——. "Arkhiv M. A. Bulgakova: Materialy dlya tvorcheskoy biografii pisatelya." *Zapiski otdela rukopisei Gos. B-ki im. Lenina* 37 (1976): 25–151.

_____. "Tvorcheskaya istoriya romana M. Bulgakova *Master i Margarita.*" *Voprosy literatury* 1 (1976): 218–53.

_____. "Opyt rekonstruktsii teksta M. A. Bulgakova." *Pamyatniki kul'tury. Novye otkrytiya* (1977), 93–106.

_____. *Zhizneopisanie Mikhaila Bulgakova.* Moscow: Kniga, 1988—2 editions, the second of which is fuller.

_____. *Novye raboty 2003–2006.* Moscow: Vremya, 2007.

Curtis, J. A. E., *Bulgakov's Last Decade. The Writer as Hero.* Cambridge: Cambridge UP, 1987.

_____. "Down with the Foxtrot! Concepts of Satire in the Soviet Theatre of the 1920s," in *Russian Theatre in the Age of Modernism,* edited by R. Russell and A. Barratt, 219–235. Basingstoke: Macmillan, 1990.

_____. *Manuscripts Don't Burn. Mikhail Bulgakov—A Life in Letters and Diaries.* London: Bloomsbury, 1991.

_____. *The Englishman from Lebedian'—A Life of Evgeny Zamiatin (1884–1937).* Brighton, MA: Academic Studies Press, 2013.

_____. *Mikhail Bulgakov.* London: Reaktion Books, 2017.

Dement, Sidney. "Architectural Details from Moscow's Sandunov Banyas in M. A. Bulgakov's *Master and Margarita.*" *Slavic and East European Journal* 60, no. 1 (2016): 87–105.

Drews, A. *Mif o Khriste,* 2 volumes. Moscow: Ateist, 1924–25.

El'baum, H. *Analiz iudeiskikh glav "Mastera i Margarity" M. Bulgakova.* Ann Arbor: Ardis, 1981.

Erykalova, Irina. *Fantastika Bulgakova. Tvorcheskaya istoriya. Tekstologiya. Literaturnyi kontekst.* St. Petersburg: Izd-vo SPbGUP, 2007.

Etkind, Alexander. *Eros of the Impossible: the History of Psychoanalysis in Russia.* Boulder: Westview Press, 1997.

Fanger, Donald. "Rehabilitated Experimentalist." *Nation,* January 22, 1968, 118.

Farrar, F. W. *The Life of Christ.* London: Cassell & Company, 1874.

Fiene, D. M. "A Comparison of the Soviet and Possev Editions of *The Master and Margarita,* with a Note on the Interpretation of the Novel." *Canadian-American Slavic Studies* XV, nos. 2–3 (Summer/Fall 1981): 330–54.

Florensky, Pavel. *Mnimosti v geometrii.* Moscow: Pomor'e, 1922.

Fokin, Pavel. *Bulgakov bez glyantsa.* St. Petersburg: Amfora, 2010.

Gasparov, Boris. "Iz nablyudenii nad motivnoi strukturoi romana M. A. Bulgakova *Master i Margarita.*" *Slavica Hierosolymitana* 3 (1978): 198–251.

Glenny, Michael. "Existential Thought in Bulgakov's *The Master and Margarita.*" *Canadian-American Slavic Studies* XV, no. 2–3 (Summer/Fall, 1981), 238–49.

Gourg, Marianne. "Gogol et *Le Maître et Marguerite.*" *Revue De Littérature Comparée* 331 (July–September 2009): 359–70.

Haber, Edythe C. *Mikhail Bulgakov. The Early Years.* Cambridge, MA: Harvard UP, 1998.

_____. "The Mythic Bulgakov: *The Master and Margarita* and Arthur Drews's *The Christ Myth.*" *The Slavic and East European Journal* 43, no. 2 (1999): 347–60.

Hayward, Max. "Pushkin, Gogol and the Devil." *Times Literary Supplement,* May 28, 1976, 630–32.

The Jerusalem Bible. London: Doubleday; Darton, Longman & Todd, 1966.

Kisel, Maria. "Feuilletons Don't Burn: Bulgakov's *The Master and Margarita* and the Imagined 'Soviet Reader.'" *Slavic Review* 68, no. 3 (2009): 582–600.

Kuznetsov, E. "Kto takoi Aleksandr Ryukhin? (Po stranitsam romana M. Bulgakova *Master i Margarita*)." *Voprosy literatury* 3 (2008): 321–35.

Lamperini, M. P. "Glosse al 23ismo capitol del *Maestro e Margherita* di M. A. Bulgakov." In *Atti del Convegno "Michail Bulgakov,"* 281–85. Milan: University of Milan, 1986.

Lesskis G. A. "*Master i Margarita* Bulgakova (manera povestvovaniya, zhanr, mikrokompozitsiya)." *Izvestiya AN SSSR (seriya literatury i yazyka)*, 38, no. I (1979): 52–59.

Lesskis, G. A., and K. Atarova. *Putevoditel' po romanu Mikhaila Bulgakova "Master i Margarita."* Moscow: Raduga, 2007.

Lovell, Stephen. "Bulgakov as Soviet Culture." *Slavonic and East European Review* 76, no. 1 (January 1998): 28–48.

Lowe, David. "Gounod's *Faust* and Bulgakov's *The Master and Margarita*." *Russian Review* 55, no. 2 (1996): 279–86.

Mahlow, E. N. *Bulgakov's "The Master and Margarita": The Text as Cipher*. New York: Vantage Press, 1975.

Mandelstam, Nadezhda. *Hope Against Hope. A Memoir*. London: Collins & Harvill Press, 1971.

Milne, Lesley. *"The Master and Margarita": A Comedy of Victory*. Birmingham: Birmingham UP, 1977.

———. *Mikhail Bulgakov. A Critical Biography*. Cambridge: Cambridge UP, 1990.

Orlov, M. A. *Istoriya snosheniy s d'yavolom*. St. Petersburg: Izd. P. F. Panteleeva, 1904.

Parshin, L. *Chertovshchina v Amerikanskom posol'stve v Moskve, ili 13 zagadok Mikhaila Bulgakova*. Moscow: Knizhnaya palata, 1991.

Pearce, C. E. "A Closer Look at Narrative Structure in Bulgakov's *The Master and Margarita*." *Canadian Slavonic Papers / Revue Canadienne des Slavistes* 22, no. 3 (1980): 358–71.

Piper, D. G. B. "An Approach to Bulgakov's *The Master and Margarita*." *Forum for Modern Language Studies* 7, no. 2 (1971): 134–57.

Pirkovsky, S. "Virtual'naya real'nost', ili tramvai na Patriarshikh." *Voprosy literatury* 4 (2004): 267–82.

Pittman, Riitta H., *The Writer's Divided Self in "The Master and Margarita."* Basingstoke: Macmillan, 1991.

Proffer, Ellendea. "Bulgakov's *The Master and Margarita*: Genre and Motif." *Canadian Slavic Studies* 3, no. 4 (Winter 1969), 615–28.

———. *Bulgakov. Life and Work*. Ann Arbor: Ardis, 1984.

Renan, Ernest. *Vie de Jésus*. Paris: Michel Lévy frères, 1870.

Rzhevsky, L. "Pilatov grekh: O tainopisi v romane Bulgakova *Master i Margarita*." *Novyi zhurnal* 90 (1968): 60–80.

Sharratt, Barbara Kejna. "Narrative Techniques in *The Master and Margarita*." *Canadian Slavonic Papers / Revue Canadienne des Slavistes* 16 (1974): 1–13.

_____. "The Tale of Two Cities: The Unifying Function of the Setting in Mikhail Bulgakov's *The Master and Margarita*." *Forum for Modern Language Studies*, vol. 16, 4 (October 1980), 331–40.

Skorino, L. "Litsa bez karnaval'nykh masok (polemicheskie zametki)." *Voprosy literatury* 6 (1968), 25–42.

Stenbock-Fermor, Elisabeth. "Bulgakov's *The Master and Margarita* and Goethe's *Faust*." *Slavic and East European Journal* 13 (1969): 309–25.

Strauss, D. F. *The Life of Jesus Critically Examined* (1835–36), translated by George Eliot. London: Swan Sonnenschein & Co., 1892.

Thayer, Charles. *Bears in the Caviar*. London: Michael Joseph, 1952.

Varlamov, Aleksei. *Mikhail Bulgakov*. Moscow: Molodaya Gvardiya: 2008.

Weeks, Laura D. "In Defense of the Homeless: On the Uses of History and the Role of Bezdomnyi in *The Master and Margarita*." *Russian Review* 48, no. 1 (1989): 45–65.

Weeks, Laura D., ed. *"The Master and Margarita." A Critical Companion*. Evanston: Northwestern UP, 1996.

Weir, Justin. *The Author as Hero. Self and Tradition in Bulgakov, Pasternak and Nabokov*. Evanston: Northwestern UP, 2002.

Wright, A. C. *Mikhail Bulgakov. Life and Interpretations*. Toronto: University of Toronto Press, 1978.

Yanovskaya, Lidiya. *Tvorcheskiy put' Mikhaila Bulgakova*. Moscow: Sovetskiy pisatel', 1983.

_____. "Treugol'nik Volanda." *Oktyabr'* 5 (1991): 182–202.

_____. *Poslednyaya kniga, ili Treugol'nik Volanda*. Moscow: PROZAiK, 2013..

Zerkalov, A. *Evangelie Mikhaila Bulgakova*. Ann Arbor: Ardis, 1984.

Index

Aitmatov, Chingiz, x
    The Executioner's Block, x
Akhmatova, Anna, 19, 31, 39, 41–42, 44,
    99, 146, 162
Akunin, Boris, x
    Azazello, xi, 56, 60, 88
Aliger, Margarita, 39
Angarsky, Nikolay, 42
Aplin, Hugh, 135, 140–141, 168
Arendt, Andrey, 42
Atarova, K., 156–157, 170
Auerbach, Erich, 53
Avins, Carol, 151, 168

Bach, J. S., 53
Bakhtin, Mikhail, 117
Barratt, Andrew, 46, 51, 55, 62–63,
    86–87, 133, 149, 152, 157–160,
    162, 164, 168–169
Beatie, B. A., 157, 159, 168
Bedny, Dem'yan, 162
Belobrovtseva, Irina, 46, 48, 77, 149,
    154–162, 164, 168
Belozerskaya, Lyubov' (Lyuba), 7
Berlin, Sir Isaiah, 133
Bethea, David, 53, 76, 126, 149, 157,
    159, 164, 168
Blake, William, xi
    The Marriage of Heaven and Hell, xi
Blok, Aleksandr, 105
    "The Artist", 105

Blyum, Vladimir, 98, 105
Bohlen, Chip, 91–93
Bokshanskaya, Ol'ga, 31, 34, 37–38,
    40, 42
Bol'shoi Theatre, 36, 39, 42
Borges, Jorge Luis, 117
Bortko, Vladimir, 148, 165
Brassard, Jeffrey, 148, 165
Brezhnev, Leonid, 143
*Brockhaus and Efron Encyclopaedic
    Dictionary,* 77
Bukharin, Nikolay, 94
Bulgakov, Afanasy, 1, 2, 76
Bulgakov, Ivan (Vanya), 5, 7
Bulgakov, Mikhail, *passim*
    Aleksandr Pushkin, 18, 21, 97, 167
    Batum, 6, 23, 25, 35–36, 44, 46,
        146
    The Crimson Island, 10, 12, 98,
        116
    The Days of the Turbins, 9–12, 22,
        90–92, 96, 105, 111
    Diaboliad, 28
    Don Quixote, 36, 131
    The Fateful Eggs, 28
    Flight, 11–12, 21, 29, 31, 36, 58, 60,
        81, 84, 116, 154
    The Heart of a Dog, 10, 12, 144
    Ivan Vasil'evich, 21, 167
    The Life of Monsieur de Molière,
        44–45

The Master and Margarita, passim.
See below for principal characters
The Notes of a Young Doctor, 3, 44
"Prospects for the Future", 5, 146
A Theatrical Novel, 8–9
The White Guard, 4–5, 7–9, 11–12,
27, 46–47, 60, 68, 81, 83, 85,
113, 148
Zoyka's Apartment, 9, 12, 68, 91
Bulgakov, Nikolay, 5, 15
Bulgakova, Elena [Bulgakov's sister],
37–38
Bulgakova, Nadezhda (Nadya), 2, 3,
37–39
Bulgakova, Varvara, 1–2, 4–7, 12, 27
Bullitt, William, 90–95, 161
Burgin, Diana, 134, 138–139, 141, 164,
168
Bushnell, John, 165, 168

Caligula, Emperor, 94
Carroll, Alexandra, 152, 168
The Caucasus [*Kavkaz*], 5–6, 23, 31, 146
Chaliapin, Fedor, 2
Chekhov, Anton, 8, 91, 113, 143
The Cherry Orchard, 143
Chudakova, Marietta, 25–27, 38–39, 43,
93, 104, 134, 144–146, 149, 154,
156, 159, 161–162, 168
Chukovskaya, Lidiya, 162
Cooper, Fenimore, 77
The Last of the Mohicans, 77
Curtis, J. A. E., 151, 159, 161–163, 169

Dante, 75, 100, 159, 168
The Divine Comedy, 75
Darwin, Charles, 2
de St Exupéry, Antoine, 93
Dement, Sidney, 160, 169
Dmitriev, Vladimir, 32
Dobranitsky, Kazimir, 161

Dostoevsky, Fedor, 12, 100, 117, 162
The Demons, 162
Drews, A., 78, 159, 169
The Myth about Christ, 78
Dumas, Alexandre, 55
La Reine Margot, 55
Dunaev, M. M., 63

Egorov, A. I., 94
Eikhenbaum, Boris, 163
Eisenstein, Sergey, 39
El'baum, H., 79, 83, 160, 169
Enukidze, Avel', 86
Erdman, Boris, 33, 42
Erdman, Nikolay, 31, 33, 42
Ericson, Edward E. Jr, 159
Ermolinsky, Sergey, 36–37, 42, 153
Erykalova, Irina, 50, 64, 85, 116–117,
149, 154, 157–158, 160, 162–163,
169
Etkind, Alexander, 161, 169
Ezhov, Nikolay, 94

Fadeev, Aleksandr, 43–44
Faiko, Aleksey, 41, 61–62
Faiman, Grigory, 146, 149
Faithfull, Marianne, xi
Fanger, Donald, 73, 159, 169
Farrar, F. W., 78–81, 84, 160, 169
The Life of Christ, 78, 160, 169
Fiene, D. M., 156, 169
Florensky, Pavel, 75, 77, 159, 169
*Concepts of the Imaginary in
Geometry*, 75
Fokin, Pavel, 153, 163, 169

García Márquez, Gabriel, 117
Gasparov, Boris, 53–54, 152, 157, 169
Ginsburg, Mirra, 133, 168
Glenny, Michael, 132–133, 136–137,
141, 158, 168–169

Goethe, J. W. von, 2, 34, 64–68, 71, 100, 102, 109, 122–124, 158, 171
  Faust, 2, 64–67, 71, 102, 109, 122, 124
Gogol′, Nikolay, ix, xii, 20, 27, 100, 111–112, 114–115, 117, 151, 154, 163
  Dead Souls, 27, 111–112, 114–115
  The Nose, ix
Gorbachev, Mikhail, 25, 146
Gor′ky, Maksim, 15, 98, 153
Gounod, Charles, 2, 30, 34, 68, 123, 152, 170
  Faust, 2, 30, 68, 152, 170
Gourg, Marianne, 151, 169
Gumilev, Lev, 19
Gumilev, Nikolay, 19
Gurev, A., 77

Haber, Edythe C., 152, 159, 169
Hall, Jerry, xi
Hayward, Max, 74, 159, 169
Hitler, Adolf, 39, 44
Hoffmann, E. T. A., 100, 108, 163

Il′f, Il′ya, 42

Jagger, Mick, xi
Jakobson, Roman, 118, 163
Job (Gumerov), 81

Kachalov, Vasily, 42
Kaganovich, Lazar, 86, 94
Kalinin, M. I., 153
Kamerny Theatre, 10
Kant, Immanuel, 135–136
Kaverin, Veniamin, 45
Kennan, George, 91
Kholodkovsky, N., 158
Khrushchev, Nikita, 44, 143
Kisel, Maria, 164, 170

Kolysheva, Elena, 26, 28–29, 31–32, 37–40, 133, 149, 154–156, 158, 168
Komsomol′skaya Pravda (*Komsomol Truth*), 43
Konsky, Grigory (Grisha), 33, 35–36, 42
Kul′yus, Svetlana, 149, 154–162, 164, 168
Kundu, Rama, 151
Kuraev, Andrey, 63, 81
Kuznetsov, E., 162, 170

Lamperini, M. P., 94, 161, 170
Lappa, Tat′yana (Tasya), 3
Lenin, Vladimir, 3, 6, 16, 23, 25–26, 38, 87, 144–145
Lermontov, Mikhail, 143
  A Hero of our Time, 143
Leont′ev, Yakov, 42, 77
Lesskis, G. A., 156–157, 170
Litovsky, Osaf, 20, 106
Litvinov, Maksim, 94
Losev, Viktor, 21, 25, 30, 32, 37, 41, 48, 67, 147, 149, 152–158, 163–164, 167
Louis XIV, King, 16, 96
Lovell, Stephen, 46, 156–157, 164, 170
Lowe, David, 152, 170
Lyamin, Nikolay, 22

MacCabe, Colin, xi
Magical realism, xi
Mahlow, Elena, 54, 87, 157, 170
Makkaveisky, N. K., 79
Mandel′shtam, Nadezhda, 19, 153, 170
Mandel′shtam, Osip, 19, 39
Markov, Pavel, 22, 36, 42, 61, 110
Marx, Karl, 13
Mass, Vladimir, 31
The Master and Margarita, ix–xiii, 1–2, 5, 11–15, 17–20, 22–26, 30, 32–33, 35, 40–46, 48–51, 53–55, 57–64, 66–68, 72–76, 79–84, 86–87, 90, 92–96, 98, 100, 102–108, 110–114, 116–117, 123–126, 130–135, 143,

146–149, 151–153, 156–160,
162–165, 168–171
Principal Characters, 61
Afranius, 33, 61, 106, 125–131, 162
Berlioz, 27–28, 38, 49, 53, 55,
64–66, 69–70, 73, 76, 86–88,
95, 98–101, 110–114, 122,
135–141
Ieshua Ga-Notsri (Jesus Christ), 49,
59, 72, 79, 96, 109, 123
Ivan Bezdomny (Ponyrev), 100,
118, 162
Matvey Leviy (Matthew the Levite),
59, 67, 73–74, 106, 109
Pontius Pilate, 80, 89, 96, 104, 109,
118–119
Woland, xi, xiii, 29–31, 33–35, 43,
49, 50–52, 54–56, 58, 61–70,
73, 81–83, 86–87, 89, 91,
93–95, 100–104, 106–107,
109–111, 113–114, 118–119,
123, 125, 135, 137, 141, 148,
153, 158, 162, 168
Mayakovsky, Vladimir, 17, 162
Melik-Pashaev, Aleksandr, 39
Mephistopheles, 2, 30, 64–68, 122
Messalina, 94
Milne, Lesley, 10, 24, 36, 54, 57, 67, 70,
79, 81, 100, 145–146, 149, 151–152,
154–155, 157–160, 162, 170
Mitchell, David, xi
Molière, J.-B. Poquelin de,
Tartuffe, 16–17, 21, 27, 44–45,
76, 83–84, 93, 96, 98, 103,
106, 116
Molotov, Vyacheslav, 54, 86
Moscow Art Theatre, 8–12, 16–18,
21–23, 27, 31, 33–35, 42, 90, 93, 96,
103, 110, 112–113
Moskva (*Moscow*), 23–24, 45–47, 54, 57,
59, 117, 132–133, 167

Nemirovich-Danchenko, Vladimir, 9
Nicholas I, Tsar, 96
Nicholas II, Tsar, 3–4
Nikitina, Evdoksiya, 38
NKVD, 34, 42–43, 88, 94, 148, 155,
161
Nostradamus, 29
Nyurenberg, A. S., 153

O'Connor, Katherine Tiernan, 134,
138–139, 141, 164, 168,
OGPU, 8, 10, 12, 15, 21, 29, 31, 42, 88,
155
Orlov, M. A., 63, 158, 170
*History of Man's Relations with the
Devil*, 63

Parshin, Leonid, 161, 170
Pasternak, Boris, 10, 19, 42, 146, 151,
158, 171
Dr Zhivago, x, 151
Paustovsky, Konstantin, 110
Pearce, C. E., 163, 170
Petelin, V. V., 153, 167
Petlyura, Symon, 4–5, 147
Petrov, Evgeny, 42
Pevear, Richard, 134–135, 139–141,
164, 168
Piper, D. G. B., 43, 54, 86, 94, 156, 158,
160–161, 170
Pirkovsky, S., 159, 170
Popov, Pavel, 12, 18, 31, 38, 41–42,
44–45, 102, 108, 111, 153, 156
Powell, P. W., 157, 159, 168
Pravda (*The Truth*), 21–22, 93
Proffer, Ellendea, 55, 57, 84, 89, 117,
133–134, 146, 149, 158, 160,
163, 170
Proulx, Annie, xi
Pudovkin, Vsevolod, 39
Punin, Nikolay, 19

Pushkin, Aleksandr, xii, 18, 21, 33, 42, 76, 83, 96–97, 100, 102–103, 143, 159, 167, 169
  The Bronze Horseman, 143
Putin, Vladimir, xiii, 147–148, 165

Radcliffe, Daniel, xi, 151
Radek, Karl, 94
Ray, Mohit, 149, 151
Renan, Ernest, 78–79, 160, 170
  The Life of Jesus, 171
  The Antichrist, 78
Rolling Stones, xi
Romanticism, 97, 103, 107–108
Roosevelt, Franklin, 90
Rowling, J. K., 63, 148
Rushdie, Salman, xi, 117, 151
  The Satanic Verses, xi
Russell, R., 159, 169
Rzhevsky, L., 54, 158, 170

Saakyants, Anna, 26, 38, 40, 48, 133, 167
Schiller, Friedrich, 136, 138–140, 164
Schubert, Franz, 107
Sharratt, Barbara Kejna, 157, 163, 170
Shebalin, Vissarion, 42
Shilovskaya (Bulgakova), Elena (Lyusya) [Bulgakov's wife], 14–15, 18, 23–26, 30–38, 40–41, 43–45, 47–48, 54, 57, 61, 67, 77, 87, 91–95, 103, 106, 115, 125, 133–134, 144
Shilovsky, Evgeny [Elena's husband], 18–19
Shilovsky, Evgeny [Elena's son], 42
Shilovsky, Sergey, 19, 34, 44
Shostakovich, Dmitry, 12, 21
Simonov, Konstantin, 41, 44–46
Skorino, L., 59, 158, 171
Smith, Hedrick, 47, 157
Smith, Patti, xii, 151
Socialist Realism, 10, 48, 98–100, 108

Sokolovsky, A. L., 65, 67
Solzhenitsyn, Aleksandr, 45–46, 132, 143, 146
  One Day in the Life of Ivan Denisovich, 45, 132, 143
Stalin, Iosif, 12, 15–19, 22–24, 33, 35–36, 42–46, 48, 54, 83, 87, 89–91, 94–96, 98, 105, 113, 132, 143, 146, 148, 161n11
Stanislavsky, Konstantin, 8–9, 103
Steiger, Baron, 95
Stenbock-Fermor, Elisabeth, 158, 171
Strauss, D. F., 78, 136, 138–140, 171
  The Life of Jesus, 171
Svidersky, A. I., 153

Thayer, Charles, 91–93, 95, 161, 171
  Bears in the Caviar, 93, 161, 171
Tiberius, Emperor, 59, 83, 90
Tolstoy, Aleksey, 7
Tolstoy, Lev, 31, 102
Trotsky, Leon, 3, 16, 86
Tseitlin, Samuil, 42
Tukhachevsky, Mikhail, 94

Vakhtangov Theatre, 21
de Valois, Marguerite, 55
Varlamov, Aleksey, 42, 53, 63, 77, 83–84, 87, 89, 92, 100, 149, 152–154, 156, 158–162, 171
Veresaev, Vikenty, 30–31, 153–154
Vilenkin, Vitaly, 42, 61–62
Vil'yams, Petr, 34, 42
Volokhonsky, Larissa, 134, 139, 141, 164, 168
Voroshilov, Klim, 54, 86, 94
Voskresensky, Ivan, 2, 4
Vulis, Abram, 46, 117

Weeks, Laura, 46, 57, 149, 152, 156, 158, 160, 162, 171

Weir, Justin, 56, 80, 116, 149, 151, 158, 160, 163, 171
Wright, A. C., 146, 149, 171

Yagoda, Genrikh, 34, 94
Yanovskaya, Lidiya, 25–28, 31–32, 34, 38–40, 43, 47–48, 65–66, 76, 78–79, 133, 149, 154–160, 167, 171
Yedlin, Tova, 153
Youmans, Vincent, 69

Zamyatin, Evgeny, 18, 43, 75, 101, 146
We, 75, 101
Zemskaya, Elena, 39
Zerkalov, A., 76, 83, 159, 171
Zharov, Aleksandr, 162
Zhukhovitsky, Emmanuil, 32, 42, 161
Zinov'ev, Grigory, 86
Zoshchenko, Mikhail, 44

Ingram Content Group UK Ltd.
Milton Keynes UK
UKHW021258090523
421461UK00025B/227